David

All the Best

Good Luck

KEEP GOING FOR IT!

By the same author

GOING FOR IT!

Keep Going for It!

Living the Life of an Entrepreneur

VICTOR KIAM

COLLINS
8 Grafton Street, London W1
1988

William Collins Sons & Co. Ltd
London · Glasgow · Sydney · Auckland
Toronto · Johannesburg

BRITISH LIBRARY CATALOGUING IN PUBLICATION DATA

Kiam, Victor
Keep going for it.
1. Business enterprise. Success – Manuals
I. Title
650.1

ISBN 0-00-215403-X

First published 1988
Copyright © Victor K. Kiam II 1988

Photoset in Linotron Times by
Rowland Phototypesetting Ltd
Bury St Edmunds, Suffolk
Printed and bound in Great Britain by
William Collins Sons & Co. Ltd, Glasgow

I want to thank my loved ones who have
been so involved and so supportive, and all
those who have helped me 'Go for it'
. . . especially my partners, the
employees of Remington who
have contributed so much.

I would like to thank Dick Lally, whose
ability to organize my thoughts and
assistance in getting them down on paper
were an invaluable aid in the
writing of this book.

Contents

Leveraging your assets: you have to keep going for it

Hello. I'm Victor Kiam. A couple of years ago I wrote a book chronicling the entrepreneurial experience. *Going For It!* was the first book I had ever written. I enjoyed it so much, I tried to buy the publishing house. It wasn't for sale. Being an entrepreneur, I settled for the next best thing. I wrote another book.

The entrepreneurial adventures in *Going For It!* ended with my successful acquisition and turnaround of the Remington Company. In an era that has been a rash of leveraged buy-outs, takeovers, and attempted turnarounds, I thought it would be worthwhile to lead off by reviewing what has happened since that purchase.

First, some quick history. Many of you are probably already familiar with the Remington story. I bought Remington from Sperry-Rand in 1978. At the time, the once-popular Remington electric shaver had lost most of its consumer appeal. Sperry couldn't wait to get the virtually comatose company off its hands. Using the leveraged buy-out, I was able to purchase Remington and begin taking the steps for its revivification.

You might recall the ads we've run. I spoofed one at the top of this chapter. They feature an unknown actor named Kiam who tells how he loved the Remington shaver so much he bought the company. It's funny. Many people believe that our subsequent success was due to the unusual approach of our TV ads. Untrue. Sir Carol Reed could have directed Sir Alec Guinness in the greatest commercials of all time and they still wouldn't have accounted for the 360 degree turn made by Remington.

That turnaround began with the Remington employees. We came in and removed all the perks and privileges that had served as walls between management and the rest of the company. The employees learned that Remington no longer had blue-collar or white-collar positions. There was only one collar: the Remington collar. Incentive programmes, benefiting every-body, were introduced. Lines of communication were opened. We created an *esprit de corps* that had been lacking in a failing company. We also painted a vista vivid with the promise of success and then got our employees excited about sharing that triumph.

With a solid team in place, our attention was turned to the shaver. We had recognized some of its problems at the outset. Sperry was a successful high-tech company that didn't under-stand the marketing demands of the shaver business. They changed shaver styles too often, leaving the public confused and retailers exasperated. Store owners and buyers were leery of stocking a heavy Remington inventory; they didn't want to get stuck when the company made its latest stylistic innovation. This hurt the shaver immeasurably. Norelco, changing its styles only rarely, was outselling Remington four to one. Stores were stocking ten times as many Norelcos as Remingtons. You couldn't blame them. They were going with the more stable product.

Remington had also got into the habit of raising its prices to keep pace with the competition. Norelco would lift its prices; Remington would follow suit. This was more than just unsound fiscal policy. It was a public relations disaster. Remington was made to look like a follower not a leader in its field.

Once inside, we reversed these trends. We took away the chrome and fancy trimmings that had inflated our shaver prices, but had done nothing to improve the product. For example, the shavers came packed in a metal case that cost us two and a half dollars and was heavy enough to inflict a slight hernia on Arnold Schwarzenegger. Unfortunately, it contributed nothing towards a great shave. An expensive, unwieldy item that was difficult for the consumer to carry, it was consigned to our scrap heap.

We also let our retailers know that our lines would be stable and that all orders would be filled promptly. One new addition was made to the line, however, but it was a positive one. We introduced the Triple Head Shaver (now known as the Triple Action Shaver), a no-frills Remington that retailed for $19.95. At the time of its debut, the lowest price Remington was selling for $34.95. The new shaver was a smash. The company sold more than half a million Triple Heads in the first year. That represented over four million dollars in gross profit. Its success played a large role in the Remington comeback. Combined with cost-cutting measures, improved distribution, the hard work of our employees, and new advertising and marketing strategies, it helped push Remington to the top of the shaver business. In a few short years, we have quadrupled employment and increased sales five-fold.

So what have you done for us lately, Kiam?

That's the pleasant recent past. What have Victor Kiam and Remington been up to lately? I'll be happy to tell you. *We've done what any entrepreneurial company must do: refused to become complacent with our success.* An entrepreneur can not stand still. If he does, those laurels he chooses to sit on will attach themselves to his backside, wend their way up and over his body, and transform him into nothing more than an inactive piece of vegetation.

We had no intention of letting Remington become part of the flora and fauna. During my first three and a half years of ownership we concentrated on the shaver business. We didn't even think about introducing any new products. Once we re-established the shaver as the best on the market, then we looked to expand our operation. A solid cash flow had been established, our market share was jumping, and the company base was strong. We were still a one product enterprise, but what a product! Now, in order to ensure our continued growth, we felt it was time to move into new territories.

That was a choice any entrepreneur would make. But how do you implement the decision? What are the obstacles to your expansion?

At Remington there was one element that would hamper our growth and it was really a toughy. As a leveraged buy-out company, you are undercapitalized. This means all inventory intensive businesses are out of bounds for you unless they grossed a sufficient profit. Why? Simply stated, if a product generated only a marginal gross profit it wouldn't have paid for you to borrow the money needed to launch the enterprise. Let me give you an example. One of the first opportunities brought to Remington was a hair dryer business. As a grooming product it was related to our shavers. Unfortunately, those dryers could only generate a profit margin of about 18 per cent. After settling the interest on the seed money loan, the company would be left with less than 8 per cent gross profit. Obviously you could do a lot of volume in dryers, but show very little on the bottom line. Your capital was being too rapidly consumed. Entrepreneurs also must avoid getting involved with 'me-too' items, products that are unabashed copies of whatever is currently hot with consumers. You have to ask yourself, what is this product's Unique Selling Proposition (The USP)? What makes it stand out among its competitors? Does it have a better motor or does it offer comparable quality at a better price? I was not convinced that our hair dryers could make these claims or that they would be decidedly different from any of those already on the market.

Leveraging your assets

Given the situation, what was an entrepreneur to do? The only possible option is to leverage off your assets. I don't want to confuse you. In the normal, financial sense, leveraging off your

assets pertains to using your tangible assets – say the land your
store sits on or your inventory – as collateral when securing
capital. I didn't have that luxury. In buying Remington I had
leveraged myself to the brink.

I had to make the most of Remington's intangible assets. In
Going For It!, I talked about the Personal Balance Sheet (PBS).
Drawing a line down the centre of a sheet of paper, I would
list my positives (willingness to work hard, sound education,
some marketing flair, fluency in several languages, etc.) on one
side and my negatives (procrastinator, hatred of paperwork,
lack of punctuality, etc.) on the other. The main thrust of
the exercise was to enable me to turn those weaknesses into
strengths. There was, however, an equally important philosophy behind this self-examination, one that I think should have
been given more emphasis: knowing your strengths, you can
see where they will lead you. My assets led me to Lever
Brothers, an international conglomerate where it seemed my
marketing skills and fluency in languages would put me in good
stead.

The PBS can be just as easily applied to a company as an
individual. Here it takes the form of an Intangible Balance
Sheet (IBS). This balance sheet has little to do with the dollar
value of a company. Instead, it measures the worth of such
things as location, the skill of your work force, and consumer
good will. Your enterprise is a living, breathing entity. It is
your baby, and the IBS can serve as its Dr Spock. Do you want
to know in which direction this growing child should be going?
Ask the IBS.

For example, a fellow has a newspaper stand not far from
my home. He has always done good business, but some time
ago he decided that he wanted to do still more. He was located
near a subway that served hundreds of commuters dashing off
to work in the morning and coming back home at night. Up
the block was a large university, many of whose students also
used that train. The stand's biggest negative was its size. There
was nothing he could do about that; zoning laws and the
high price of New York real estate prevented the owner from

physically expanding. The stand's greatest positive was its location and the unused, albeit limited space in the inner back
portion of his booth.

Aware of these factors, the stand owner made several choices.
First he brought in a line of cigarettes. He correctly reckoned
that many of his customers would run out of cigarettes overnight
and that he would be the morning's first opportunity to quell a
nicotine fit. Size restrictions dictated that he stock only the
most popular brands. Cartons were kept stored in a box on
the floor of the booth. Samples of these wares were kept
prominently displayed. Catering to the students who bought
his newspapers, the owner installed wire shelves in his stand's
inner rear wall. These were lined with inexpensive items such
as ballpoint pens, erasers, and pencils. To call attention to these
he put brightly coloured signs on the stand's overhang. Business
grew dramatically. With his increased profits, this entrepreneur
had larger, plastic windows installed in the stand, enabling his
customers to get a better look at his full line of merchandise.
The owner is now dickering to buy another stand across town,
to be run by a cousin. All this was the result of the IBS he drew
up for his enterprise. Using its strengths and recognizing its
weaknesses, he has turned the newspaper stand into a personal
and financial triumph.

The biggest plus on the Remington PBS was obvious: the
Remington name. Remember, we weren't concerned with the
inventory or the value of our factory. I was focusing on our
intangible assets. We were spending an awful lot of money
advertising our shavers. Each commercial or ad was also celebrating Remington. That name and the quality it now stood for
had a real value. This meant that any venture launched under
the Remington umbrella was automatically enhanced by the
association.

To take advantage of our name, I wanted to launch a product
that could be closely tied in with the shavers. We developed a
combination beard, moustache, and hair clipper. This was a
product with a built-in USP: it was the only grooming product
on the market featuring three separate clipping functions. All

the other clippers on the market came with numerous attachments. It took an instruction book, two guides, and a translator to figure out which attachment performed which task. Our product wasn't such a puzzle. It took up less space on the consumer's grooming shelf and performed all three functions without fuss. Retailers loved it because it was three products combined to form one stockkeeping unit. It didn't wreak havoc with their inventory. It also commanded less space for storage. Retailers were also thrilled with the way it jumped off the shelves and into the hands of consumers. Being our first grooming product other than the shaver to carry the Remington name, we were especially pleased with its reception.

One segment of the business already bearing the Remington brand was our service centres. I decided to do an Intangible Balance Sheet on them and this was the result:

INTANGIBLE BALANCE SHEET
Subject: Nineteen Remington Service Centres

Liabilities	*Assets*
1. Money losers	1. Goodwill engendered by service centres
2. Require a parts inventory, bleeding our cash flow	2. Tied to long-term leases at what was now a low rent
3. Tied to long-term leases in now rundown neighbourhoods, customers afraid to visit	3. An in-house staff of expert service-people
4. In-house staff not trained in sales	

I was working under many of the same conditions as that news-stand vendor I mentioned. Short of closing the shops down – which I couldn't do because the centres were a necessary part of our business and the buy-out of our leases would have cost us a bundle – I had to deal with the limitations of a physical space. Looking at our list, we attacked our problems. The long-term lease liability cancelled itself with a low rent. I solved the inventory question by carrying the stock for all nineteen stores in our Bridgeport plant. This created more room in the centres and allowed our staff to concentrate on shaver repair, rather than the shipping of spare parts to dealers.

Next we needed to improve customer traffic. At the time, Remington had 19 per cent of the shaver business in the US. Service centre customers were being drawn from that slice of the consumer universe. Yet, we had the technology and could get the spare parts to service our competitors' products as well as our own. This was of great convenience to the consumer; many of our competitors would do servicing only through the mails. Enabling them to simply drop them off at our shops doubled our service centre business.

With the numbers moving up, we decided to train the service centre staff as salespeople. Now whenever someone brought in a Norelco to be fixed, the salesperson would try to get him to try the Remington option. These employees became so confident we felt we could introduce a line of products to be sold exclusively in these stores. We were transforming the service centres into retail outlets.

Choose the right product

In picking the product line to be launched in these outlets, I followed the example set by my friend the news-stand owner. I looked at the service centre's clientele. It was 90 per cent male. We were already offering shaver accessories such as replacement foil heads. We were about to introduce a cleaning lubricant for the shavers and a powder stick, designed to keep the beard dry and stiff for an even closer shave. But we wanted to offer a line that represented a small but significant break from the shavers.

We tried several items including cigarette lighters and key

chains. None of them took hold. Finally, I found just the thing we were looking for in Canada. The discovery was something of a fluke. I had walked into a cutlery store in Toronto. The shop was nothing but wall-to-wall knives. I had not come in hunting for a business venture. To be honest, I wasn't looking for anything more than a good nail clipper. *But when opportunity knocks, the entrepreneur is always home.* I was so fascinated by the focus of this speciality shop that I started quizzing the manager. He said that knives were an interesting business. Generally a customer didn't buy one knife, he bought five or six. Most importantly, the bulk of his customers were males.

There was no way of telling how the shops would fare in the United States. For whatever reason, hardly any stores in my country carried cutlery exclusively. Stores that sold knives kept a limited variety of stock. They carried the incomplete lines of only two or three major brands. You could buy a company's steak knife, but they might not carry that same manufacturer's utility blade. This was uncharted territory. The entrepreneur, a modern pioneer, can think of nothing more attractive. We decided to do a market test of the cutlery line in three of our service centres. They went through the roof. We expanded the operation to include all our shops. Our salespeople were tutored until they became cutlery connoisseurs. We augmented the knives by offering knife-honing and key-making services. Certain stores were told to place greater emphasis on particular types of knife. For instance, in coastal regions we did a large business in maritime, fishing, and scuba knives. In the landlocked Mid-west, our displays featured utility knives. We were leveraging our assets. In this case, the location was the asset. We tailored the stock to meet the demands of the area.

The response of these changes was such that those nineteen shops have grown to eighty-five. This proved something I had always believed. Just by building on your strengths – using them to offset your liabilities – and paying attention to your market you can turn a big loser into a winner.

Experts don't always know

We've exported that cutlery business to the UK. Remington
had had four service centres in England; they have become six
retail centres. The English experiment was not without its risks.
We were told that the British did not, as a rule, spend a lot of
money on knives. European marketing experts claimed that
the British would rather use a one-pound kitchen knife to cut
a magnificent piece of beef than spend a few extra bob on a
more elegant blade. One Englishman told me, 'Victor, you
have to understand. We don't care how quickly the blade
works, how it looks, or even if it cuts particularly well. All we
want to know is, "will it cut the meat?" ' Manufacturers told
us the same thing. Everyone we spoke with told us to forget
the English market.

There comes a time when an entrepreneur has to follow his
own instincts. You have to ignore the experts. I did a bit of
research on my own and came away convinced that upmarket
knives hadn't found a niche in the English market for one very
good reason: no one had bothered to try to establish one. The
English consumer had been fitted to a stereotype that had been
accepted by an entire industry. I wanted to challenge that idea.
We started offering our cutlery line in one store in Bristol.
Guess what? The experts were wrong. The English loved our
knives. Not only are we now selling our knives there, but we
have negotiated to get full distribution rights from all the great
knife distributors around the world. We will be the knife
distributors for the UK, selling not only in our own stores but
in other shops as well.

As an entrepreneur, you're going to run into more than your
share of naysayers. By his nature, the entrepreneur is often
cutting against the grain of popular opinion. You can't reject
experienced advice out-of-hand. You can give it a certain
amount of weight before coming to a decision. However, you
also can't allow it to overwhelm your gut feelings. Investigate.
Take the time to find out the cause or source of contrary
opinions. That negative feedback can be a plus. It should force

you to look deeply into the heart of your venture and to take that view with a clear and critical eye. If your investigation convinces you the experts are in error, damn their torpedoes and full speed ahead. If we had listened to the experts, we would never have launched in England. A valuable business would never have got off the ground.

Entrepreneurial synergy

The best ideas don't just materialize out of the ozone. They can come as the result of a synergy. One idea spawns another or is merged to a second concept to create a third entity. Remington now had outlets possessing an inventory of attractive male items. We had an impressive mailing list built on the warranty cards from our shavers. We also needed to make our cutlery available to those millions of consumers who didn't live near a Remington store. The list, the inventory, and our need combined to become the Remington mail-order catalogue. In turn, having a catalogue forced us to look for an even wider range of products.

The first catalogues featured speciality shavers, accessories, and cutlery. We've increased our selection to include beer steins, pens, leather goods, jewellery, and – a product line with as strong a USP as I've ever seen – Samurai ceremonial swords. If a Ninja's favourite weapon isn't a unique gift item, I don't know what is. These catalogues have grown into a formidable business. Four years ago, the turnover of the shops and catalogues was roughly three million dollars. The turnover for the last fiscal year was over thirty-two million. It's still climbing.

The hidden USP

In choosing a new product or venture, its USP isn't always obvious. You can have a wonderful snow-tyre, but unless it outperforms all of its competition, it is still just a wonderful snow-tyre. In such an instance, *your marketing concept can be a product's most powerful USP.*

We found this to be true when the success of the cutlery and catalogues persuaded us to launch a second product line. Again, we wanted it to be male oriented. Someone suggested we jump into travel products. I found a supplier, but I was leery. I wasn't sure the items were substantially better than anything already being sold, though I knew they were at least as good. This USP had to represent something other than superior quality. We went out and did some research. We found that while these products – alarm clocks, electrical conductors, steamers and travel irons – were available, consumers couldn't find them under one roof. They had to mill through six or seven departments or stores to put together a decent travel kit. Boy, did the lightbulb go on. We brought the products together in a self-contained display unit in a single location. They were labelled Remington Travel Plus. The ease of purchase was the USP and it made the products especially attractive. Since introducing that line, Remington has acquired a company whose travel products are rated number one throughout the world. We are now the largest company in the travel appliance business.

Building this business has not been easy. One problem we're still wrestling with is that created by multiple buyers in larger stores. Certain of these stores will have a clock buyer who deals with nothing but clocks, and an iron buyer who works exclusively with irons. There wouldn't be any one buyer authorized to buy a travel kit embracing these and other items. The clock buyer also resented having someone else offering travel clocks in another department. The iron buyer would raise the same squawk. Some stores try to solve the problem by separating the kit and offering the items in different departments. That violates our USP. Remington has been adamant about keeping the kits whole and in one section. As retailers see how well the approach works, we're bringing them around to our point of view. Nothing sells better than success.

Entrepreneurial teamwork

In *Going For It!* I described a practice we instituted at
Remington to improve employee communications. We held
Friday morning coffee meetings. About a dozen employees,
representing all levels including management, would meet for
coffee and Danish pastries and discuss a topic pertinent to the
company. Over a period of time, each one of our employees
has an opportunity to participate at least once. We want our
employees to share in our entrepreneurial adventure. These
coffee meetings are their forum. They can ask questions, air
criticisms, and make suggestions. These meetings are designed
to give everyone a sense of participation. But they also do much
more than that.

Management does not have a lock on great ideas. *As a
business's leader you want entrepreneurs working for you on
every level.* You can encourage this by giving your employees
a forum, allowing their ideas to be heard and given serious
consideration. The best feedback they can possibly get occurs
when one of their concepts grows into something tangible. For
example, one of these brainstorming sessions was attended by
a young woman from our assembly line. She said very little
during the first three-quarters of the meeting. Then a fellow
employee made a product suggestion. He did a lot of painting
and often had to paint around glass. No matter what he did,
some paint would always run down and harden on the pane. It
was a holy terror to remove. You had to scrape it off with a
razor blade or some similar instrument, all the while hoping
you didn't damage the glass. The process was time consuming
and exhausting. They started to kick around the idea of an
electric scraper. It would run on the same principle as our
shavers.

While they were focusing on this subject, that young woman,
unaccustomed to speaking in front of groups, found herself
inspired. She timidly raised her hand and said, 'You know three
months ago, I was in the hospital for an operation. As part of
the pre-op procedure, the nurse had to shave me. I got nicked.

The wound wasn't particularly large, but it was enough to get them to postpone my surgery. They couldn't risk the possibility of infection. This company's business is shavers. Isn't there anything Remington can do about that?'

Everyone in the room got excited. A pre-operative shaver! What a marvellous avenue to explore. We researched the hospital-hygiene market and discovered it was still in the dark ages. No one was being shaved electrically; patients still had to submit to the horrors of blade and cream. Soon after this meeting, the company started developing a medical shaver. It would be used in hospitals and doctor's offices. Having heard of our plans, 3M offered to join us in the venture. Remington would manufacture and 3M, already a giant in the medical field, would distribute. We came up with a project and put it through FDA clinical testing. The result was a shaver that virtually eliminates any possibility of nicking. Its head is disposable for sanitary reasons. Surgeons use it on a patient once and then throw it away. The doctors love the implement. Cutting the hair at a perfect length, it prevents the growth of ingrown hairs. These hairs can be a major annoyance if located near an open wound.

The hospitals only have to buy each shaver once. The repeat business is in the disposable heads. One major hospital in the US is using 20,000 heads a month and this year we expect to do over three million heads worldwide. That little product has given us a foothold in the medical field. We are actively looking to acquire a small medical company. Remington is also busy developing new mechanical and electrical products specifically for hospital use. One is an off-shoot of the disposable shaver head: a throw-away electric shaver. It will be run by a battery. The battery charge will last for six weeks, much longer than the average hospital stay. When the power runs out, the shaver is thrown out. We are also working on a shaving version of 'Star Wars'. This will be a shaver for the handicapped. Set on a track and using laser beams it will allow quadriplegics or anyone who has lost the use of their hands to shave themselves.

All of these ideas are spin-offs of the hospital shaver. They might not have happened if Remington hadn't created an environment where a young assembly-line worker could feel comfortable sharing her ideas with upper management. By the way, that idea for a paint scraper did not get lost in our enthusiasm for the hospital shaver. The concept was researched. It wasn't viable. The small size of the market and the cost of the blade made it an unpromising product. A follow-up was done with the idea's originator. We wanted him to know we had tried to turn his concept into reality, but that it wasn't for us. Knowing the consideration we gave his idea can only encourage him. It was a heck of an idea and I want to keep him thinking. Who knows? He just might come up with the next great Remington product.

Entrepreneurial teamwork, part two

As an entrepreneur, you want your executives to share your approach to business. You don't want them seeing life as a long cafeteria line leading to a mundane menu. Have them think of it as a *grande bouffe*, glimmering with golden trays overladen with opportunity. You want these people to do more than just feast on the delicacies, you want them to bring something to the party. A case in point is the story of the pool alarm.

The Canadian government had awarded a grant to two engineers. It called for the development of a device that would cut down on the number of drownings. Canada had suffered an unusually high number of such deaths. Tragically, most of the victims are children. The grant represented an entrepreneurial answer to the problem on the part of the Canadian government. The two engineers were up to the task. They created an alarm that emitted an easily heard warning whenever an object weighing eight pounds or more fell into the water.

It was easy to see this product's USP. Nothing like it was being sold anywhere. By a happy coincidence, one of the inventors was a neighbour of our Canadian company's president. He was shown a prototype of the gizmo. Immediately recognizing the pool alarm's potential, he started the process of acquiring the rights to it for Remington. We are currently selling it throughout the world. The president might have had a harder time netting the product in other companies. He could have been caught up in the bureaucratic red tape and political backbiting. Before it could be straightened out, a more entrepreneurial company – one supporting its executive's in-itiative – would have made off with the goods.

Seeing the tree for the forest

Sometimes the next great product or idea can be right under the entrepreneur's nose, only he doesn't see it. He needs an outside influence to place it in a proper perspective. Not too long ago, I was in Washington DC to take part in discussion with other businessmen and politicians. The main topics centred around the trade deficits and the fluctuating dollar. During one of my exchanges on the telephone, a US senator changed the subject, saying, 'Victor, I use your shaver. I like it a lot but I have one problem with it. I have an annoying amount of excess hair in my nose and ears. I can't shave inside either of those two places; shavers are too big. Have you got anything that can help me?'

I knew we had some small item that was being offered in our retail stores, but I wasn't sure it met the senator's needs. Returning to our Bridgeport factory, I called in Lee Feist, the gentleman in charge of our retail department. I asked him what we had that would meet the senator's needs. He showed me a Heath Robinsonesque device featuring a small crank on the side of a cylinder with cutters at the top. I looked at it and asked, 'Do we sell many of these?' Lee said, 'You bet. We have them in forty stores and we're going to sell about 10,000 of them this year.' My God, that was 250 a store, almost one a day! It was quite a number.

I sent one down to the senator. He replied with a gracious thank you note and a cheque for the product. He had it wrong.

It was I who should have been sending a letter of thanks to him. I hadn't realized how well this little item was doing nor how much people really needed them.

I couldn't get the clipper out of my head. Calling in our engineers, I showed them a model and said, 'Look, we're selling these things like they're the latest hit by Bruce Springsteen. Is there any way we can make an electrical version?' I wasn't making this suggestion merely for the sake of modern technology. I wasn't satisfied with the way the current model performed. It took a lot of elbow grease to crank the apparatus. The manual turning also made the user susceptible to cutting. You couldn't stop the thing in mid-crank, so if it grabbed hold of your skin, you could suffer a pretty good nick.

The engineers worked on it. The result was an electrical version that trims you without exertion. A safety device automatically cuts off the motor at the cutter's first touch of skin. We've introduced this model in our catalogues. The nose clipper is already the catalogue's second biggest seller. It's just hitting the retail market. We don't have any conclusive numbers yet, but we have large hopes. It's funny. If not for the senator, it might have been months before I knew what a hot item the clipper was. It was such a tiny part of our business. That one conversation led me to a real revelation and gave this company another potential blockbuster.

Is the door closed? Open another!

One of the other products we tried to introduce was an air purifier. It would rid your room of dust, pollen, smoke and other impurities. I thought it was pretty spiffy. I couldn't wait to show it off at the annual housewares show in Chicago. Couldn't imagine anyone offering anything quite like it. Talk about having your enthusiasm dampened. When I got to the show, I found no less than twenty-five different manufacturers hawking their version of the air purifier. I thought, 'My God, I'm going to be lost in the crowd here. There's too much competition.' I wanted to pack my tail and my air purifier between my legs and go home.

I know I've often preached that when an entrepreneur finds the door closed, he's got to find a way to bang it open. This, however, was an unusual situation. If I rammed the door ajar, I might not like what I found on the other side. It could be like opening up Dracula's crypt. The market was going to be so overcrowded there wasn't going to be any way to make a decent profit. Realizing this I thought, 'Hold on. This entrance is locked, and now I doubt I want to waste time trying to find its key. I still believe in the product. Why not try another door? The air purifier hasn't been introduced in Europe. We would have heard about it. All the manufacturers are at this show. I bet they're so busy trying to sell the US and Canada that they're not paying any attention to the other side of the Atlantic.' What's an entrepreneur to do? Leave the housewares show and return to his hotel. I spent the rest of the afternoon calling all the major Remington accounts in England. My calendar became glutted with appointments.

The next day, I drove out to the airport, hopped on a plane and took my sample across the Atlantic. My competitors were cutting each other's throats in Chicago; I was working my buns off in the UK. By the end of the week, it had been placed in all the major stores. Today, Remington is number one in the air purification business in England. I think we tried the right door.

Drawing the line

There were a large number of products that we chose not to pursue. Some of them were tempting. We rejected them because research showed their market was too narrow. Others were downright wacky.

I remember one in particular. Its inventor had been referred to me by a mutual friend. This friend had said, 'Victor, you must talk to Robert. He's always coming up with ideas and he has one now that he thinks is a world-beater.' Okay. You're an entrepreneur. You're supposed to be in the world-beating business. I agreed to see this chap.

About two weeks later, the inventor meets with me and my engineers. He tells us a little bit of something about himself and then says, 'Let's get down to business. I have a product here that is going to revolutionize the industry. I just know you won't believe it when you see it.' With that, he opens up a container and takes out what looked to be a watering can with a flashlight taped to the side of its nozzle. The reason it looked like that is because that is exactly what it was.

He was right. None of us could believe it. My engineers just sat there trying to hide their quizzical expressions. Finally, after a few moments of throat clearing, I looked at the beaming inventor and asked, 'What's it for? Watering the garden at night?' He replied, 'Oh, no. That's to see where the water is pouring. You can't always tell if you're actually covering the intended area of a garden or flower bed.' I can be dense at times but I just had to ask, 'Well can't you just feel the ground with your hands?' That silenced him for a moment. Then he said, 'Sure you could do that, but then you'd get your hands dirty.' I didn't need to do any market research on this baby. I already knew that most people who garden like to get their hands dirty. It's part of the experience. When I told him this he looked at me as if I had grown an extra head. He couldn't believe that I couldn't see the genius of his invention. The inventor said, 'You just wait and see. This is going to be the biggest product on the market place. I'm taking it to your competitor.' He may have been bluffing. We'll never know. The last time we checked, the illuminated watering can hadn't replaced the hula hoop or Rubik's cube in the hearts of world-wide consumers.

Right around that time, we rejected a product that did have merit. A fellow brought us a food vacuum. This was a glass bell fitted over a glass plate sided with rubber grooves. Having placed food on the plate, you covered it with the bell and used a suction pump to pull out all the air. The bell was then locked.

The food retained no moisture in this vacuum. You could keep it fresh indefinitely. We researched the product. In America, we came up against a spendthrift mentality. They'd rather not go through the trouble of vacuum packing food, even if it saved them money. They would just throw the leftovers out.

We didn't give up on this idea. We decided to research the European market. Generally, Europeans tend to be less wasteful than Americans. The overseas test killed it. The average European kitchen is smaller than its American cousin. This product was about eighteen inches tall and twelve inches wide. It took up too much counter space. We found the best market for it would be in lesser developed countries where food storage was a problem. They, however, couldn't afford it. We rejected the food freshener. It proves that sometimes a Unique Selling Proposition isn't enough. This product had a fabulous USP. It just wasn't strong enough to overcome American profligacy or European space limitations.

You sometimes have to ask yourself how long a product's USP will last. A chap brought us a variation of a hot plate. This was a smaller version. It would automatically shut off once the food or beverage placed upon it had reached a desired temperature. When that temperature dropped a few degrees, the power returned. This seemed like a great product, particularly for offices. A person could heat up a cup of coffee and then maintain its temperature throughout the day. Wow! Here was a product that would enhance coffee drinking, one of the great rituals of Western life. It was also economical. You would no longer have to throw out and replace cold half-cups of coffee.

As we took a closer look at this creation, our enthusiasm waned. This was really little more than a hot plate with a heat responsive timer. It was the result of already known technology. Therefore, we would be unable to protect it with a US patent. We felt the heater's market outlook was glowing. But only in the short term. Within months, there would be fifty knock-offs of ours, all at lower prices. Remington is an advertising-intensive company. If we took the product out, the company was going to back it to the hilt. We didn't want to spend the time and effort building up a business for someone else. There are entrepreneurs who love to grab the short-term success. Nothing wrong with that. They introduce a new product at a maximum margin, make their money, and then bow out as soon as the market is glutted with imitators. Remington like to look at the long haul. Our kicks come from building businesses. This heater was a great idea. We still had to pass.

Remington had to make a similar decision on another interesting idea. A fellow brought me a leather saddlebag. At first, I thought he had mistaken me for Roy Rogers, but then he explained that the saddlebag wasn't supposed to be thrown over a horse. It was designed to fit over a briefcase. Serving as an overnight case, it meant the user only had to carry one item when off on a short trip. The saddlebag would hold pyjamas, a couple of shirts, a few ties, and toiletries. The inventor offered us an exclusive on what I thought was a neat item. Unfortunately, the exclusive was worthless. Even though it was a fine concept, at base it was nothing more than a saddlebag adapted to a new use. Remington didn't have any way of protecting the idea from copiers. We tried to create an additional ingredient that would bring it under the sanction of the patent laws, but we came a cropper.

I'm looking at a product now that has a chance. An automated jar-opener. Have you ever bought a jar of spaghetti sauce or pickles and found yourself in traction after trying to open the darn thing? They are so well sealed by mechanization they would give a Houdini fits. This is especially true in the States. The rash of product poisonings has engendered an understandable caution in the food and drug industry. No one wants to be the next Tylenol.

Women find the jars especially trying. Women also form the bulk of the kitchenware market. This device is going to make their day. It has a gripper that electrically twists off the jar top. Nothing to it. That gripper adjusts to various jar sizes. The technology behind its adaptability is something that can be protected. A patent search is already in progress. We already know there is a market for it. The tool is a natural fit with the can opener. If our investigation works out you might be seeing the Remington jar openers by the time this book is out.

Sometimes a product is victimized by having too much technology. I was acquainted with two entrepreneurs, Rick O'Malley and Don Hamer. Their corporation sold premium products. They would sell things like drinking glasses bearing pictures of rock stars. Companies would buy them and then give them away in promotions. They did a nice business.

One day, a supplier called them with a proposition. He had acquired the rights to a garbage-bag clip gun. Shaped like a weapon used by Rambo, it discharged a metal clip. You could fire it at the twisted neck of a plastic garbage bag and seal it for disposal. O'Malley and Hamer are both entrepreneurs. When an opportunity comes into their sights, they react as heat-seeking missiles. They asked the supplier to send over a sample.

They both liked the look of the thing. O'Malley, being the wackier member of a zany duo, decided a test was in order. First, he took an ordinary, full to bursting, plastic garbage bag. He sealed the neck with the gun and then swung the bag around the office. Vigorously. When he was finished, he was so dizzy he couldn't walk for ten minutes. The bag had held fast.

As soon as he recovered from vertigo, he put the clip gun through another drill. O'Malley has often proclaimed that he likes to get close to a product. He proved it in this instance. Going down to his building's cellar, he came back with an industrial size garbage bag. He placed it on the floor. Then he crawled into the bag and assumed a fetal position. Hamer clip the bag shut. O'Malley spent the next five minutes trying to push the clip off from the inside. It was quite a sight. A secretary came into the office and found Hamer sitting at his desk, calmly reading an inventory, apparently oblivious to the large black bag rolling back and forth across the office floor. The only sound heard was emitted from the bag. It was O'Malley yelling, 'Jesus, what a great product!'

The boys fell in love with the contraption. They negotiated a deal with the supplier, giving them an equal share in the rights. This covenant contained one important stipulation. The two had to sell 10,000 units in ninety days or the full rights would revert to the supplier. Neither of them saw this as a problem. They thought the clip gun was such a winner, vendors would be knocking their doors down with orders.

No such luck. Sixty days into the agreement, they hadn't sold a unit. Rick and I happened to be meeting over an unrelated matter right around this time. He told me about the clip gun and asked, 'Do you have any idea who might be interested in this thing?' I suggested that Remington take a look at it. It seemed as if it might fit in our catalogue.

Rick and Don sent over a sample. It turned out to be everything they promised. Unfortunately, it also carried a high price tag. Too high. With import duties and two mark-ups, the gadget couldn't have been sold for less than $10.95. Extra clips would cost $3.95 a bag. In America, we have a variety of manually operated garbage-bag seals. Some are plastic; others composed of thin wire. All are free with the purchase of the bags. Using them is fairly easy. We didn't think that consumers were willing to pay the price to bring the process into the mechanized age. We had to turn the guys down. The final thirty days went by in a blur. No sales. Apparently other possible distributors shared our sentiments. They ended up surrendering the rights back to the supplier.

Climbing Pike's Peak, or entrepreneurial kismet

Sometimes the marriage of an entrepreneur and a venture is little more than fate. A product that has received a good deal of attention was brought to me by its creators. As you've seen, that wasn't unusual. How I ended up with the worldwide rights to it, on the other hand, is quite a story.

A little over two years ago, I received a call from a Canadian chap. He said, 'Mr Kiam. My name is Geoffrey Pike. I am an entrepreneur and, like yourself, have acquired a company through a leverage buyout. I have a product that is simply sensational. We think you're the man to sell it and we would like to show it to you as quickly as possible.' The call came on a Thursday. I was heading to Europe on Sunday.

Explaining this to Mr Pike, I said we could get together on my return. He wasn't having any of it. He said, 'Look, surely you can give me an hour or two on Saturday?' As it happened, I did have two hours open that day, but I didn't intend to devote them to business. Mr Pike, though, was insistent. He said, 'Look just give me two hours. You won't regret it. If after that time you don't think this is the greatest thing in the world, I'll not bother you again. You'll love what I have to show you. There's nothing like it.' Woh baby, now there was a brightly painted vista. His unrestrained enthusiasm won me over. I also liked the sense of urgency he brought to his pitch. He made it seem as if Remington would be missing the product of the century if we didn't meet that weekend. I made an appointment to meet this ball of fire and two associates. One would be his chief engineer, the other his company's president.

The three of them arrived promptly. Mr Pike had his product in a canvas bag. Before they had a chance to say very much, I presented them with a Remington disclosure agreement. Pike refused to sign. He responded with a confidentiality form of his own. I wouldn't sign his.

Such an odd stalemate. For a moment, it looked as though we would spend the whole two hours haggling over these protective covenants and might never get to see the bloody thing they were protecting. Finally, I suggested a compromise. I would agree to sign his confidentiality form provided it excluded everything Remington was either already in or planning to enter. To my surprise, he agreed.

I ticked off the categories – personal care, grooming, cologne, and apparel among them. I went through every business I could think of, and Pike still said they bore no relation to his product. This exchange accomplished two things. It made me sanguine about signing his form and it made me maddeningly curious to see what the deuce they were trying to sell.

I couldn't wait to get a look at this mircale machine. Mr Pike had other plans. Without so much as glancing at the canvas bag in his possession, he asked if he could have a cup of coffee. His engineer asked for a glass of grape juice. The president opted for a coke.

I served them and sat down, certain Mr Pike would unveil his creation. Wrong again. Mr Pike stood up, casually sipping his brew, and then suddenly spilt the majority of it on to a patch of carpet. The engineer stood up and said, 'You know, I really don't like grape juice. I think I'll just dump it on the rug.' With that, he emptied his glass on top of the spreading coffee stain. The chairman followed his friends' example with his coke.

What was I to make of this? I found myself trying to humour these fellows until the boys with the butterfly nets appeared. The carpet was a technicolour mess. None of this seemed to perturb Mr Pike. He took his contraption from its canvas home and plugged it into the wall socket. The machine had a suction nozzle on one end with a clear plastic front. Mr Pike set the nozzle on top of the stain. Within seconds, I'm watching this goop being sucked out of the carpet. The excess moisture was soon gone. Only a colourful blotch remained.

Mr Pike attacked that problem with the other side of his machine. It squirted some detergent on the spot. An attached brush sloshed the liquid cleaner into a nice froth. The suction device was then reapplied and bingo! No more stain. I was impressed, but Mr Pike wasn't finished. He asked me if we had a particularly stubborn spot anywhere in the apartment. We sure did. It resided on our living room rug. For ten years, we had kept its presence hidden with a strategically placed chair. Professional cleaners had taken regular turns with it. No amount of scrubbing could persuade it to vacate the premises. Not too many Ahabs wanted to tangle with this Moby Dick of stains, but Mr Pike was an entrepreneur. He loved this sort of challenge. He got to working on the spot and had it all scooped

up within minutes. I couldn't believe it. This stain had been
with us for so long, I almost wanted to hold a memorial service
for it.

Flabbergasted by the results, I told the three men I was
interested in acquiring the rights for Remington. Remington
agreed to put up the capital for development and to perfect the
design. We would test the product, and if the results were
satisfactory, sell it around the world. Mr Pike agreed to a deal.
It had only one hitch. Remington could distribute the cleaner
only in the United States, Australia, New Zealand, and the Far
East. Geoffrey was going to keep the Canadian rights and
Electrolux, the vacuum cleaner company, was apparently about
to be named as European distributor.

I was disappointed. We were increasing Remington visibility
in the European market. This seemed the perfect product for
our continued expansion. Still, I was more than willing to make
do with what I had.

The machine was christened the VicVac. We brought it to
retailers in April 1986 with the promise of a September–
October launching. I took it out on the first round of sales calls.
Though I am busy running Remington, I often like to participate
in the selling of our products, especially the new ones. I was
particularly excited to take the VicVac on its rounds. I wanted
a first hand look at how clients responded to it. The first account
we called on gobbled it up at $37 wholesale. That was a nice
start. At that price, however, the margins wouldn't allow us
much advertising. So I turned to my salesman and said, 'Gee,
it sold pretty easily here. Let's raise the price to $40.' Another
quick sale. We kept raising the price with each succeeding
customer. By the end of the day, we found we could sell it for
$52. Accounts still thought that was a great buy and it gave us
a tremendous amount of money for advertising.

Shortly after the VicVac's US launch, I attended a meeting
of major European retailers in England. I brought along a tape
that chronicled what Remington stood for and what we were
up to around the world. The VicVac was featured on the tape.
The European retailers flipped. They rushed me asking when

they could order their VicVacs. That was frustrating. I told them, 'You should be talking to Electrolux. They have a representative here. We've only got it for the United States.' With that, I left for my hotel room and a good solid hour of banging my head against the wall.

Instead of that indulgence, I decided to accompany the president of our English company to his office. I was being overwhelmed by a good case of entrepreneurial persistence. I turned to the president and said, 'My God, I just know we could sell the heck out of this thing if we had it in Europe. I've got to give it at least one last shot. Let's get Pike's number at your office. I'll call him from my hotel.'

We got back to my room at about 7 p.m. My wife Ellen and I chatted. I looked over some mail. We made arrangements for dinner. Finally, I said to my president, 'Let's make the call.' I grabbed the number from my wallet. Before I could put my hand to the receiver, the phone rang.

It was the switchboard operator. Someone was calling from CBS for an interview. I told her to put the caller through. Seconds later, I was being greeted by a familiar voice. It was Geoffrey Pike! He had used the CBS ruse to ensure that the hotel would put the call through. I was in shock. I thought I had just walked into a Steven Spielberg fantasy – 'Business Encounters of the Third Kind'.

I said, 'Geoff, you won't believe this, but I was just about to call you. This very minute! I have something to discuss with you.' Pike replied, 'Don't talk. Let me say something first. It can't wait. How would you like to have the VicVac for England and all of Europe?' A sudden chill tap-danced up my spine. This was getting scary. He proceeded to explain that Electrolux had been sitting on the product for too long without coming to any decision on it. Geoffrey Pike was a mover. He was through waiting. He liked the aggressive way Remington had handled the product in the US and wanted to throw in with us. All the way.

I wasted no time coming to an agreement. When it was concluded, Geoffrey said, 'Great. Now that that is out of the way, what did you want to talk about?' What could I say? I didn't think anyone would believe this. I replied, 'Oh, nothing important, Geoffrey. Just thought I'd call to see how you were doing.' When I hung up, I sat down in a trance. My English president and I just stared at each other. I was awed. Remington and the VicVac. I guess it was fate.

Over the past six years, Remington has come to mean more than just shavers. Besides the ventures mentioned we have entered into the machine-washable necktie business, and we've introduced a designer cologne. A new shaver, the Ultimate, was brought out in 1987. Shavers, VicVacs, pool alarms, colognes, and neckties. What's it all mean? Simply this: the entrepreneur works hard to build a company into a success. He's pleased by his good fortune, but never lulled by it. Remington's willingness to expand proves that we approach new business with the same entrepreneurial zest that led to the original purchase and turnaround of the company. This is essential for any company hoping to survive in today's market.

We'll pursue any avenue in trying to improve the company. Nothing is sacrosanct. Not even our advertising. Remington has had continued success with our commercials. Over the years you may have noticed some subtle changes in them. Despite this, the commercial is basically the same one we've been running since I took over the company.

I read and answer every letter addressed to me. Some correspondence concerns my ads. Many of the writers seem to think the commercials would be better if they were to star in them instead of me. They're probably right, but since no one has given a compelling reason to take my place – a USP – I've resisted their suggestions.

Recently, however, I received some advice from a celebrated source. During a sojourn to California I was introduced to world champion wrestler Hulk Hogan. The Hulk is apparently a Remington fan. I asked if it was because it gave his face such a close shave. He said that was one reason, but that he was especially enamoured of how easily it could shave the hair off his entire body! Hulk liked the sleek look. The lack of body hair made it especially difficult for opponents to get a firm grip on him.

Hulk admired the shaver so much, he offered to join me in a commercial. Mr Hogan is about 6 foot 7 and weighs over 300 pounds. If there is an ounce of fat on his sculptured frame, it is hiding in his wrestling boots. I've seen him throw 300 pounders around as if they were frisbees. I gave his suggestion serious consideration. I haven't come to a decision yet: I'm not sure a shaver's ability to whisk off all of your body hair is a USP with a broad-based appeal. Also, using a wrestler in my ads would be a radical departure. It would certainly be entrepreneurial. Hulk and I could take turns reading the commercial copy and then we could finish in unison proclaiming, ' . . . shaves you close as a blade or your money back!' Of course, we might just have Mr Hogan drop by your house to pick up any returning shavers!

Failures?
Everybody has them!

It was nice reviewing some recent successes. Sounds as if life for the entrepreneur is filled with nothing but triumph. Don't kid yourself. History shows that Thomas Edison went through over 5000 different filaments before discovering the one that made his light bulb a shining reality. He didn't let those first several thousand mistakes dissuade him from his task. You must have the same fortitude. You are a pioneer. Failing will be part of your adventure. *Show me the person who has never failed, and I'll show you someone who has never taken a risk. I'll show you someone who is not an entrepreneur.*

You can't be half-pregnant

On the other hand, show me someone who learns from his mistakes and keeps persevering, and I'll show you an entrepreneur. Everyone experiences failure. I've certainly had my share of turkeys. I am, after all, the fellow who failed to see the full commercial potential of a product called Velcro. That adhesive fabric now serves as the base for a multi-billion-dollar industry. I had a chance to be a partner in it when Velcro was little more than an idea. It was something I really wanted to do. I let friends and colleagues talk me out of it. They all thought I would be crazy to leave Playtex, a company where I was doing so well, and tie my fortune to this untested product. I learned from that mistake. *When your guts tell you to move forward with a project, don't be swayed by the doomsayers.*

Those same people warned me off Remington twenty years later. Who knows? I might have listened to them if I hadn't remembered the advice they gave me on Velcro.

Time for a little trivia quiz. Have you ever heard of the Catholic Record Club of America? No? You mean you haven't heard of the company that launched 'We're Going to Have a Cookout at Your Cremation'? Don't worry. You won't be ostracized by the 'in crowd'. They haven't heard of it either. That record club was a Victor Kiam rocket that never got airborne.

It was about 1955. I was fascinated by the sudden proliferation of record societies. A music lover, I had joined the RCA club. It sent out a monthly catalogue, inviting members to choose discs from its vast library. Every conceivable musical style was represented: classical, pop, jazz, folk, and early rock. It even included records produced by labels other than RCA.

After months of receiving their catalogue. I realized something. This club and its competitors were broad-based. Each offered the same general music mix. I thought there might be room for a club that would go after a niche market. This was a generally sound idea, but exactly what kind of club could it be? It couldn't contain any of the elements already offered by existing associations. That would detract from its USP. No, it had to be something that no one else was offering. This was a tall order. It takes a variety of skills to be an entrepreneur, but creating a new form of music out of thin air is not, thank heavens, one of them.

As it turned out, I didn't have to be quite that inventive. Record clubs were not the only thing catching the American public's fancy in the mid-fifties. Religion had come to television. A leader of this phenomenon was Bishop Fulton J. Sheen, a Catholic prelate. His hourly show was watched by millions across the nation. I felt this new religious fervour could be translated into a business. A friend – someone already in the music business – and I put together a proposal for the Catholic Record Club of America. The organization would be aiming at a very specific group: religious music fans. In addition, it would offer albums featuring lectures by the leading Catholic orators of the day. Actors, appearing on other records, would read famous religious works. This was going to be my first entrepreneurial effort outside corporate confines and I thought it looked like a zinger.

Jumping right in, we put together a mock catalogue. Many of the records were obscure, but some of them were well-known works such as Bing Crosby's 'Ave Maria'. The company obtained a mailing list comprised of people who regularly bought religious items and took pains to bring together a high-powered board of directors. Everything seemed to be falling into place. Even the Catholic Church played a role. After hearing our plan, they agreed to give the club its – if you'll pardon the expression – blessing. This official sanctioning did not come free. The Church was to receive a cut of the profits on every record sold. I liked that. The priests and their representatives were fair, tough businessmen. They taught me that you could find entrepreneurs anywhere and that they didn't necessarily have to come clothed in Brooks Brothers suits.

An informal board meeting was convened before our launching. First topic on the agenda: who would run the actual ongoing business? Minutes after airing the question, I thought, 'Woh, not so fast, now. Don't everybody volunteer at once!' I mean no one stepped forward. It didn't take very long to realize I had made a terrible mistake. This board of directors was high-powered all right, too high-powered. Not one member – including my recording expert friend or I – had any time to run our new enterprise! We were all too occupied with our full-time careers.

The company had to make a decision. It either had to find someone to take the club's helm or dissolve. The quest began immediately. Unfortunately, it was doomed by two factors. First, none of us had time to conduct a thorough search. Second, the few candidates we did unearth were unwilling to chance involvement with what they perceived to be a risky idea.

We were about to abort. Then RCA, having heard of our concept, came forward and offered to buy it. We sold. I probably should have been elated at making money on my first sizeable venture. I wasn't. RCA had bought little more than an idea, an unfinished catalogue, a mailing list, and Church approval. The club itself was still an untried, unproven commodity. Having been forced to sell too early, none of us realized a meaningful profit. We did however pick up a valuable lesson: you can't be half-pregnant. An entrepreneur must be able to give his enterprise a full commitment. If I really believed in the club's viability, I should have at least taken a leave of absence from my job at Lever Brothers, and given the thing my best shot. It's a lesson I've never forgotten.

Best laid plans . . .

There are going to be times when your best idea is going to be a victim of circumstances. A friend of mine, fellow in the marketing business, had heard that a major American tobacco company wanted to do a sports promotion. Sports have always been an attractive advertising opportunity. In America, despite our free market and freedom of speech, there are certain products that active athletes cannot pitch. These athletes are considered role models for American youth and are discouraged from setting anything resembling a 'bad example'. Cigarettes and other tobacco products are further restrained by a ban preventing their being advertised on TV or radio. Not only are tobacco companies unable to use players as spokespersons, they are also banned from buying commercial time during events featuring these athletes.

There is a slim loophole around this limitation. A company can sponsor a televised event. It is still unable to advertise during its broadcast. It cannot use the event's participants in its advertising. It *can* have its name tied to a sport by financial support. Witness horse racing's Marlboro Cup, or the Virginia Slims Tournament in women's tennis.

Having heard of the tobacco company's search for a sports promotion, my friend approached it with an idea: a tennis yearbook. This manual would be a review of the past year's major tournaments and a preview of the upcoming tennis season. It would feature statistics, records, full-colour photos, and, most importantly, interviews with star players.

The company loved the idea. By featuring pictures of the athletes on the cover and highlighting the interviews, they could form a legal, indirect relationship with the players. After review by the promotions department, the concept moved forward. It grew bigger at each step of the corporate ladder and the company was soon considering an order of six million copies. My friend was already counting his profits. You can imagine his disappointment when the idea collapsed.

Apparently, the company felt the best way to distribute the book was as an on-pack. The paperback would be attached to a carton of cigarettes. Everybody thought this was brilliant. Everyone, that is, except for one of the company's marketing executives. He came to a meeting armed with a ruler. Measuring the book's thickness, he pointed out that every four copies meant one less carton of cigarettes shipped to the vendors. One less carton shipped. One less carton displayed. One less carton sold. With an order of six million books, the vendors would be stocking over a million and a half fewer cigarette cartons. This was not the sort of mathematics companies like to hear.

Suddenly the concept lost its lustre. It met a firm rejection. The idea was still solid, but it was done in by its own logistics. Shortly after the turndown, my friend told me, 'I really made a mistake there. I was so caught up looking at the advantages of the programme, particularly the advantages to me, that I didn't really pay close attention to the disadvantages. If I had taken a better look, I would have recognized the problem before making the proposal. Then, I would either have suggested an alternative route of distribution or come up with an entirely different idea. I just didn't consider the needs of the sponsor or his market.'

In any negotiation, you have to know what the other side wants. Sure, it may be a super idea for you. But what makes it sizzle for the fellow across the table? Do a balance sheet on your concept. List its weaknesses and strengths from the other side's point of view. Build your proposal around the plusses and then do everything you can to eradicate or soften the negatives. Had my friend done this, he might have anticipated the shipping problem up front. He could then have offered either a new plan of distribution or a different version of his idea.

Coincidentally, I had once found myself in a similar situation with a tobacco product. A gentleman by the name of Bill Stengel had brought an item to me that seemed best suited for a magic act. A self-lighting cigarette. It was normal in every aspect, except for a small bit of sulphur residing in its tip. When struck against a rough surface, it lit without matches. This was terrific. You could light it in almost any weather. Gusty winds had no influence on it. You wouldn't have to worry about running out of matches or lighter fluid. I thought the cigarette would be particularly useful for hunters, sailors, and outdoorsmen. Invented by a gentleman named Decapitano, it had been christened the Deca. Stengel had an opportunity to pick up the rights for it and he asked if I would like to get involved as part of a joint venture. I agreed.

Bill and I took the creation to two large tobacco companies. One did an enormous business in snuff and chewing tobacco, but had only a small percentage of the cigarette trade. It was excited by our idea. The Deca seemed to be a unique vehicle that could sizably increase the company's cigarette market share.

The second company was one of the tobacco business's leaders. It was similarly intrigued, but for different reasons. Aware of its position, it wanted to be first with any item that might have a major impact on its industry.

Both companies researched the product thoroughly. Both gave it the thumbs down. The reasons for the rejections were simple. Their research showed that smoking a cigarette was ritualistic. The lighting of that smoke was an integral part of the process. Smokers, creatures of habit that we are, are loath to abandon or change this initial step to nicotine pleasure. The research also found that when a man reached over to light a woman's cigarette, the act was fraught with sexual overtones. The striking of the match or flicking of the lighter was often the opening note to the mating dance. Heavy stuff. Our reaction was, 'Fine. Then market the Deca as a cigarette for outdoorsmen!' Not a bad comeback. Unfortunately, we discovered that these findings had only had a minimal impact on the decisions of both companies. The biggest reason for their rejection was fear. The two corporations were scared to death of the Swedish match cartel. They were certain that the introduction of any self-lighting brand would put their other cigarette lines in bad odour with the cartel. All those free match packs accompanying the cigarettes bought in vending machines would suddenly disappear. Add in the research results and you can understand the company's reluctance to buck the cartel.

We took the rejections in stride and tried to sell the product to several other companies. No dice. Everyone liked the Deca, but the feature that gave it a USP was the thing that made it anathema to an industry that wouldn't risk the wrath of the matchmakers. An entrepreneur has to have the courage of his convictions. We were convinced that the Deca was a hell of a product. You also have to know when you're licked. We now knew that no company would agree to distribute it. Bill and I dropped the Deca.

Okay, your big idea has met an untimely death. You're grieving. You're depressed. How long do you stay down? About two and a half minutes. There is no better therapy for the pain accompanying rejection than to throw yourself back into your work. I started by examining the presentation we made for the Deca. Where did we go wrong? Was there any way to salvage the enterprise? If such an examination discloses a chink in your proposal, perhaps some tinkering will improve it. If it illustrates that you've done all you can, then it's time to turn the page and move on to something else.

Satisfied that the Deca's turndown was unavoidable, I sought the balm of a new idea. It could have been months before another attractive opportunity came along. However, in this case I was lucky. Another venture presented itself just as the Deca was put to rest. It came in tropical wrappings.

I had visited Bermuda on several occasions. During these trips, I had become quite friendly with the island's inhabitants. Bermuda had a racially mixed population, about two-thirds black and one-third white. A prosperous island, it probably had the best social relationship of mixed races found anywhere in the region. Despite this, there was no university of any kind for anyone, regardless of race. Most of the white families sent their children to universities in either the United States or England. The majority of blacks and low income whites could not afford this luxury.

I became fascinated with the idea of founding a University of Bermuda. The island already had a number of leverageable assets. Its people were an industrious group who, given the opportunity, would probably place a premium on higher education. An old navy base featuring buildings that were ideal candidates for classrooms and dorms could be bought for a song. Its locale, alive with crystal-clear calm seas and balmy breezes, would attract young people from other countries. I thought American students would find our offering particularly compelling. The timing certainly seemed right. Four-year colleges in the US were grossly overcrowded and junior colleges had sprouted like dandelions. These were two-year schools that offered students the hope of eventual transfer to a regular college. Ours would also be a two-year school, featuring a solid education and all the amenities this stunning island had to offer.

I found several Bermuda-based businessmen who were willing to invest in the venture. They thought it was a worthwhile idea. They also believed it would create an atmosphere conducive to their doing business on the island. With their backing, I contacted a man who came highly recommended, the president of a medium-sized junior college in the United States. This fellow had won high marks for running an outstanding learning centre at a considerable profit. His academic credentials were impeccable. With his portfolio, the money, and a sound business plan in tow, I was ready to seek government approval.

Bermuda's Superintendent of Schools relished the idea. They arranged to have us present our plan in a session of the Bermuda Parliament. I actually had to wax poetic over the idea on the country's legislative floor. I think I do a pretty mean sales presentation, but no one has ever mistaken me for Sir Winston Churchill. Somehow, I managed to stumble through without embarrassing myself before this august body. The net result was a charter endorsed by Bermuda's Governor General.

We were pumped and ready to go. Then I became victim of a good news/bad news story. The good news was that I had suddenly been given an opportunity to buy the Benrus Watch Company. The bad news was that this would prevent my giving a full effort on the school's behalf. None of my investors had the time to take over the reins either. Remembering the Catholic Record Club of America, my options were clear. I immediately resigned as head of the group and named the college president as my replacement. That was a mistake. The president was an educator, not a businessman. He didn't know how to move the project off square one. That wasn't his fault, it was mine. Eventually, the charter lapsed and the idea died. It was later done by some other group. Another lesson learned. It's not enough to delegate. You have to put your enterprise into the hands of the right people. If I had made a better effort to find someone who really knew his way around a profit and loss sheet, we probably would have opened the school.

Ahead of your time

By his very nature the entrepreneur is an innovator. He doesn't follow fashions, he sets them. Unfortunately, you will have times when you are too innovative. You think you're bringing the word to the faithful, but the faithful's ears are filled with cotton.

When I was with Playtex we introduced the world's first

machine-washable bra. Revolutionized the industry. Before its debut, bras had to be washed by hand. Our new version was so successful – we sold ten million in the first year – we decided to take a look at our girdles. We found that women rarely washed their girdles. The girdles were hard to clean and just couldn't stand up to repeated washings. As a result, the used girdles quickly became soiled and odorous. These wrecks had to be liberally doused with colognes and perfumes before they were made suitable for wearing. Knowing this gave me an idea for what was later known as 'The Dirty Girdle Promotion'. It became part of the Playtex legend because it was the only marketing idea in the company's history that nearly caused its creator's arrest.

The concept was simple enough. We chose the Stone and Thomas department store in Charleston, West Virginia, as our first test-market outlet. The public was offered a girdle trade-in. You brought in your tired, dirty, old girdle and we gave you a four-dollar discount on the purchase of a brand new Playtex model. Vic Kiam, innovator at large, was sent down to conduct the test.

We erected a large container in the Stone and Thomas corset department. On the first day, the women came as a swarm. Girdles were flying through the air, most of them landing in the container, but a few probably struck some hapless buyers. We did terrific business. In fact, business was too good.

I had planned every aspect of the promotion with the same meticulous eye for detail as the fellows who set up D-Day. The only difference being, once my troops hit the beach, I didn't have the means to move them inland. I hadn't made arrangements to have the dirty girdles picked up during the day. It never occurred to me that we would get such a large turnout.

On the second day, a noxious air settled over the corset area. Somebody maintained consciousness long enough to call the sanitation bureau. Within the hour, three burly representatives of that department made their way across the floor. They were accompanied by a large police officer. Eyeing the delinquent container, one of the men asked, 'Who's in charge here?' I replied meekly, 'I guess I am, sir.' He shook his head in disgust, turned to the officer, and said, 'Book him.' Book him! Oh Lord, welcome to my nightmare. There was a storeful of customers, newspapermen were waiting outside, and I was about to be a martyr for Playtex. I thought, 'Hey, I know I'm an entrepreneur. I'm supposed to stand out. But there's got to be a better way of getting attention than this!'

Fortunately for Mr and Mrs Kiam's little boy, the officer was a touch more laid back than this hard-eyed civil servant. He talked with the three gentlemen. They decided to let me off with a summons for creating unhealthy conditions in the city. I was given a $100 fine. They also made it clear they wanted me and the girdles out of town by sundown.

All right, I had a lemon. The promotion started well, but ended in disaster. What kind of lemonade could you squeeze from this? An image kept coming to me. It was that container of used girdles. I thought, 'This is obviously a problem for women. Maybe we can do something about it?' You're an entrepreneur. You recognize a need, you try to come up with a product or service answering that need.

I went down to a store in Miami to conduct further investigations. I had deliberately picked a city with a tropical climate. This locale's heat and humidity translated into heavy perspiration. The resulting problem of feminine odour was so pronounced that once a woman tried on a girdle, she had to buy it. The store wouldn't take it back. This was embarrassing for the store and the customer. I was also positive that it was hampering girdle sales.

I got together with the Playtex ad agency, Young and Rubicam. They hired a psychologist to interview women on their hygienic needs and his report convinced us that a new business had been discovered. We developed a group of cosmetics to be named 'Body Magic'. The line included an after-bath tingler, a powder, a body lotion, and a feminine deodorant. All were applied with an aerosol spray. The feminine deodorant was the line's primary USP. It was the first product of its kind.

Playtex ran limited tests on the products and the results were overwhelmingly positive. We couldn't wait to launch. Then the monkey wrench came flying into the works. It was tossed by Mr A. N. Spanel, Playtex's chairman of the board. He insisted that we place the new line in either our accounts' 'notion' departments, where small items for women such as sewing materials, hangers, potpourri etc. were sold, or in the corset sections. At the time, these represented the traditional Playtex outlets. We were barred from selling Body Magic anywhere else in the store.

This was a mistake. Body Magic was a cosmetic line and we wanted to sell it in cosmetic departments. We did everything we could to change Spanel's mind. I pleaded with him to let us do a broad test of the market, allowing it to determine where the line should be sold. If I did this once, I did it twenty times. Spanel was sent daily memos and was beaten over the head with the idea at every opportunity. We weren't being obstinate merely out of a love for our own concept. The entrepreneur, especially in the corporate environment, has to check his ego at the door. You have to ask yourself, 'Is this good for the company?' We felt it was. Body Magic would have brought Playtex into a whole new market, one that no other corset company had explored.

Mr Spanel could not be persuaded. He was one of the great entrepreneurs. As founder of Playtex, Spanel had introduced marketing concepts, products, and ad campaigns that had innovated the industry. This was a risk-taker. But he did have some blind spots. Though he loved to implement new ideas, Spanel felt that Playtex already had a basic, strong distribution base. He didn't want to tamper with it. He saw the introduction of a Playtex product in the cosmetics department as a risk. It could mean weakening our relationships with the buyers in either the corset or notions departments. Spanel wasn't about to do that.

Playtex brought Body Magic out over my protests and with Spanel's restrictions. It posted tremendous sales for about six months. Then every major cosmetic company jumped into the market. They, of course, sold their lines in the cosmetic departments. We got wiped out. My associates and I had created a new market, but the company had been unwilling to capitalize on it. This was quite depressing. It stands as a defeat that can still rankle me. With good reason. Every now and again, I run into some executive from Revlon or Alberto Culver. Invariably, they pat me on the back and say, 'By the way, Kiam, thank you so much for building one hell of a business for us.' Through gritted teeth I tell them, 'You're so very welcome.'

If you're an entrepreneur in a corporation, you are likely to run up against your own Spanels time and time again. You can't let it discourage you. Go back, salve your wounds, and get ready to assault their petrified attitudes with your next great idea. It's been my experience that eventually you will be given the opportunity, even if it's just to shut you up. Playtex gave many of my more entrepreneurial ideas a chance to fly. Fortunately, the concepts did just that. If you are an entrepreneur and your company doesn't give you any chances to explore risks, you'd better consider finding another situation.

A common error

Bill Constanza is in the dilemma described above right now. He was a full partner in a small, successful advertising agency in New England. The company – alias the CC Agency, for the purposes of this story – was formed in 1984 and did $1 million in billing during that first year. By late 1986, business had quadrupled.

A large conglomerate – we'll call it Diehard Associates – was the firm's major client. It, and its affiliated companies, represented almost forty per cent of CC's business. CC handled all of Diehard's big campaigns. This gave Bill an opportunity to hobnob with the company's president, board chairman, and leading executives.

Constanza is an impressive fellow. Whenever a campaign seemed in trouble, Constanza would solve the problem. For example, Diehard wanted to set up a national ad campaign built around charge-free telephone numbers. These numbers would be advertised in national periodicals and on TV. Consumers would be asked a question requiring a yes or no vote and the poll would be tied in with the company's latest product.

From the very beginning, the campaign provided nothing but headaches. There was the expense of the national phone line, the high costs of national TV advertising and nation-wide print ads. The price tag was becoming more than the budget could absorb. A fundamentally solid idea was about to be nickled and dimed to death.

Constanza went to work. Doing some fast research, he discovered that it would be more cost effective to get national coverage on a region-by-region basis. Bill could arrange deals with each of the regional phone companies and buy local print ads. This not only lowered the bills, it also allowed Diehard to maintain tighter control on the campaign's demographics. The phone promotion went through without a hitch.

One week later, CC tackled another Diehard emergency. This time, the company needed a print ad. For reasons too complex to chronicle, they had to have it done immediately – as in yesterday. Constanza and his partner, Ray Calo, wrote the copy in less than two hours. They hired a photographer and models, and scouted a shooting location. Constanza even acted as prop man for the shoot. Within forty-eight hours the photos were finished and the ads were being processed. It was a first-rate job. Had it been bungled, a national promotion would have been postponed, and possibly shelved. Constanza had saved Diehard's bacon.

These were entrepreneurial solutions and they bowled Diehard over. It decided to make the CC Agency part of its big happy family. An offer was made to Bill and Ray. They would join Diehard as vice-presidents in charge of advertising and promotion. As they learned Diehard's business, they would be dealt a hand in marketing and public relations. In return, they would each receive base salaries of $100,000. This would be augmented by bonuses and profit-sharing incentives. A sweet deal, especially for a company that had only been in existence for just under three years.

Calo, a bachelor, turned the offer down. He walked off with a nice buy-out for his share of the agency. Constanza, married with twin sons and a third child on the way, grabbed the security the offer represented.

Bill has now been with the company for a year. In addition to his base, he picked up a $15,000 bonus and is due for an equal sum from his profit-sharing plan. The company loves his work. It is thriving, and its success makes his position that much more secure. Bill is miserable.

When he got hooked up with Diehard, Bill figured they were as entrepreneurial as he was. Once in, he found he had been operating under an illusion. Since Diehard had always appreciated his troubleshooting, he thought they would allow his freewheeling approach to influence their ad campaigns. No way. Diehard had a preconceived notion of how their ads worked. Constanza was allowed to deviate only when obstacles arose. Whenever he asked why the company had to follow a certain line, he was told, 'Because that is how we've always done it and that is what has always worked.'

Bill also found the corporate structure unpalatable. He was used to informal brainstorming sessions with Ray at all hours of the day. At Diehard, he was chained to a system of boring meetings and duelling memos. One afternoon, he tried to drop by the office of the guy in charge of marketing. He wanted to have a quick chat about the direction of the company. Since Bill didn't have an appointment, his sudden appearance nearly caused cardiac arrest in both the marketing director and his secretary.

Being an entrepreneur, Bill was turned off by corporate politics. It seemed as if most of the executives spent an inordinate amount of time avoiding failure rather than risking success. They cared little about the company's growth. As long as their pay cheques cleared and no one was able to accuse them of making even the tiniest mistake, they were happy. There is no way an entrepreneur can survive in this environment. Bill now realizes that all the security in the world can't replace that entrepreneurial sizzle. He is looking to make a move. His family has adopted a strict budget. A large part of Bill's earnings are accumulating in a savings account, and he is already in discussion with Ray and his former cronies. Despite the salary and the perks, I think a vice-president's slot will open up at Diehard before the year is out.

Bill made a mistake getting involved with Diehard. That's understandable. It's easy to be dazzled by monetary rewards and the seeming safety of a position with a prosperous organization. But before signing on, you have to be sure you're not entering into an agreement with the Devil. Take a look at the company's public face. Is it an enterprise that always seems to be forging new ground? Talk to the company's personnel and clients. Find out how the corporation reacts to innovation. Make sure you can fit. An investigation of a few hours can save you a lot of grief.

Riklis 1 Kiam 0

I've always advised fledgling entrepreneurs to join companies in a 'line' position. This means you want a job that produces results that can be measured on the bottom line, such as salesman. You need to have a measurable impact on the company. Don't worry about salary. The financial rewards will come. Whatever route you're on should lead to the top of the company.

You want to be president of every enterprise that employs you. That's the ultimate. If you miss – and there can be, after all, only one president – you should still reach a pretty high level. I wanted to be president of Lever Brothers. Had I stayed, I like to believe I would have made it. I also wanted to be president of Playtex. I came close. I was on a fast track until outside forces derailed me. Losing the opportunity to reach my goal was one of my biggest disappointments.

In 1967, I was president of Playtex's Sarong division. Sarong had been a rival girdle manufacturer. I had helped Playtex acquire the company and had been installed as its head. The Playtex president – and my immediate superior – was the dynamic Harry Stokes. Playtex itself was a subsidiary of the Stanley Warner corporation, a movie theatre company owned by Si Fabian and his brother-in-law, Sam Rosen. Rosen and Fabian had acquired the company in 1953 as part of a diversification programme. Now they were getting on in years, I thought they might consider selling the company.

Al Peterson, the head of our US company, joined Mr Stokes and me in making a proposal to Rosen and Fabian. This had to be delicately handled. I mean you couldn't exactly barge in on Si and Sam and say, 'Look guys, neither one of you are long for this world, so we think it might be a good time for you to sell the company.' Instead, as in any good negotiation, we concentrated on what was in it for them. I said, 'Gentlemen, you're both past seventy. We're sure you might want to consolidate your estate at some point. If you ever do, we have a plan for the selling of Playtex that should maximize your benefits. It will also present the best opportunity for your employees.'

Contrary to what you might think, neither man was offended. They were pragmatic businessmen. In fact, they thanked us for showing so much concern for the company. They also promised to read our plan.

We had proposed selling the company to Avon Cosmetics. Avon was the number one cosmetics company with massive door-to-door distribution. Playtex was number one in girdles and bras. We could give Avon a vital entry into the retail world through department stores, notion shops, and discounters. Avon would also have been able to augment Playtex by marketing some of our products door-to-door. It seemed a good synergy. Al Peterson – a crackerjack executive not given to superlatives or patting his own back – thought the proposal was brilliant.

Unfortunately, I don't think either Si or Sam gave it much consideration. They did come to a decision to sell shortly after our meeting. They did not come to us or Avon. Instead, they turned the transaction over to the Boston banker who had arranged their original purchase of Playtex.

That gentleman arranged to sell the company to one Meschusalem Riklis. This prospect didn't please me. I felt Mr Riklis was more of a financial operator than a business builder. His history seemed to indicate that he bought companies only to sell them for a quick profit. Nothing wrong with that. However, entrepreneurs are interested in more than just a fast dollar. If all you want to do is increase your capital, do the world a favour. Play the horses. Take a gamble on the stock exchange. Don't pass yourself off as an entrepreneur. Entrepreneurs want to build businesses, to take them beyond their perceived potential.

Playtex's continued growth was my number one priority. I doubted it would rate as high under a Riklis stewardship. The welfare of the employees was another strong concern. If Playtex underwent a radical change in direction, there could be a destabilizing effect on everyone in the company.

As a corporate stockholder, I was also unhappy with the price Riklis was offering: about fifty-five dollars a share. Playtex was as successful as any company you could name. Almost every one of our divisions stood at the top of its market. I felt the company was worth much more than Riklis was offering.

I called Harry Stokes. We found we shared the same feelings. At thirty-seven years old, I was a novice in high finance. Naivety breeds confidence. I was positive we could come up with the money to beat the Riklis offer. Harry suggested we convene a meeting of like-minded executives.

We invited Al Peterson. A good choice. He had joined us in our proposal to Fabian and Rosen. I also judged his business philosophy to be diametrically opposed to this particular take-over. My last call went to an executive vice-president named Stan Youmans. Wrong move. In *Rumpole of the Bailey* you are taught never to ask a witness a question if you're not sure of the answer. The results can be disastrous. In attempting this sort of clandestine operation, never ask anyone to join unless you're certain of where they stand. Youmans's response to my invitation was a curt, 'No, I don't think I can make that meeting.' I didn't have to be a breaker of codes to decipher that line. It meant trouble.

We proceeded with the meeting anyway. I told Harry and Al that I was certain Youmans was about to throw in with Riklis if he hadn't done so already. After thinking about it none of us was surprised, making my mistake seem all the more glaring.

The meeting opened with an outline detailing my opposition to the Riklis bid. To my amazement, Peterson disagreed with my assessment. He felt we had no way of knowing what Riklis would do with the company after the purchase. More importantly, he doubted we could attract a better offer. Al didn't think our risk-reward ratio looked very promising. He decided to sit this one out.

Stokes and I were on our own. We decided we couldn't afford to approach the usual financial markets for capital. There was no way of going down to Wall Street without our actions becoming public knowledge. Instead, our proposal was taken to Avon, our original choice. They shot us down. We then called on some friends possessing contacts in the corporate investment world.

One of them, a fellow named Ed Williams, was the executive vice-president of the Schlitz Brewing Company. Owned by the Uhlein family, it was the number two brewery in the US and it was looking to diversify into other consumer products. Williams thought Playtex offered some intriguing possibilities. After speaking to me, he put together a meeting with the Uhleins.

Harry and I were brought to the estate of Bob Uhlein – the Schlitz chief executive officer (CEO) – by a company helicopter on a rainy Sunday evening. A meeting of the family was convened two hours after our arrival. The most respected family member was Uncle Irwin. Owner of 15 per cent of the company, he had been Bob Uhlein's corporate predecessor. At first, I directed a good deal of our presentation towards him, since I thought his voice could help sway the others.

This was probably my second mistake. Uncle Irwin was eighty-seven years old. He really didn't have much enthusiasm for this sort of affair. I'm bombarding him and the others with charts, graphs, facts and figures. Uncle Irwin responds by dozing off during most of our dog and pony show. He seemed intent on punctuating my talk with the worst snoring you've ever heard. That wouldn't have been so awful if he had stayed asleep. He didn't. Every five minutes or so, he would wake up, and announce: 'When you lay down with dogs, you get up with fleas.' Then he'd nod off again. It was frightfully encouraging. Making it worse, he made this withering pronouncement with the timing of Perle Mesta, America's legendary society hostess. It always seemed to cut through the room right as I was making a particularly telling point. For example, I would say, 'And Playtex has gone through twenty-five years of sustained growth, proving . . .' ' . . . when you lay down with dogs, you get up with fleas.' Arf!

Somehow, we got through the presentation without my strangling Uncle Irwin. The family voted to take up the matter at a full board meeting one week from the following Monday. Harry and I were encouraged. We felt we had made a pretty good pitch, despite Irwin and his dogs. From words spoken after our meeting, we felt we already had Bob Uhlein in our corner.

The presentation before the board of directors went smoothly. Uncle Irwin was on good behaviour. When it was over, we were asked to wait outside while the matter was put to a vote. There were only twelve people being polled so I figured we'd have a decision in about fifteen minutes. Boy, did I have a lot to learn. Four hours later, we were called back into the room.

The result had been a tie. I've often heard athletes say that playing to a tie is like kissing your sister. It doesn't quite make it. I've got news for them. Their assessment is generous. The feeling you're left with is that of an ill-used rope after a tug-of-war. You're pulled by elation because of the closeness of your dream, you're wrenched by depression over the proximity of disappointment.

Bob Uhlein told us he would push for us. He also explained that the person with the tie-breaking vote was on a trip to Europe and would return for a second vote on the following Monday. Bob told us we needn't bother to come back. He would call us with the result. I thanked Bob for his support and thanked God the tie-breaking vote wouldn't be cast by Uncle Irwin.

Perhaps it should have been. The board turned us down a week later. Harry and I scrambled to find other investors. We pitched Scott Paper. No interest. We went to Darrel Ruttenberg of Studebaker. He had recently merged his company with Worthington Pump. Darrell just couldn't see acquiring a corset company after having just bought a pump manufacturer. He felt the businesses were too diverse. On Thanksgiving Day, we brought the idea to Nate Cummings of Consolidated Foods. The decision to meet with him on a holiday was entrepreneurial. We wanted to stand out. On a normal business day, we might have been one of ten companies on his agenda. An early Thanksgiving meeting guaranteed we'd be his only business meeting of the morning. Our enterprise didn't sway him. He rejected our proposal.

Looking back, I can now say we took the wrong route in this attempted acquisition. There was a group of companies that could have been approached that would never hear about the opportunity because we didn't call on them. We had felt limited in our choices by our decision to conduct this as a clandestine operation. Major error. Within twenty-four hours of our initial proposal to Schlitz, Riklis and his associates knew exactly what we were doing. He didn't need Mr Youmans to tell him. Though we didn't know it at the time, you couldn't keep something like this a secret.

Right after we had left Schlitz, its financial officers were phoning investment bankers, asking them for information on us and Playtex. It didn't take long for word to hit the street. Apparently, the only two people who were unaware of the attention our actions were receiving were Harry and I. Two babes in the wood. In the financial world, if one more person than you knows your secret, it is no longer a secret.

I now realize that we should have made our intentions public from the outset. We should have gone to the institutions that had invested in Playtex and had seen a healthy return on their money. We were the people who had built the business; they would have backed us. That might sound like conjecture. It's not. Months later, I was in the process of buying the Benrus Company. One of the investment firms involved had held a financial stake in Playtex. I told him how we had fought to hold on to the company. He said, 'Yes? Well, why didn't you come to us? Hell, we would have backed you to the hilt.'

I wish we had been wise enough to have known that then. Riklis took over the company. A week after the acquisition, Stan Youmans – Playtex's new CEO – called me into his office and simply said, 'Too bad, old boy.' I knew what that meant. One, it was too bad that you picked the wrong side and two, I am the new head man and you, Mr Kiam, will be working under me. If, of course, you're working here at all.

In early Roman history, when a coup against the emperor failed, the plotters lost their heads. Fate was only slightly kinder to our Gang of Two. It was strongly suggested that I seek employment elsewhere. I left Playtex in mid-January 1968. Sixty-five year old Harry Stokes was forced into early retirement. Al Peterson, having kept himself above the fray, was moved to the corporate staff of Riklis's other entities. Stan Youmans was rewarded with the company's top spot.

It was a bitter ending. On the surface, I took my departure with my usual equanimity. In reality, I was shattered. I felt as if malignant elves were prancing about my stomach, shredding my innards with razor blades. My career with Playtex had lasted thirteen years. In the marrow of my bones I had never doubted that I would one day be company president. Everything I had accomplished there seemed to affirm that opinion. When I was forced to leave, it seemed as if my world had come to an end. I had to start all over.

I must admit it gave me very little satisfaction to see my

predictions about Playtex come true. Once Riklis took over, Playtex's growth just about came to a halt. Youmans was a cost-cutter. Under his regime, the company reduced their investments in advertising, marketing, and development. Everything that had made Playtex the giant that it was had been truncated. The company tried to coast on its past reputation. Not good enough. Market share and profits dropped off dramatically. Riklis began dismantling the company. He sold divisions, merged Playtex with another outfit, then disposed of some more pieces. Finally, he sold the whole company to the Swift Packing Company. That gave us a chuckle. Throughout my tenure with Playtex, we had had an indelicate nickname, the 'Meatpackers'. Now the company had been sold to one of the largest meatpacking firms in the world.

I have to admit something. Despite my failure to pull Playtex out of the Riklis grasp, I'm glad I made the attempt. Yes, my approach was haphazard. I should have modified it. But I'm glad Harry and I took a stand. The entrepreneur has to have values. These values can only be defined by how strongly you're willing to fight for them. The most important thing to us was the company's continued growth and the happiness of the employees. When we felt these were threatened, we couldn't turn our backs. Playtex meant too much to us. As it turned out, my failed attempt to take over the company was one of the greatest experiences of my life. It was the start of an education. Our shortcomings forced me to be better prepared for participation in the world of finance. It also made me look for new opportunities. Without this temporary failure, I might never have become 'The Man Who Bought the Company'.

A haunting failure of the soul

I've often said that the entrepreneur can't measure his success with mere dollars and cents. He also can't always find his losses in the red ink of a bottom line. Believe me. The greatest failure

I've ever had didn't cost me a dime. It just took a huge chunk out of my soul.

It began while I was still with Playtex as head of Sarong. I was calling on the buyer for a large department store in Brooklyn, New York. On the way up to her office, I noticed a sizable crowd had gathered on one of the selling floors. They had been drawn together by a baby-faced young salesman hawking a manually operated kitchen utensil that did everything. It sliced, diced, mashed, and juiced meat, fruit, or vegetables. The salesman demonstrated it with all the nimbleness of a top-flight surgeon. His hands were flying in twelve different directions at once. This chap really put on quite a show.

His implement was made out of tin. It couldn't have cost more that $1.25 wholesale. This fellow was selling them for ten dollars each and with the way the crowd was reacting you would have thought he was giving away gold. He sold out his entire stock in less than ten minutes.

When he was finished, I approached him. I found out his name was Bobby Dugan. We exchanged small talk for a few minutes and then I said, 'Boy, you are a sensational salesman. If you can get people to buy this gizmo, you can sell anything. Take my card. If you ever want to change your job, give me a call.'

He came to work for me about six months later. His first territory included Brooklyn and the Bronx. These were not prime locales. The stores were small, a large number of them had bad credit, and few of them carried our complete line. He did a superb job. Within six months the area had gone from perennial loser to a prosperous territory. Less than a year after that, Bobby was named district sales manager for New York State.

By the time I left Playtex, Bobby was a regional manager in charge of half the country. He had married a beautiful model and they had an adorable little boy. He eventually moved over to Puritan Fashions as executive vice-president in charge of sales for one of its larger divisions. From all appearances, you had to conclude that Bobby Dugan was living the American dream.

Bobby called me one day. Since last hearing from him, I had taken over the Benrus Watch Company. He congratulated me and said, 'Vic, I'm going to go into business for myself, too. I want to run some thoughts by you and get an opinion.' He was going to go into the direct-mail clothing business. The idea was to pick an area, invite housewives to a fashion show in a local hotel, and provide them with food, drink, and entertainment. He would later take orders and money for the clothes modelled in the show. The concept had jumped past the planning stage. Bobby had contracts with several suppliers and had already chosen two cities as test markets. Those first shows were scheduled for Syracuse, New York and Columbus, Ohio in February.

I thought it might be a worthwhile venture, but I warned Bobby that he had better make darn sure that his test was run properly. Syracuse and Columbus were not ideal places to test anything in February. Both cities were prone to heavy snows. Bobby's financing was small; the majority of it was his own capital. The tests would eat up most of that money. It was easy to see that it would only take a slight glitch to halt this enterprise before it really got started.

Bobby didn't share my view. He said, 'No, I think this is the right way to go about it. I don't want to wait. Vic, I've been working for companies for fifteen years and it's time to be my own boss again. I'm so sure this is going to work that I'm going to resign from Puritan next week.'

I felt this was an error. Bobby had a family to support and there was no reason why he couldn't run these tests while staying with his company. Most of the preparation could have been done over the phone at night. Working at it only part-time, he still could have given the run-through a full shot. If the tests proved positive, then he could disconnect the umbilical cord. Should they fail, he could keep collecting a salary until he could afford another test or find a different venture.

I hated to put any dents in his enthusiasm, but I was trying to be realistic. Bobby responded by promising to think over my recommendations. He said he'd get back to me with his final plans.

I didn't hear from him for five months. I subsequently learned that he had followed his original strategy. Bobby left Puritan and ran his February tests in Syracuse and Columbus. On the day of his exhibition, an unforgiving snowstorm blanketed Syracuse. No one came to the event. Bobby lost every nickel he had in the venture. On top of that, he had accepted money from the people who had given him orders at the Columbus test. Their cash was used to cover some of the expenses for the aborted Syracuse run. Now he didn't have the capital to fulfil his customers' orders or to give them a refund.

Bobby's life became unhinged. Lawsuits for non-delivery of goods were being processed. He had fallen behind on the payments for his estate in Connecticut. He and his wife had separated and Bobby was desperate for a reconciliation. The guy needed help. He called me and asked for a job.

Benrus had a jewellery division, the Wells Company. We hired him to sell women's jewellery to accounts in Long Island. It was Playtex all over again. Bobby just set the region on fire. Within three months he was the best salesman we had. He had gone through a rough time, but he still had the magic and I was positive things were going to turn out fine.

Then one morning, while driving to the barbershop, I was listening to a news broadcast. It was the usual potpourri of mundane events until the announcer said, 'Connecticut police are investigating the murder of Alicia Dugan and her maid in Mrs Dugan's palatial Greenwich home. Mrs Dugan's young son was found crying but unharmed in his playroom. Both women were killed by gunshots in the back of the head. Police are trying to locate Mrs Dugan's estranged husband Robert. They are not yet calling him a suspect in the crime.' I nearly drove off the road.

As soon as I reached the barbershop, I called the president of Wells, told him what had happened, and pleaded with him to track Bobby down. He found him calling on a customer. I met with Bobby. Still in shock, he assured me he had nothing to do with the crime. He continued to protest his innocence to the police, but he was unable to supply them with a coherent alibi. The police grilled him for hours. When they were finished, he was booked on suspicion of homicide.

Bobby spent a month in jail. This portion of his ordeal ended when he was released for lack of evidence. He was still a prime suspect in the killing. The police restricted his movement to three states – New York, New Jersey, and Connecticut. He could visit his son, who had been staying with Bobby's parents in Florida since the arrest, but such a trip would require police permission.

We had to fill Bobby's job during his absence. When he returned, we gave him a new position representing Christian Dior – our line of jewellery and leather goods for men – in New York City. Talk about admirable performances. Here was a chap under suspicion for homicide. He was separated from his only child who was living with his parents. The region he returned to had recently lost all of its key accounts. Didn't matter. He built the business back up from nothing. I don't believe I've ever seen a better natural salesman.

During all this, I had taken an interest in a trading company in Kuwait. I needed someone to go overseas to run it. This was a sales-oriented company. The job demanded the talents of some-one who was skilled in opening up untried territories. I thought to myself, 'Holy Christmas, of all the people we have on the payroll, the one guy who can run this thing is Bobby Dugan.'

I asked Bobby if he'd be interested in the position. He wanted it badly. However, he doubted the police would allow him to travel to Kuwait. I said, 'Look, why don't I call the chief of police. I'll explain the conditions of the job and we'll even look into posting bond for your return. We'll let him decide.' I should explain that I was willing to take a certain amount of responsibility for Bobby, because I was certain of his innocence. He had already given me his word that he had had nothing to do with the crime. My instincts told me he wasn't lying.

I made my case to the chief a few days later. The first thing he wanted to know was Bobby's present whereabouts. I told him he was working out of New York while awaiting this decision. That information turned out to be wrong. Bobby *was* working out of New York, but not today. Without telling the police, he had gone off to Florida the previous afternoon – violating the conditions of his release – to visit his son. He had mentioned to me that he might possibly go to Florida. However, when the chief asked me where he was, I assumed Bobby had changed his plans. It didn't occur to me that he would have left without telling the police.

The chief said he wanted to think the idea over and that he would get back to me on the following day. About an hour later, I got a call from the manager of our New York office. Twelve cops had come barging in looking for Bobby Dugan. They had a warrant for his immediate arrest. I was frantic. Now assuming he had indeed gone AWOL, we tried to reach Bobby at his parents'. No luck. We left word with anyone who might see him to make sure he got in touch with us immediately. We didn't hear a peep. That night I was driving home. Once again the radio brought sad tidings. Bobby Dugan had been arrested in Miami. The police had already arranged his extradition back to Connecticut.

Have you ever been smacked between the eyes by a sledge-hammer? That's how I felt when I heard the news. My first thoughts were, 'This is my fault. My phone call triggered all of this. If I'd just kept my mouth shut and not thought about Kuwait, none of this would have happened.' I hadn't foreseen the tempest my request would cause. As soon as the chief heard the word Kuwait, he probably had visions of Bobby disappearing overseas, never to be seen again. Bobby's turning up in off-limits Florida only confirmed his suspicions.

Bobby's bail was set at $1 million. We couldn't raise it. He was placed in a Bridgeport Connecticut jail. When I finally got to see him, he had been in prison for three weeks. It had been harrowing. Bobby was not a big man. He was baby-faced, slim, and almost pretty. The prisoners welcomed him as easy prey. He had been beaten and raped. Two of his front teeth had been knocked out of his head.

We put up money for the defence. The lawyer won his release, again on the grounds of insufficient evidence. It had taken nine months. Though out of jail, Bobby's freedom of movement was again restricted. The state had held the case open and Bobby was still the number one suspect.

The Saturday he got out of jail, I picked him up at the prison. Bobby was beside himself. Claiming to need the protection, he said he was going to buy a gun. He was frightened that some of his fellow inmates, since released, would come looking for him. It was as tragic a thing as you would ever want to see. His eyes no longer glowed with confidence. The effervescent salesman, a guy who could sell flying lessons to eagles, was gone. In his place was this beaten shell whose furtive gaze saw menace in every shadow. I didn't know what I could do for him. I took the afternoon off and spent the entire day with him. We went to see my son in a tennis tournament. I thought that would be good therapy. His parents and son were down in Florida. Bobby was all alone and I wanted to create a family atmosphere for him.

We spoke for hours. By dinnertime, his mood was unchanged. He described the horrors of prison in graphic detail. When I told him that was behind him he said, 'Yes, it is. And I'll never go back there again.' There was nothing vehement in the declaration. It was just a simple truth laid bare.

We gave him his old position with Dior. He threw himself into his work. Meanwhile, the investigation of the Connecticut police failed to furnish any further evidence against him. In fact, stories were now circulating that it had been the maid, not Mrs Dugan, who had been the target of the hit. The maid had apparently worked for figures in the drug trade. She had allegedly stolen something from them, either drugs or money, and the killing was their retribution. Poor Alicia Dugan had merely been in the wrong place at the wrong time. It looked like Bobby was in the clear. Six months after his release, the direct-mail clothing venture came back to haunt him. He had never settled with his customers. We had offered to cover those obligations, but it didn't make a difference. The case was coming to trial.

The results of the hearing were disastrous. Bobby told me

that the judge had promised to throw the book at him. I tried to calm him. I couldn't believe that he would get too harsh a sentence for what was a relatively small mistake. After about an hour of commiseration, I said, 'Trust me Bobby, everything will work out. You have to hang in there.' He cried, 'Vic, it's got to be all right. I just can't face jail again. I can't.'

I had to go down to the Virgin Islands the following afternoon. I was testifying before the Islands' legislature on the question of watch tariffs. Midway through the testimony, the bailiff tapped me on the shoulder. There was an urgent call for me from the US. I asked if he could take a message. He shook his head and said I had better answer the phone immediately. It was the New York police department. Bobby Dugan had committed suicide. He left a note proclaiming his innocence, but declaring he couldn't spend another day in prison.

When you're an entrepreneur, business demands such a large portion of your life. Always remember that any business you're involved with revolves around human beings. Try not to forget that life has the unseemly habit of taking the most vibrant souls and stripping them down to their most naked frailty. When that happens, you have to put the contracts, the appointment books, and the ledgers aside, and give of yourself. Completely.

I honestly believe I did that with Bobby. When he needed advice, money, a job, or just a shoulder to lean on, I had made myself available. But a nagging voice in me charges that I let him down in the end. I'm the guy who has always said business is where you are. My business should have been with Bobby that weekend. I should have listened better when I saw him that last time. I should have recognized the desperate patter that was the final moments of his tap-dance towards the abyss. Maybe I could have found the right words to soothe him. Maybe I should have brought him with me to the Virgin Islands. Maybe I should have cancelled the trip and helped him make it through that hellish final weekend.

Maybe.

There is no greater failure than maybe.

CHAPTER THREE

Selling,
more selling

The entrepreneur is always selling something: an idea, a service, or a product. Business is a game, a lifelong Olympics. Selling is the easiest event to score. At the end of the day all you have to do is ask yourself, 'Did I get the order?' More times than not, the winners answer 'Yes!'

Every sale is a point in your favour. Those of you who have, or are trying to obtain, the entrepreneurial spirit have a distinct advantage over your competitors. The entrepreneur is a risk-taker, daring to be creative. So many people approach selling as just another job. They do everything by rote and their paltry pay cheques and inability to rise on the corporate ladder are direct results of their ho-hum approach.

Don't be afraid of bringing some pizzazz to your work. Sometimes this can take the form of humour. Twenty years ago, when I was with Benrus, I was trying to convince the buyer for K-Mart, the world's largest seller of timepieces, to place more of our watches in his stores. He was already carrying some of our products, but we were his smallest selling line.

I had just taken over the company and wanted to improve our standing with this important client. It had the potential to be a prized account. An appointment was arranged with the buyer. He was a medium-sized, wiry fellow named Bruce Weill. This guy was one ball of fire. Having been with K-Mart for over thirty years, he worked fourteen hour days as a matter of habit. He loved what he did. Companies place a high value on executives of this stamp. They know if they ever lose them it will take three or four people to fill the vacuum. They also treasure his opinion. I knew if I could get Bruce behind Benrus, he'd be a powerful ally.

I liked dealing with Weill. He could be abrupt and quick with his judgements, but his position demanded decisiveness. I enjoyed that because Bruce never wasted your time. He also wasn't a buyer who placed a strong emphasis on personal relationships. Often a buyer depends on a clique of salesmen: having done business with these chaps for years, he feels comfortable with them and is loath to entertain any new faces. Bruce didn't care if you'd been dealing with his company since the time of the Big Bang or were the newest kid on the block. If you represented an item that could earn profits for his company, he would see you.

I was confident that the right approach could sell Bruce on our watch lines. Upon meeting him in his office, I started to go into my presentation. I must say I thought I was scintillating. I trotted out samples and painted a vista of future business that was blinding in its promised magnificence.

Bruce sat through my performance without uttering a word. As soon as I was finished he said, 'You're a newcomer to the watch business, aren't you?' I admitted I was. He continued, 'I thought so. You see, you don't really understand our customers. Let me look at your shoes.' This was not the usual request I encountered at the end of a presentation. In fact, it seemed more than just a bit strange. I thought, 'My God, I'm a president of a company. How can he ask to see my shoes? What does he want to do, see if they are polished to a spit shine?' I was tempted not only to show him my shoes, but also to tell him where he could put them. Then I thought of the large number of outlets this gentleman represented. Without saying a word, I lifted my feet for his inspection.

Glancing at them, Bruce said, 'How surprising. They're just plain leather.' Puzzled, I asked what was so astonishing about that. He explained, 'I expected them to be made out of alligator or some other exotic hide. You see, your watches are priced for the alligator-shoe customer. Most of our customers wear tennis sneakers. I like your watches. The styles are attractive and I know they keep good time. But if you want to sell us, you have to price them for the tennis-shoe consumer. Until that happens, I can't buy them from you because our clientele won't buy them from us.'

That was discouraging, but for the entrepreneur, every rejection is only temporary. If you keep your ears open, today's turndown can bring the opportunity to score more points tomorrow. Bruce had done me a favour. When an account is that clear in his objections, he has given you something tangible to overcome.

I left Weill's office and headed back to Benrus. The next few days were spent in brainstorming sessions. We needed to create a lower-priced watch that retained our product's style and timekeeping ability. This was not an easy problem to solve. It wasn't as if we could merely lower our prices for this one privileged customer. Had we done that, our other accounts would have had our heads for paperweights. No, if the cost was going to drop for this large chain, it was going to drop for everyone. After running through the numbers in every possible combination, we finally hit on a solution.

We had been preparing to launch a national TV campaign and had figured the cost of this advertising into our mark-up. Common sense said that the TV ads would be useless if we didn't have enough outlets carrying our lines. We decided to reduce the amount to be spent on those commercials. We also made some minor changes in the watch construction. For instance, we went from a five micron gold plating to a three micron version. The switch did nothing to alter the product's attractiveness or performance, but it did save us some money. Combined with the major adjustment in our TV marketing mix, we were able to trim our gross profit margin from thirty-three to twenty per cent.

Three weeks after the price drop, I called on Bruce Weill. Knowing his love of brevity, I had created a way to get my message across while using as few words as possible. I entered his office, pulled up a chair, and plopped my feet up on his desk.

Bruce seemed stunned. He was probably about to ask what the hell I was doing, but my shoes caught his attention. They were tennis sneakers. He broke out laughing and I said, 'Bruce, since I was last here, I've been wearing these and thinking about nothing else but your customers. I think I understand their needs. Let me show you our tennis-shoe watches at their tennis-shoe prices.' Bruce liked my presentation. More importantly, he liked our new price tags. He gave me a large order and his company became our largest account.

This presentation was a good ice-breaker. A few laughs go a long way towards making a potential client comfortable. In this case, the joke served a more important role. It immediately told Bruce we had heard his message and had given it our attention. It told him we hadn't given up. This was the key. If we had passively accepted his initial rejection without attempting to solve the pricing puzzle, we would never have opened the account.

Throughout the years, I don't know how often I've heard salespeople complain about accounts that were particularly hard to crack. You'd ask them why they can't make the sale, and they'd say, 'I don't know. I guess he doesn't like our product.' That may be, but it's also possible you're not listening to the buyer. If all you hear is the rejection, you're probably missing valuable clues. *Don't be afraid to ask why you're not getting the order*. Have the buyer be as specific as possible and write down every comment he makes. Then approach that list the way you would approach the Intangible Balance Sheet we mentioned earlier. Turn those negatives into positives! You still won't be able to satisfy everyone. Nobody can. But you will see a dramatic change in the number of noes that turn into yesses.

It's not always going to be easy. You have a product, service, or a programme. You know that it is the greatest thing since peanut butter. You run up against a buyer or customer who just doesn't share your enthusiasm. His reasons are vague and he's unresponsive to any suggestions you make. In your heart you know that his store is the perfect outlet for your merchandise. If this is the case, it might very well be necessary to go over the buyer's head. My friend, this is one of the most critical situations in selling. It must be delicately handled.

I was up against these circumstances very early in my career as a salesman for Lever Brothers. We had just come out with a wrinkle remover called Ayer Magic. Every buyer I called on thought it was a great product. Every buyer, that is, except an elderly gentleman – call him Moe Kates – who represented Gray Drugs. When I asked Kates why he wouldn't order Ayer Magic, he replied, 'No reason. I just don't think it's much of a product.'

That was all he would say. Now, I know I told you to examine any clues you get during a rejection, but I think you'll admit even Jane Marple would have a hard time with this one. I went back to Kates several times, and always left with the same response. I did write down, 'Doesn't think it's much of a product,' but what could I do with that? Have Kates lobotomized until he docilely accepted anything I stuck in his hand? I didn't think that solution sounded very promising.

I had to come up with something. Gray's was potentially my biggest account and a failure there would have been damaging. I took a hard look at Ayer Magic. Was it everything I thought it was? Every other buyer I had sold it to seemed to agree with my assessment. Thumbing through their purchase orders I thought, 'This is ridiculous. These results prove I have one hell of a cosmetic here.' Certain I was right, I called Gray's merchandise manager Robert Meachum. I said, 'Mr Meachum, I have a product called Ayer Magic. It's going great guns throughout the region. This cosmetic has been presented to your buyer three times and he doesn't see any merit in it. I think he's wrong. Gray's is missing out on a tremendous opportunity here and I would like you to review this decision.' I requested a meeting with Meachum for the next afternoon and insisted that Kates be invited.

Once in Meachum's office I said, 'Bob, I admire and respect Moe. I've worked with him for eight months and think he is a real pro. But what we have here is a simple difference of opinion. I want to present my programme, let Moe air his objections, and then let you be the arbiter.' Then I made my pitch. I showed him what Ayer Magic could do, pointed out how there was nothing like it on the market, and showed him how other accounts had enthusiastically greeted the product. In selling, this is known as 'painting the vista'. I was enticing the customer with a picture of the product in all of its potential glory.

When I was finished, Meachum turned to Kates and asked him why he was against Ayer Magic. For the first time in my presence, Kates explained that he was introducing a new cosmetic with Revlon and that he doubted the store could get behind two big promotions simultaneously. Meachum asked if they were similar products. They weren't. Meachum replied, 'Well, Moe, normally I would agree with you about supporting two promotions at once. But this Ayer Magic is something brand new and different. It could really be exciting. I think we ought to try it. You and Vic should get together and see if you can't work out a programme.'

That's exactly what we did and it was such a big success that after a while Moe forgot that he had ever had any objections to carrying Ayer Magic. Let's look at what happened here. First, I examined the product to make sure I wasn't fooling myself on its viability. Then, I went to the buyer's boss, but insisted Kates be brought into the meeting. You don't want anyone to get the impression you're sneaking around behind the buyer's back. No matter what the outcome, you will probably have to be dealing with that buyer in the future. You don't want this person as an enemy.

At the start of the presentation, I tried to smooth things over by complimenting Kates. That bit of ego massage and my calling the matter nothing more than a difference of opinion took some of the edge off our dispute. Finally, when I made the presentation, I was ready for anything. Every piece of information I needed to make my case was at my fingertips. This was so important. If you jump over a buyer's head, you want his boss to believe you had just cause. A dazzling, well-informed presentation will go a long way towards accomplishing this.

Of course, your best evidence will be the product itself. You have to believe in it with all your heart. If you have any doubts about it at all, don't try to trump the buyer. Understand the risks. A failure will see you hit over the head with 'I told you so's' for as long as you call on the account. You'll never be able to go over his head again and you'll be hard-pressed to sell the buyer on any other new ideas. If, however, you know you have a winner, go get them. A success will heal any wounds suffered by the buyer's pride, and it will make him more receptive to any programmes you bring him in the future.

I've always maintained that the entrepreneur has to stand out from the mob. Tennis shoes and jumping over a buyer's head when the situation calls for it were, in a sense, offshoots of that philosophy. You can't be afraid to put yourself on the line. However, don't get the idea that the entrepreneurial salesman is given *carte blanche* to exercise his creativity. Be as wild and wacky as you want in the planning stages of any concept. Stretch your imagination to the limit. But when it comes to the actual fulfilment of a programme, you have to ask yourself, 'Does this help sell the product? Will it be cost and time effective?' Importing twenty hula dancers from Hawaii to accompany you while calling on an account might set you apart from your competitors, but will the expense lead to a loss? Will the hoopla get you the order or is it just gossamer hype?

Wells, the jewellery division of Benrus, had a salesman named Dick Dotson. A bright, personable fellow, he was a crack operator. He did have one problem. No matter what an account asked him to do, no matter how extravagant, Dick would do it. He would hire fashion models to walk through the stores wearing our jewellery. Another time, he gave away a free bottle of perfume with the purchase of any Benrus item. These small promotions were costly and they did nothing to increase his bottom line.

Once a large account told him they didn't want to carry the same jewellery as their competitors. They asked if all the pieces we sent them could have at least a subtle difference from those sent to other stores. For instance, if an ornamental gold leaf on a bracelet went from left to right, they wanted the leaves on their bracelets to go from right to left. Dick should have told them it was impossible. He had some leverage. Our jewellery line was a best-seller for this retail chain and they were as interested in making profits as we were. Instead, he said, 'No problem. We'll custom design stuff specifically for your store.' That was just great. Our factory was going to be suddenly discombobulated by the new, separate line. This would wreak havoc on our inventory. Because these items would be for one customer, the volume would be very low and our margins were going to get shot to pieces. Even if we sold every piece, we couldn't make money.

Dick and I had quite a row over this one. I listened to his reasoning, took a look at his plan, and overruled him. Then, I took the time to explain my thinking. This was a creative guy. You can't have him racing off with every promotional zephyr that blew his way, but you also do not want to suppress that terrific mind of his. A fellow like this has the makings of a master marketeer, he just needs direction.

I told him that there had been one thing essentially wrong with all of his recent promotions. It wasn't the expense. You can justify a short-term decrease on your bottom line, if the long-term results are sufficiently beneficial. I wasn't all that upset that the programmes had been duds. Minor failures like the perfume give-away should not discourage the entrepreneur. They should, though, make him examine his methods.

Hiring the models wasn't a bad idea. It was a common practice in our industry. Bedecked in our latest pieces, they would parade throughout the store, and entice customers into the jewellery department. But since everyone else was doing it, without Dotson coming up with a creative new wrinkle – which he hadn't done – the promotion lacked a USP. In addition, Wells jewellery was not ultra-chic. It really shouldn't have been showcased in such a high-fashion promotion. Dotson made another mistake by hiring the models to work from store opening to closing, six days a week. There just wasn't enough customer traffic to justify this expense. On certain late nights, he could very well end up with more models on the floor than shoppers. If you were going to launch this programme, it should have been targeted for a day when it could reach its maximum audience. Saturday and certain weekday afternoons would have been better choices. You could have reached more customers in a concentrated time period and maximized the return on your marketing dollar. As it was, the pithy increase in business could not offset the expense incurred by the promotion. Again, it wasn't an awful premise. But even the best concept is worthless if it lacks proper execution.

The perfume give-away was a bomb. I believe in give-aways when they are used to introduce products to the public, act as a market test, or lead directly to an additional sale. For instance, we once gave away charm bracelets. With each one, we also gave the customer two free charms. Do you know how naked a charm bracelet looks with only two trinkets dangling from it? This give-away was almost guaranteed to compel the customer to buy our full set of charms. In another example, Remington recently brought out a powder shaving stick. It is made to stiffen whiskers for an even closer shave. We introduced and in a sense market-tested the item by including a sample with every Remington shaver. The consumer could try it and, if he liked it, purchase additional sticks for future use. Dotson's free scent promotion did not have this advantage. We were not in the perfume business. The programme did not introduce a new product. Had it increased our volume, which it hadn't, most of the additional profits would have been wiped out by the cost of the perfume. It was just a bad idea.

After our meeting, Dotson took a different track. Every programme he proposed was created with the idea of bringing the public to the product. Sometimes this involved nothing more than physically enhancing the display of our merchandise. Other programmes featured special prices for jewellery sets. Pieces bought as part of a group would cost less than pieces bought individually. The profits were affected only marginally and this was outweighed by the increase in volume. That's the sort of promotion you have to love.

I mentioned earlier how going over a buyer's head was one of the most critical situations you would ever face. Here's another toughy: taking over a territory from a popular salesman. Some people have such dynamic personalities that they become as important as the product. To many of their customers, they *are* the product. There is no telling what can happen when these buyers are confronted by a new face. It's very hard to transfer personal loyalty.

When I took over Sarong girdles for Playtex, I met with our district manager in Boston. His name was Joe Rafter and he was seventy-three years old. His sales force was made up of three other guys: Eddie Kramer, who had been with the company for forty-six years, Howard Hunt, a thirty-seven-year man, and Freddie Gibbons, who had twenty-four years of service. The others referred to Freddie as the new man. If you included Joe, the four of them had been with the company for over one hundred and sixty years!

You can imagine the relationships these fellow had built up with their accounts. Howard Hunt was especially well loved. Whenever he went into a store he gave every salesperson and buyer a stick of chewing gum. It was his calling card. People would come up to him and say, 'Howard, don't you like me anymore? You haven't given me any gum yet!' Howard would hand them a stick, chat about the weather, and then make a sale. I knew these boys could not go on for ever. When it came time for their retirement, the company had a chance to be in a hell of a fix. How on earth do you replace a lifetime of good will?

We formulated a plan. I asked each of the four to inform us of their retirement four to six months prior to the fact. As soon as they did, I would give them a hand-picked replacement. The new salesman would travel around with the veteran and get to know his accounts. Eddie Kramer would go up to a buyer and say, 'This young boy is going to be taking over for me when I retire in a few months. He's a good man and I've taught him everything I know. See that you take care of him or I'll come back to haunt you.' Howard Hunt had his replacement handing out chewing gum. It made for a nice smooth transition.

When I was with Lever Brothers, I took over a territory from a living legend. Harold Paine had been with the company for over thirty years. He was forced out of action one day when he fell in his bathtub and injured his back. I was moved into the breach. Harold had the same strong ties to his buyers as the four sunshine boys in Boston. Unfortunately, his injury kept him from introducing me to his long-time friends. Realizing this, Harold called each one of his accounts and explained why I was taking over the territory. He told them to be nice to me. Believe me, they were and it made my first selling experience a lot easier than it might otherwise have been.

One of the things I learned in that early time was to keep parts of my predecessor's system intact. We drew up a list of every account's foibles. If Harold had coffee with a particular buyer on Wednesday, I continued the practice. Eventually I would exert my own personality, but only after establishing myself with the accounts.

Of course, if you're taking over from a popular salesman who has been fired, your task becomes that much harder. Like the loss of a loved one, accounts can take the dismissal of a friendly salesman very badly. All you can tell a disgruntled buyer is, 'Look I know you loved Barry. I loved Barry, too. But for reasons not known to you or me, he's no longer with the company. I had no part in that decision, but I promise I will do as good a job as Barry did, if not better.' Then work your buns off to deliver and hope time really does heal all wounds.

It's going to take a while. I learned that the hard way. We had a salesman at Benrus – Bill Whitson – who was practically the king of Lower Manhattan. He made over 100,000 dollars a year and would call on accounts in a chauffeur-driven limo. Talk about calling cards, this one was several steps ahead of a stick of chewing gum.

I went into Benrus with Al Peterson. He was very conscious

of our bottom line and when he got a gander at Whitson's earnings he nearly had apoplexy. Al figured we could hire three salesmen for what we were paying Bill. I said, 'Yes, but this guy has been with the company for over forty years. He know's the buyers and their families. We have to protect those friendships.' Al wouldn't hear it. All he thought about was how three salesman could cover three times the territory of one. The sales force was my domain, but I respected Peterson's greater experience. I acquiesced to his decision.

What a catastrophe! The first thing Whitson did was sign on with a competitor. We lost every large account in Manhattan. They figured that they had lived with Whitson for forty years. He was family. If our company was going to treat him so shabbily, they weren't going to do business with us. The three salesmen who replaced Bill couldn't even earn their keep. We ended up with one man for the entire territory and he did less than 20 per cent of the business Whitson had delivered.

I learned two things from this. First, in selling, treat relationships as if they were precious gems. Second, never think you can save corporate funds by merely cutting loose a large salary. Don't worry about what an employee is making. What is that person's value to the company? You will often find the person was worth every single penny he earned and more. As an entrepreneur, I want to see everybody on our payroll making as much money as possible. If they are enjoying an enormous success, so is the company.

Taking over from a popular salesman is hard enough, but taking over from someone who has been ripping-off his accounts brings a whole new set of problems. When I was a regional sales manager with Playtex, we employed a chap named Ralph Carney. He had to have been the hardest working salesman I'd ever seen. On the few occasions when we called on accounts together, he would pick me up at 6.45 a.m. We'd be on the customer's doorstep before the store was opened. I always recommend that salespeople make the most of their day – don't even stop for lunch. Eat on the run and use that valuable time to call on accounts. Carney took this philosophy one step further. He wouldn't eat at all. His entire waking day was consumed by his drive to get the orders.

Every week, he led all the other salesmen in our region in volume. He didn't seem to sell any large orders to any single customer, but he had a remarkable consistency. Every store he called on would buy one of everything. In the trade, this was known as 'selling ones' and it was not an uncommon practice. Stretched out over a fourteen-hour day the sales mounted up. When I asked him why he used this method, he explained, 'I have a daily goal. I want to sell one of every item we have to every account I call on. That way they have a complete range of our merchandise. The stuff moves very quickly, so I get immediate reorders on my next trip back. I think it's a good way to gradually build up the business. The total volume is impressive, but none of my individual customers feels that he's been squeezed by a hard sell.'

This made sense, but I later found out that there was another reason why Mr Carney was so bent on selling ones. We had a big promotion earmarked for late September. During his last few trips prior to the campaign, he accumulated more orders than ever. I mean his volume went through the roof. He wanted all these orders tied in with the autumn promotion. This meant they would be processed and delivered after 25 September. On 25 October, we gave Carney his monthly commission cheque. Naturally it included all those sales we had processed for him in September. It was over $12,000. In 1958, the average American worker was earning slightly more than half that amount as a yearly salary. The day after cashing this cheque, Carney shocked everybody by resigning. He offered personal reasons as his excuse.

Personal reasons, my foot. Less than a week after his resignation, we started to receive an unusually heavy number of returns. It went on for days. Almost all of the merchandise came from Carney's territory. I called on the accounts to find out what the problem was. I was afraid that there might have been a product defect that our quality-control people hadn't caught before shipping.

It was nothing like that. Instead, each of the accounts claimed they had received more bras and girdles than they had ordered. Checking the paperwork against our shipping files, I couldn't see a discrepancy. Each purchase order showed four of each item had been bought and signed for by the account.

I called on several buyers with this proof of purchase. When they took out their own records of the transaction, we found they matched ours. In every store, I received the same reaction. The buyer would scratch his head and say, 'I don't care what I signed or what these say. I did not order four of everything. I always buy ones. Why would I suddenly change?' After hearing this same story two or three times, I started to sniff an noxious smell. It was emanating from Carney's documents.

I thought back to the last time I had gone out with him. He was very meticulous. Whenever he got through with a sale, he would go over the order with the customer and verify exactly what had been bought. As he ticked off each number he would put a check mark next to it. Then he would have the buyer sign his slip. Examining these purchase orders carefully, I soon realized what Carney had done. He had followed his usual procedure. Only this time he used a tiny L-shaped check mark and he had slashed it through all of the ones. This transformed the ones into fours! He did this with every damned order. No wonder his sales had quadrupled. No wonder he had been so quick to resign.

All his accounts were overloaded and we now had to contend with one angry group of accounts. I called in Fred Talbot, the fellow who had replaced Carney. I told him what had happened. There is only one thing you can do in a situation like this. Your company's reputation is at stake and you know how much value is to be placed on that. You have to be honest with your accounts. Then pray that they understand.

We called on each of the injured buyers. Before anyone had an opportunity to throw something at us, we explained we weren't looking for new orders. We had come to pick up their returns. Then we showed them the signed forms and explained how they had been fleeced. Realizing the mistake was partially

their own made them that much more forgiving. Taking back
the extra stock ensured we were restored to their good graces.

Funny thing. During this minor tempest, one fellow in St
Joseph, Missouri got as overstocked as anyone, but he didn't
seem to mind. He paid his bill without complaint. From all
appearances, he must have been doing some business. Fred
and I called on him one afternoon.

We were looking over our merchandise when he joined us
on the storeroom floor. We told him we were his Playtex
representatives. He said, 'Ah, Playtex. You boys make this
item here.' He pointed to one of our more well known models.
I proudly replied, 'Yes sir, we do. That's our Living Bra!' He
answered, 'Well, for you it may be living, but for me it's a dead
duck.' I broke up. It turned out he was just as overladen with
undergarments as his competitors, but had been too timid to
say anything. He explained, 'Well, the temperature can get up
there in August when I made this order. After it arrived, my
records confirmed I had signed for the purchase. I figured the
heat must have gotten to me, so it was my headache.' Poor
guy. He had a small shop and was stuck with enough inventory
to last him for a decade. We took back all of his overload too.
If your customer thinks he's been had, you have to make him
happy. He is your lifeline to growth and profitability. We could
have looked at the matching records, seen all those bogus fours
and said, 'Tough. If they didn't want them, they shouldn't have
signed for them.' We could also have slit our wrists. It would
have had the same result.

As a salesperson, keeping the customer satisfied is your chief
responsibility. Getting the order is your goal, but you're not
going to reach it without that customer or buyer's help. It's a
basic fact of business. Yet, I've seen salespeople violate this
ancient bromide time and time again. Then they wonder why
they aren't enjoying success.

Teddy Barnes is a copywriter I've worked with on occasion.
Let me share a story he recently told me. Teddy's staff is always
expanding. As his operation becomes more computerized, he
is constantly investing in new software. One day he needed a

program that allowed him to place the information stored in his computer in orderly files. Without it, the computer's access time would be markedly slowed. He was told about a piece of software that not only maintained a streamlined system, it would also retrieve any material that had been accidentally deleted.

He picked this little marvel up at a newly opened computer shop, we'll name it Blotto Computers, around the corner from his office. It cost $35.00. He brought it back to work, slipped the disk into his PC, pressed his keyboard and . . . nothing. The program didn't work.

On his way home that evening, he took the software back to Blotto. The salesman put it up on his computer and got the same result. A blank screen. The salesman checked and found there weren't any replacements in stock. Then he turned to Ted and sniffed, 'Here is the phone number of the manufacturer. The best thing to do is to call them and tell them what happened.' Teddy couldn't believe his ears. He said, 'I bought the software here and I am bringing it back to you. You see it doesn't work. I want my money back!' I should mention that Teddy is the sort of chap who believes you can get more with a left hook and a kind word than just a kind word. The cavalier attitude of this salesman was pushing him towards his usually low boiling point.

Recognizing this, the salesman called over his store owner. The boss was a fat little guy who looked like the Michelin man dressed in a Hawaiian shirt and Jack Nicholson sun glasses. He told Teddy, 'I'm sorry. But store policy is that we don't give refunds.' When angered, Teddy has eyes that would put the fear of God into Clint Eastwood. He turned these lasers on the boss and said, 'I don't give a damn about your store policy. You are the owner. You are the store policy. Give me back my money or I'll stuff you into your cash register.' As negotiations go, this was one hell of an opening gambit. The owner reached over, took Teddy's software, and again placed it in the store's PC. Another blank screen. Noticing Teddy's ham-like fists, the owner said, 'Well, I guess we should give you a refund.'

Teddy shook the owner's hand and left with his money. When he told me the story he said, 'You know I was really pleased that this store had opened so close to the office. Its prices were excellent and I was going to be needing a lot of software. It's really too bad because I will never walk into that store again. Not too long ago I bought a program at a different shop, a member of a large chain. Their stuff is more expensive than Blotto Computers. I had a problem with it. It required a colour monitor and I have a monochrome. My fault. I didn't read the packaging thoroughly. I brought it back and started to tell the salesman about the mistake I had made. He would have been perfectly within his rights to say tough luck. Instead, the salesman stopped me in mid-explanation. He said, "Mr Barnes, it's no problem. This happens all the time. Would you like a credit, an exchange for another product or your money back?" I took an exchange. I was so impressed with the way I was treated, that I've been a regular customer of this store ever since. It doesn't make any difference that their software is often slightly more expensive than their competitors. I'm willing to pay a few extra dollars because I know they stand behind their merchandise.' Teddy then told me that he had already spent over $6000 in that store. Blotto lost that business over a $35 piece of software. A little bit of courtesy and caring. It goes such a long way.

Making the customer happy has to be your first priority. I was recently visiting London and stopped into a local store to buy some magazines. The person behind the counter didn't smile, offer any help, or seem to know very much about their stock. I came away without making a purchase. A few days later, I stopped into a different shop. The salesperson greeted me with a warm hello, helped me with my selection, and – without being asked – offered me some idea of when certain American publications were delivered. When I'm in London again, which shop do you suppose will get my business? The answer is obvious.

The old saying 'Any job worth doing is worth doing well' had to have been conceived by an entrepreneur. Too often, we see people who think of themselves as trapped in mundane jobs. How absurd! They are not trapped by the job, they are trapped in their own attitudes. There isn't any reason why you can't put colour into the drabbest of jobs and turn it into an entrepreneurial springboard.

A young woman started out as a clerk at an American department store. It is the closest thing we have to Harrods. She was one of over 2000 clerks working at this large store. Along with her usual duties, she made it a point to learn the whereabouts of every department in the building and what merchandise it featured. When a lost customer turned to her for assistance, they weren't sent to the nearest directory. They were given clear instructions to aid them in their search.

Two months into the job she was assigned to the quilt department. This woman spent as much time as possible talking to the buyers and soaking up their experience. Any salesperson calling on her department represented another opportunity for improvement. She would ask him a series of prepared questions in an attempt to learn everything she could about the product she was representing. During her lunch break she read books and trade magazines on quilts, fabrics, and weaving. This was a remarkable display of enterprise for a young clerk. Did these exercises make her a better salesperson? Did it get her noticed by her superiors? You bet it did. She rose rapidly, becoming first an assistant buyer and then a full-fledged buyer. At her rate of progress, it wouldn't surprise me if she were running the entire store some day.

Doing the best job you can might often have unexpected benefits. One day my wife Ellen went out shopping for shoes at one of her favourite stores. For whatever reason, she just couldn't find anything that struck her fancy. The salesman lugged out enough pairs to shoe Imelda Marcos for a lifetime. Ellen felt awful. The poor guy worked so hard and put so much time in with her, yet he didn't make a sale. You know it had to beat the heck out of his commission for the day, but he seemed unperturbed. This fellow was as gracious when Ellen left as when she had first entered the store. When she said how sorry she was for not buying anything, he said, 'Please, don't worry about it. I'm only sorry we didn't have a shoe for you. Do come back again soon and give us another try.'

When Ellen got home she couldn't stop raving about this salesman. She was so impressed with his enthusiasm, energy, and utter professionalism. Not to mention his patience. At the time, we had just opened an Italian jewellery business. We were desperate to find a top-notch salesperson to help launch our line in the United States. After hearing Ellen sing this chap's praises, I said, 'Look, if he's really that good let's go back to the store and try to hire him for our business.'

We did exactly that. This fellow accepted our offer and then did a sensational job. Built the business right up. Within a year and a half, he left our company for another position that could pay him more than double what he was making with us. We were sorry to have him go, but we were happy for him. He's gone on to a number of tremendous successes. It just goes to prove that an entrepreneurial approach to your job can yield surprising rewards.

That salesman is a rarity. I believe one of the big problems in retail stores today is the lack of customer attention. Too often I see salespeople standing behind their counters as if they had taken root. They are all waiting to be asked for help. The customer doesn't bite. One or two might growl on occasion, but that shouldn't prevent you from approaching them.

If I were working in a shop, I wouldn't let a customer leave without going up and letting them know I was there to assist them. Don't come on like a hurricane. You don't want to intimidate them out of the store. But give them something more than the cursory, 'Can I help you?' How often have you been asked that by a salesperson? If you tell him 'I'm just looking,' what's the usual reaction? Most salespeople I've said that to disappear quicker than Jumping Jack Flash. It's almost as if they've glad they don't have to deal with you.

Instead of using this mundane line, go up to the customer, and say something like, 'Hi, my name is Victor and I'm here to help you. I think you'll find we have a lot of nice things here

today. Take your time to look everything over. If you have any
questions at all, please feel free to ask me.' Now you've given
the customer a human presence to deal with. You've shown
an enthusiasm for them and your merchandise without being
pushy. Try this the next time out and see how it works. I think
you'll be amazed at the results. I don't know how many times
I've heard people complain, 'I went into the store to buy
something, but nobody seemed to want to bother with me so I
left.' Every time an order walks out the door, you're losing
points that are going to be hard to win back.

Talking with your customers will also give you an insight into
their needs. Since an entrepreneur is often a trail-blazer, this
can be especially vital when he's attempting to introduce a new
idea or concept. The greatest product in the world has no value
if you can't find someone to buy it. You have to know your
market.

That point was driven home for me when I was president of
Sarong. Our girdles featured a patented criss-cross that gave it
an extra firm hold. Another company made a knock-off of the
girdle and was underselling us by offering its version in discount
basements across the United States. We sued it for patent
violations. The dispute slowly crawled through the courts while
the copycat continued to slash into our sales.

I wanted to best this company in its own neighbourhood.
Neither Sarong nor Playtex, its parent company, had ever
bothered with the bargain-basement business. I decided we
would launch a new lower-priced girdle called the Tahiti. We
put together a marketing programme for the product and chose
Litt's, a department store in Philadelphia, for its introduction.
Litt's had one of the largest bargain basements in the country
and it was one of our most valued accounts.

Its merchandise manager was a fellow named Al Ritchie.
He was a real no-nonsense type who was quick to let you know
where you stood. I called on him, showed him our samples,
and then started painting a vista. I told him we weren't going
to run the usual basement ads. We were going to shoot splashy,
four-colour, full-page ads featuring Polynesian models wearing

our girdles. Very upscale. These ads were going to run in *Harper's Bazaar*. When I finished what I thought was a grand presentation, Al looked at me and said, '*Harper's Bazaar*? You're going to advertise a basement girdle there? Fellah, you must be cracked.' After assuring Al I was quite sane, I explained that I was an entrepreneur and that I wanted to do things differently. He said, 'That may be true, but this is as ridiculous an idea as I have ever heard. My customers have never even heard of *Harper's Bazaar*!' I thought that was an exaggeration. I figured even if you didn't read the magazine, a person had to have at least heard of it. When I told Ritchie this he replied, 'You think so? OK, let's go to the basement and find out.'

We go out to the floor and Al stops the first woman he sees. She was five feet tall and five feet wide and dressed like Rosie the Riveter. 'Madam,' Al says, 'this gentleman and I are conducting a survey. We'd like to ask you a few questions.' He then asked her how long she'd been shopping in Litt's basement (about ten years) and why she was such a regular customer (she liked the prices). Then it was my turn to ask the big one: 'Miss, have you ever heard of *Harper's Bazaar*?' This haughty look came over her face and she peered at me as if I was some new kind of insect. She said, 'Of course, I've heard of it! It's a deadly disease!' I looked over at Al. He could scarcely suppress his laughter.

We made the same inquiries of several other customers. They weren't any better at identifying the magazine than Rosie. In fact, her guess probably came the closest. Case closed. We did launch the Tahiti, but as a basement-priced line without the highfaluting fashion image. It did very well and put a real dent in that other company. If I hadn't taken the time to listen to my account and ask a few questions of his customers you would have probably read about the Tahiti in an earlier chapter. The one on failures.

Talking to your customers is an ideal method of building a strong business relationship. I used to call on one buyer who was a football fanatic. Before dropping in on him I would bone up on all the latest football statistics and standings. We'd start off by chatting about the fortunes of his favourite team, then we'd get down to doing some business. Another account was represented by a fellow who was quite an outdoorsman. A quick reading of *Field and Stream* let me shoot the breeze with him. These little chats created a pleasant atmosphere for selling. They also made me something more than just an impersonal tradesman hungry for an order. I was a compadre with similar interests.

Knowing what to talk about is easy. Just listen attentively to the other person, ask a few questions, and you'll find out what his interests are. Knowing what not to say can be tricky. Generally the traditional conversational taboos of polite social gatherings – sex, religion, and politics – apply to business. Let me tell you the story of a salesman who forgot this. He talked himself out of one sweet deal.

He represented an office-supply dealer and had been working for months on a potentially large sale to an international conglomerate. In his final meeting with the company's buyer, he struck the motherlode. He was given every indication that he would leave with a whopping order.

During a lunch break, he and the buyer passed the time with some chitchat. Nothing earthshaking. Just the usual gab about weather and business. Suddenly, out of nowhere, the salesman starts talking about the Iran-Contra hearings. He goes into a blazing diatribe about how the Congress was abusing Colonel Oliver North, and how the colonel was a great patriot. He went on for a good ten minutes.

The salesman had been accompanied to the meeting by an assistant. This perceptive chap kept trying to shush him. Failing that, he looked for a table to hide under. When the bombast subsided the meeting reconvened in a suddenly arctic atmosphere. The poor boob did not get his order. It seemed the buyer was not an Ollie North fan. To the contrary, he thought what North had done was immoral and he was leery of doing business with anyone who could so heartily endorse the colonel's actions. He also didn't want to have an account handled by someone who could exhibit such inappropriate behaviour. The salesman learned a hard lesson. In business, keep all small-talk small. Stay away from controversial subjects. They have no place in business. You never want to be in a situation where you win a debate, but lose the order.

I once said a few things I shouldn't have to an account. It cost me dearly. I had been trying for quite a while to sell a certain large retail chain on Remington. The account carried only Philips shavers and, for some reason, wouldn't let us in the door. Occasionally, the buyer would order a smattering of our products just to prove they wouldn't sell. Well, of course they didn't sell. You can't expect any item to move if you don't back it with a full commitment. If you had walked into the shaver department of this store, you would have seen a wall devoted to Philips. The few Remington shavers would be buried in some drab little corner. This didn't strike me as a very fair test.

This was an important account. Establishing strong Remington presence in its stores would have been quite a plum. Finding the buyer's attitude frustrating as hell, I finally decided to take the bold step we discussed some pages back: I was going over his head.

I thought I might have a bit of an advantage with this risky move. Some time before, as president of Benrus, I had done business with the company's chairman, an older man who now took only a semi-active role in the company. We had gotten along just fine. His son was the company's CEO. Hoping to trade off on some old family ties, I called the young man to plead the Remington case. I introduced myself as someone who had dealt with his father and said, 'I've been trying to sell our product to your buyer for over a year. I believe I have the best shaver on the market. We are backing that claim with a major advertising investment. I'd like an opportunity to come in, show you our product, and lay out our strategy. I think we could be very good for each other.'

The first thing he asked me when I finished was, 'I think I might be interested in seeing you. But, first, tell me who you've been dealing with?'

I said, 'George Frazier, and he's my biggest problem!'

'He is, why?'

'Because he is one of the stupidest, most opinionated buyers I've ever run into. I keep bringing him product and programmes and he won't even discuss them. He keeps saying no, but offers no explanations.'

The CEO cleared his throat and said, 'Well, you also don't understand something else.'

'What's that?'

'That stupid, opinionated buyer is my brother-in-law!'

Oh.

It took quite a crowbar to dislodge my foot from between my lips. I think I lost three toes during the process. I still don't know what took hold of me. I guess I had been swallowing a lot of bile while trying to deal with the buyer and it had to be purged. No matter, I should have used the perfect scenario drawn up when I dealt with the head of Gray's drugstores. If I had kept the scathing, personal remarks to myself, praised the buyer to the skies, and then presented our dispute as a simple difference of opinion, I think I would have had a decent hearing. We might have had a sale. Instead, we were banned by the buyer for more than three years. As long as he retained his position, we couldn't even get an appointment. It taught me something I've never forgotten: never, ever blast an employee or a co-worker when you're dealing with an account, no matter what the provocation. Once you do, you've jumped into a mined harbour. It's only a matter of time until something explodes.

Throughout much of this chapter, I've said or implied that you have to keep the customer satisfied. You do. However, you should never let anyone use you as a doormat. My wife runs a company called the Friendship Collection. It is the largest importer of jewellery from the People's Republic of China in the US. About three years ago, it was approached by a department-store chain – call it Bigstore's – to put together a mammoth promotion. It required our flooding the chain's over forty stores with a huge selection of Friendship jewellery.

The company asked to be billed on consignment. Every thirty days they would settle up with us on whatever they had sold. I'm usually against consignment. I've always believed that you should make an account pay for its merchandise as soon as possible. Let them share in the risk of moving the item. It increases their incentive to make the merchandise a success.

Despite this, it seemed like a good idea to make an exception in this case. Bigstore's was a prestigious account, a trend-setter. If we made a big splash there it would receive widespread publicity throughout the industry. This would have to impact favourably on our business with other stores. They would be clamouring for our lines. We decided to go along with their request.

We developed a marketing and advertising programme with Bigstore's. At the end of the first month, we sent them a bill for what they had sold. Six weeks went by without payment. We sent them another invoice. This time it reflects their current balance plus the amount past due. We don't hear a thing. When we call the company's accounts payable department, we receive the eighties version of that old standby, 'Your cheque is in the mail.' The manager tells us, 'Oh, I'm sure we've approved that payment. Your cheque must be in the computer.' He assures us it will be forthcoming.

We accepted this and went right on shipping merchandise. The stuff was selling like crazy, and we became so caught up in its success that we no longer pressed to collect the balance due. The Friendship Collection was doing so well, we assumed it was in Bigstore's interest to keep us happy. We also thought of Bigstore's as an established, trusted name in the business. You can expect your bigger clients to fall behind in paying. Their sheer size often ensures this will happen and you make allowances for a prized customer. You do want everyone to pay on time. If you offer terms of net thirty and you get paid in ninety, you are undoubtedly going to suffer a bit. However, it's not a tragedy as long as you do get paid. We knew we'd get our money and, after a while, we did.

Sort of.

Nine months into the relationship, I was going over Friend-ship's accounts receivable. We had sent Bigstore goods worth a total of $400,000. They had, as promised by that manager, sent us a cheque.

One cheque.

For $322.87

Of course the first thing I wanted to know was where did the eighty-seven cents come from? The next thing I wanted to know was the whereabouts of our $399,677.13!

I called Bigstore's jewellery buyer and asked him the same question. He said, 'I can't believe that hasn't been paid yet. Let me check with our merchandise manager and one of us will get back to you.' Between the two of them I got the royal run-around for the next three months. When I called to ask why we still hadn't been paid, the buyer explained that they were trying to pull together the sales records of each individual store to make sure our billing was accurate. I knew I was in trouble then. That sort of undertaking could take for ever, and that's if they were doing the job quickly. Of course, I didn't think they were doing the job at all.

As an alternative, we offered to wait till the end of the year, when the figures would be easily lifted from Bigstore's annual chain-wide inventory. Those numbers would arrive in less than two months.

When they came in, Bigstore claimed they showed a wide disparity between what they owed and what we billed. They alleged we had failed to deliver some of our goods. The mer-chandise manager refused to pay us a cent until we produced proof of delivery for every single shipment to each of the chain's forty stores.

That took six months. We'd now been dancing with these fellows for more than a year and a half. The promotion was going great guns but it was tearing our insides out. We produced the evidence substantiating our claims and presented Bigstore with a bill for the full amount. You'll never guess what they did. Looking at the invoice, a Bigstore executive said, 'If you're going to give us a statement for this kind of money, we don't want to do business with you. Our records don't agree with yours.' I had presented them with documentation supporting every figure on our invoices. These forms were signed by his employees, but this bozo was acting as if the numbers and signatures didn't exist.

Now what do you do in a case like this? As a salesman, your cardinal rule is to bend over backwards to satisfy a customer. Never do anything to destroy a relationship with a valued account. Well we had bent over backwards. All that did was allow Bigstore an opportunity to twist the stiletto in a bit deeper. If a customer is going to do that, don't worry about the relationship. You haven't got one.

We sued to recoup the debt. The threat of that action forced them to settle with us for a figure close to our original claims. We haven't done business with them since and don't expect to do any in the future. It was quite an account to lose. That's all right. Our company made the right decision. We got our money and our decisiveness won us a lot of respect throughout the industry. Shortly after we split with Bigstore's, a rival chain gave us a better deal on an even bigger programme. And this time we got paid on schedule.

I'm often asked what makes a successful salesperson. Energy, self-confidence, confidence in whatever you are selling, an enthusiasm for your current job and its potential for growth, an ability to get along with people, and a thick skin to handle rejection, these are the primary ingredients; you combine them with good old-fashioned hard work. Since you want to get to know as much about your customers as possible, it also pays to be observant. It is often the unspoken things that can tell you the most about a person. I'd like to close this chapter with an example of what I mean.

Every year, when certain forecasts weren't met, Benrus had to unload its excess watch inventory. Some styles would be discontinued and we would have a number of odd lots that were unattractive to retailers. The cost of storing these unwanted pieces was punitive. There were few places that would buy the extra stock. One man who operated in New York's Bowery became the watch dump site for the entire industry. His name was Tiny Grossman.

Tiny was 6 foot 3 and must have weighed a good 350 pounds. He would sit in his ramshackle office at a battered, old desk and drive the toughest bargains in the business. An ancient sign written in Yiddish hung on the wall directly behind him. The first year or two, I tried to make a few dollars in our negotiations. I'd think, 'The watches cost us fourteen dollars. I'll ask for twenty dollars a watch and settle for eighteen.' I quickly learned I was dreaming.

Tiny would look over the pieces. Blowing cigar smoke in your face, he'd ooh and ah over their fine craftsmanship. He'd tell you they were the most magnificent watches he'd seen all year. Then he'd offer you ten dollars apiece.

We're talking about 100,000 watches at a clip. That worked out to a $400,000 bath for Benrus. I'd do everything I could to persuade Tiny to up his offer. My pleadings did the trick every time. Tiny would move his price all the way up to $10.25. That was his final deal. What could I do? Tiny was the court of last resort. I'd take his cheque and use it to dry my tears on the way home.

This went on for four years. Finally, after once again being drubbed, I asked Tiny if he didn't have any pity for us. He pointed to the sign in back of him and said, 'Can't you read?' I couldn't read or understand a word of Yiddish, so I asked him to translate. He said, 'That's my philosophy. It says "Your hernia is my blessing!" ' Great! All this time that placard had been staring me in the face. If I had just bothered to have it translated earlier, if I had paid more attention to Tiny's environment, I'd have had an insight into the man. It might have helped with the negotiations. You just can't tell what a difference this might have made.

Why, I might have even got him up as high as $10.50!

CHAPTER FOUR

Business is a game, but not everyone plays by the rules

I've often told novice entrepreneurs, 'Business is a game. Play it to win.' That advice is not, however, licence to pursue victory at all costs. The player who will double-deal to win has no place in my game. He is not an entrepreneur. An entrepreneur loves challenges and risks. What sort of thrill can you possibly get from winning a contest you've rigged?

In playing by the rules, however, you mustn't ever forget that you will sometimes run into business people who lack your integrity. Be alert! A well-fanged viper can take a healthy chunk out of your entrepreneurial dream. That reptile can cost you money, ruin an enterprise, or, worst of all, destroy a reputation. I know. I've been bitten. Fortunately, I've come out of these skirmishes relatively unscarred. I'd like to tell you about four of them.

The opera ain't over till the fat lady sings

One of my first encounters with this brand of snake occurred during my early days at Remington. We were expanding our overseas operations. Under Sperry, the distribution for our shavers in Italy was handled by a Mr Belmudo. He had won this right by making a very questionable deal with Remington's Italian representative, Mr Crassi. Mr Belmudo was slipping under-the-table payments to Crassi. These gratuities often came as cash, but would occasionally take the form of a trinket, like a Mercedes Benz. You ever try to slip a Mercedes Benz underneath a table? That must have been one large piece of furniture.

Sperry, of course, was unaware of the arrangement. Nothing in Crassi's past suggested he was capable of this sort of skullduggery. When he told Sperry that Belmudo was the man to distribute the shavers in Italy, the company took him at his word. It assumed Belmudo was a first-class distributor. Sperry had no way of knowing that Belmudo didn't know a thing about the appliance business. He had run other, unrelated companies with little success and saw the Remington deal as a chance to finally make good.

To manage the business, Belmudo wanted to hire a mysterious Italian beauty named Madame Destazia. During her initial meetings with Belmudo and Crassi, she represented herself as having contacts at the highest levels in the Italian government. Her credentials were impeccable. So impeccable, in fact, that no one could verify them. Among other things, she claimed she had been an administrator under the Italian Secretary of State and had been a paid government consultant for the last ten years. She also claimed her job involved the handling of sensitive information, requiring her to work under deep cover. Therefore, if anyone asked the government anything about her, they would deny she ever worked for them. Well, it's not every day you get to hire one of John le Carré's characters to run your operation. Crassi agreed to Destazia's coming on board.

Belmudo named her as his company's managing director. She took over the distributorship just as I took title to Remington. Our first days on the job were somewhat dissimilar. I arrived in Bridgeport in my faithful old car, dressed in what I hoped was a tasteful but unextraordinary business suit. The only piece of glitter on me was my watch. Madame Destazia showed up for work in Italy in a block-long Rolls-Royce, bedecked in mink from head to toe, and dripping with enough precious stones to make the Liz Taylor collection look paltry. If this woman was playing a part, she was certainly playing it to the hilt.

Remington's Italian operation came under the jurisdiction of our English managers. In a first meeting with them, Madame Destazia overwhelmed these chaps. She laid out a plan that utilized all her connections. It vowed to make Remington Italy's number-one shaver in a short time. That was quite a promise. When it was made, Remington commanded less than 10 per cent of that country's shaver market.

She worked out a deal with the English representatives that required our shipping an enormous amount of product. As a rule, Remington gives its distributors terms of net ninety days. You have to pay for the shavers within three months of their delivery. Madame Destazia wanted net 180 days. My English managing director cabled her request to me. I refused. He called me and said, 'I'm convinced this woman can triple or even quadruple our business. However, she'd be building the business from almost nothing and feels she needs these terms to make a go of it. I've seen her plan; I think she's worth the risk.' I still wasn't convinced, but he kept the pressure on until I finally gave him the go-ahead.

We shipped her order. The first results were miraculous. She claimed business had immediately shot up to almost six times over what it had been the previous year. Every cable from Italy brought news of even greater sales by them and orders from us. After the four months, our market share had zoomed. My managing director was more than just a little pleased with himself. His monthly reports from England would often carry five pages on Italy and only a few paragraphs covering the rest of Europe.

We had shipped Destazia's order in early July. By the end of the year, the invoices, now totalling almost $400,000 were coming due. We didn't receive a farthing. Letters were sent to Destazia and Belmudo demanding payment. Their response was a purchase order for an additional $100,000. They hadn't paid for a single shaver and they were trying to order several thousand more!

By now, the managing director of our English company was feeling a bit uneasy. He sent a representative down to Italy to demand either immediate payment or the return of the shavers. The rep was picked up at the airport and whisked off to Mr Belmudo's warehouse. Once there, he was brought to the Remington holding area by Madame Destazia. There wasn't a shaver in sight. Madame Destazia gushed, 'You see, we have sold them all. That is why we need another order and we need to have it soon.' Though the sight of the bejewelled Madame Destazia revelling in her triumph was dazzling, our rep was able to maintain his senses long enough to ask a simple question, 'If you sold all the shavers, where is the money?' Destazia giggled and said, 'I've been naughty. I gave our customers longer terms than I should have. Their payments are only just starting to trickle in, but there is no need to worry.' With that, she produced a small mountain of invoices indicating payments due. They seemed to back up everything she was claiming. To put our man even further at ease, Destazia wrote out a cheque to Remington for $10,000. She said, 'Here take this as a sign of good faith. It is not a company cheque. I have so much trust in my clients and this enterprise that I have drawn it on my personal account. But please, ship me that order. We have a growing business here, but it is a fragile one. We must keep it moving or our momentum will die.'

What could the rep do? He didn't want the company to be ripped off, but at the same time he couldn't risk destroying everything Remington had accomplished in Italy. Torn by doubts, he called our managing director in England and explained the situation. He was told to deposit the cheque in the Remington account. If it cleared, the company would ship Madame Destazia's order.

The cheque did not bounce. The order was sent and we drew up a schedule of payments for the rest of the monies owed. The first deadline came. The first deadline passed. No cash. This time, we sent a private detective and a lawyer to Italy for a surprise visit. Finding Madame Destazia at the warehouse, they asked to see her books. Madame Destazia couldn't have been more gracious. She brought them to her office, gave them espresso and pastries, and allowed them access to all of her records. She then explained that she was about to have lunch with her accountant and that she would return with him as soon as they had finished. That meal has to be in *The Guinness Book of Records* as the longest lunch in history. It must be still going on because Madame Destazia was never heard from again. She just vanished.

Sifting through her records, we discovered that she had indeed sold all those shavers and had received payment. However, the corporate account showed almost none of the money due. It looked as though Madame Destazia had apparently given herself one whopping commission. We later found out that she had kept very little of the swag for herself. She had donated the bulk of the proceeds – over $200,000 – to the La Scala opera house. We also found out how she had been able to turn the business around so dramatically. She had been selling the shavers for less than she was paying for them! Destazia, travelling about in her limo, would deliver them personally to the retailers and accept payment in cash. Talk about bizarre twists, this one absolutely boggled my mind.

With her gone, we sued Belmudo for getting us in this mess. He immediately declared bankruptcy. We couldn't pierce his corporate veil and the court held he had no responsibility as an individual. It was just as well. Despite his shady dealings, Belmudo was an innocent in this case. He had been taken for a ride by Destazia and found himself ruined.

We went after Crassi for his under-the-table dealings with Belmudo. He claimed he was an American citizen and could not be sued in Italy. We pursued the case in the US. The court ruled that since the entire transaction had taken place in Italy, he had to be sued over there. Catch-22. Crassi got off scot-free, but his reputation suffered irreparable damage. Both he and Belmudo had been burned because they were already playing a crooked game. The kickbacks to Crassi were evidence of this. Their satisfaction didn't come from jobs well done; it came from lining their purses. They were made to order for an operator like Destazia. Remington took its lumps because we were blinded by the opportunity. Destazia had painted the Trojan Horse of vistas. When you're an entrepreneur, you don't look a gift-horse in the mouth. You look behind its ears, peer up its nose, and take it around the track a few times. Madame Destazia, in offering to make us the top shaver in Italy, had followed a practice of Chairman Corleone. She had made us an offer too good to refuse. When someone comes along offering to give you the world, that's when the alarm bells should sound off and the red lights should start flashing. You shouldn't shy away. However, make sure you have all your questions answered before proceeding. We should have insisted that Madame Destazia back up her curriculum vitae with tangible references. We also shouldn't have varied our terms. If we had monitored the programme more closely, we might have avoided a mess that hurt everyone involved. Everyone except Destazia and, of course, the opera company. It ended up giving the good Madame an award as one of its most outstanding patrons of the arts.

A most expensive parking ticket

Parents often tell their children, 'Tell the truth. I don't care what it is you've done wrong, you will only make it worse by lying.' It's true. If you make a mistake, own up to it. Tell your boss you spilled hot coffee in the lap of your most important client. He'll understand, even if the scorched client doesn't. Covering up your mistakes with lies won't change reality. It can only cost you your self-respect, the respect of your peers and your job.

I recently saw an example of this in one of my companies outside of the United States. The fellow involved was a good fellow and a dynamite salesman. Let's call him Tim Burke. His boss – Mr Tiptop – was a meticulous fellow, living and dying by the book.

Mr Tiptop had a rule. If you were out on a sales call and

were stuck with a parking ticket, it was your bad luck. One day, Tim was calling on a major client. This meeting lasted longer than he had anticipated. When he got out of it, he found that his car had been ticketed. The fine was $25.

Mr Burke had not made a sale at his meeting, so perhaps frustration coloured his reaction to the ticket. Whatever the reason, he decided that Remington was going to pay for his mistake.

Tim knew, of course, that he could not claim the money in his expenses. At least, he couldn't enter it as reimbursement for a parking ticket. So he got around this technicality by claiming he had taken a buyer, Miss Sales, to lunch that day. He recorded the cost of the meal – wouldn't you know it was $25 – and put in an expenses chit.

Have you ever heard the blues song that proclaims, 'If it weren't for bad luck, I wouldn't have no luck at all'? It's called 'Born Under a Bad Sign'. Tim Burke may not have been cursed at birth, but he was sure living under a bad sign on this particular day. It so happened that his boss had been on the phone that afternoon and had spoken with the very buyer that Burke had claimed he was taking to lunch. The call had nothing to do with Tim. Mr Tiptop was just making some general inquiries about the account. At the end of the chat, Miss Sales mentioned that Tim Burke was supposed to be calling on her that day. At four o'clock.

When Tim handed in his voucher, it listed the bogus lunch. Seeing it, Mr Tiptop thought, 'Now this is odd. I spoke to Miss Sales at two. She had just come back from lunch. She made no mention of having it with Tim, and in fact said she expected to see him at four. Either she is a crazy, a world-class eater, or Timothy is fibbing.' He called Miss Sales and asked if she and Tim had gone out to eat. No. Summoning Burke, he asked him to explain the entry. Tim hemmed and hawed, but finally told his boss the truth. Tiptop let him off with a stern reprimand. An embarrassed Tim left the office, thinking the incident was behind him. It wasn't. All business associations are built on trust. With this small infraction, Burke had planted

doubts in his boss's mind. He had undermined their relationship.

Over the next few months, Mr Tiptop kept a careful eye on
Tim's expenses. He was looking for the slightest discrepancy.
It didn't take long to find one. The company was holding a
sales meeting in another city on a Monday morning. Tim was
booked into a hotel room for Sunday night. For reasons that
remain fuzzy, Tim missed his Sunday flight and didn't arrive at
the hotel until Monday afternoon. His room was given to a
different individual. By the time Tim joined the meeting, it
was already half over. Burke should have called his boss and
admitted his error. Instead, he panicked.

Tim was supposed to be in town on Sunday evening for a
Monday morning meeting. Tim was expected to include a
receipt for his room in his expenses report. The absence of that
statement could tip off his boss that he had missed his flight.
Burke covered up by taking the bill for the hotel meeting room
and placing it in his expenses report. The idea was to trick the
company into believing it represented the charge for his own
unused quarters.

This thin charade held up for about five minutes. In going
over the expenses for the entire meeting, Mr Tiptop wondered
why the company hadn't been charged for a meeting room.
The hotel was not a philanthropic organization; they had always
billed Remington in the past. He called the establishment and
asked what had happened. The hotel manager replied, 'Oh yes,
you've been billed as usual. In fact, Mr Burke picked up the
statement and said he would take care of it.'

Tiptop then phoned several people who had attended the
conference. The truth came out. This time there was no reprimand. Burke was told to clean out his desk. Neither of his
missteps were terribly serious. A $25 parking ticket and a
missed meeting are not two of life's great tragedies. It was the
lack of candour that finished Tim.

*

Another gift-horse

Wouldn't you suppose that getting a cheque for over two million dollars was a cause for celebration? Ordinarily it would be. However, a cheque made out to Victor K. Kiam for something more than that amount was not drawn under ordinary circumstances.

Sitting in my office on a rainy Friday morning, I was going over the copy for our latest Remington commercial. That exercise was interrupted when my secretary informed me I had a phone call. This caller's name was unfamiliar, so I asked that she take a message. The fellow on the line wouldn't have that. He explained that it was an emergency and that he had to speak to me immediately.

Emergency? Thoughts of accidents and ambulances crowded my head. I jumped on the phone and was greeted by a pleasant, modulated voice saying, 'Mr Kiam, you don't know me. I work on Wall Street. I was walking to the office this morning and, well, I don't know how to say this exactly, but were you expecting a cheque anytime soon?' That seemed a simple enough question, but I didn't have an answer, the volume of business is so great it's often impossible for me to keep track of every minor transaction. I said, 'It's possible. Why do you ask?' He replied that he had found a cheque made out to me. The caller had snared it just after a stiff wind had sent it fluttering up Wall Street.

After first thanking him, I said that the cheque could be for almost anything and that he should send it to our accountants. I was all set to switch him over to them when he said, 'Well, Mr Kiam, I really don't want to put it in the mail. You see, it's for a very large amount.' I asked him how big a cheque it was. In round, dulcet tones, he chimed, 'It seems to be for two million, two hundred and sixty-three thousand dollars.'

You can appreciate how the figure gave me pause. I don't care how busy we were, if someone owed us that much money, we would have known about it. The note was a cashier's cheque. This meant it could be cashed anywhere by anyone, so long as it had been endorsed by me. I needed to think. Asking the fellow for his office phone number, I promised to call him back in twenty minutes.

At this point, I had two alternatives. I might get back to this chap, give him a generous reward, and then cash the cheque in a hurry. Couldn't do it. I knew darn well that I wasn't due a cheque for that amount from the bank. This would have been accepting the money under false pretences.

The second alternative was far more viable. I called a friend in the banking business. When I first phoned, he thought I was pulling his leg. Couldn't blame him for that. Having been assured I was serious, he said, 'The first thing you must do is have the cheque picked up from this guy. Now as long as you're certain that this isn't some legitimate payment you've forgotten about, you should also call the bank. I suggest one of their agents should make the collection. If you like, I'll also send over one of my lawyers and a security guard to witness the transaction.'

The transfer took place and was duly recorded. That afternoon, the bank's security chief called, thanking me for my prompt response in the matter. He also asked that I not mention the incident to anyone. The bank was apparently conducting an internal investigation and was unwilling to risk the scorching glare of publicity. It knew that would damage its inquiry. When I asked if I could give a reward to the man who had found the cheque the chief said, 'No, that won't be necessary. You stay out of this. We will take care of the gentleman. Then I think it would be best if you forgot this ever happened.'

How could I do that? I mean this was a cheque for over two million dollars, not 44 cents! Over the next four months, I had my lawyer periodically call the bank to find out what had occurred. We couldn't learn a thing. Finally, the truth came out as part of a major scandal. Employees at a particular branch of this prestigious institution had been issuing cashier's cheques in the names of famous people. They would be endorsed and then cashed. The scam had netted these con artists almost twelve million dollars before they were apprehended. A bit of

Sherlock Holmes in me prefers to think I had a tiny hand in their capture. I must say I still can't believe these people thought they could get away with it. The incident only proves that some people are greedy enough to try anything. It also taught me a lesson in the disadvantages of being too well known. Of course, I suppose the perpetrators may have been giving me a most left-handed compliment. After all, I didn't notice them signing the Philips president's name to any of those cheques.

The galloping venture capitalist

Some years after leaving Remington, Harry Stokes was considering an investment in a company that produced ship fittings. He was receiving some assistance in this enterprise from a young venture capitalist named Tom Barron. Harry was very impressed with this man. He often told me, 'Vic, if you're ever looking to raise some money for a project, this is a fellow you should meet. We're getting together with him next week and I would like you to be there.' I always treated advice from Harry like the Sermon on the Mount. Though Harry didn't know it at the time, I was already involved in a project requiring some venture capital.

My deal was in the formative stages. It involved purchasing a company called Maui Divers, a maker of fine coral jewellery. Located in Hawaii, they had a government licence to operate a submarine. This sub carried two passengers. It would patrol the ocean floor searching for coral. Reaching a reef, it would use two crablike claws to cut the coral. The now severed prize would be dropped into a basket attached to the sub and carried off to be transformed into delicate pieces of jewellery. The government licence was exclusive. No other company was allowed to mine those oceans for these exquisite skeletons.

The venture-capital group looking to back this investment was giving me a rough time. I felt they wanted too much equity in return for their money. Their stubbornness and Harry's recommendation made Mr Barron a very attractive figure. I accepted Stokes's invitation.

As it happened, Barron and I were practically neighbours. He owned a brownstone less than six blocks from where we made our New York headquarters. Barron kept his business offices on one floor. When I got there, the joint was jumping. Secretaries were bustling back and forth, the phone never stopped ringing. It was all very impressive.

I was greeted by Mr Barron. A tall, bearish-looking fellow, he smoked a cigar and appeared rather soft-spoken. When he did speak, you got the idea that he was giving you 'The Word'. He was like an oracle. Before the meeting with Stokes and his partner got underway, we discussed the Maui venture. Barron agreed that the project had possibilities. He said he would examine it further and get back to me with some suggestions.

About this time, a deal came along that stole my attention from Maui Divers. It was Remington. That project consumed most of my time for the next few months. After its completion, I ended up getting involved with Harry and his nautical venture. Stokes was living in Tucson, Arizona. His partner lived in Connecticut. Barron had provided the financing. Since Barron's home was practically right next door to my own, I began to see Tom on a regular basis. We would often breakfast together while discussing the ship-fitting venture.

Besides going over the Stokes project, Tom was always bringing me other ventures. One of the first was a company that imported fine European wood carvings. Its owner was a gentleman who had no formal business training. He had done amazingly well on his own. Looking to expand the operation, he now needed both financial and managerial help. I thought he had a heck of a business, but I wasn't interested. This didn't deter Tom. It seemed as if he was bringing me a new idea every other week. I have to admit I loved his energy and enthusiasm.

One day he called me at my office. He said, 'Victor, I'm selling my country home and I'm taking out a second mortgage on my brownstone. I have a super deal and I need capital fast. You've got some idea of the different things I have my finger in. I am fully extended at the moment. The mortgage is more than enough to cover what I need, but I won't get the money until that deal is closed. That will take too much time. I need about $20,000 to tide me over.' I was about to tell him that my own finances were tight – the Remington purchase after all was not a small one – but he had already anticipated me. He said, 'Victor, I wouldn't want the money from you. I'm going to apply for a loan to be paid back in six months. I was wondering, first, would you recommend a bank and, second, would you be the guarantor for the loan?'

I had just received a loan on behalf of our Friendship Jewellery Company from the New Jersey bank. I called the loan officer and said, 'I know this fellow who wants to borrow some money short term. He's in venture capital and he's working with some friends of mine. At the moment, he's borrowed up to his ears and is not sure he can get any more credit. Would you look over his papers? He's getting a second mortgage soon and the loan will be paid off. If you won't lend him the cash directly, I'll guarantee it.' That was not a bright decision on my part. By offering to cosign for the loan, I was giving the bank the perfect out. The loan to Barron was risk-free if they had me ready to take full responsibility for the entire amount.

The loan officer agreed to interview Barron. He called me the day after the meeting. 'You know,' the banker said, 'this is an impressive fellow. He's into so many different things. He showed me his projects, we've looked at the value of his house. We'd like to give him the loan, but with all the projects he's got going, we would indeed like you to be the guarantor.' I acquiesced. At the time it wasn't a hard choice to make. Tom seemed to be running a well-organized and thriving company. I trusted him. In fact, I trusted Tom too much. Just as a matter of sound business procedure, I should have obtained a lien against his house. It would have given me access to his money if he failed to make good on the loan. That's hindsight. Instead, I cosigned the loan without obtaining any legal means of redress if Barron defaulted.

I didn't pay any further attention to the transaction. Remington was commanding all of my time and concentration. Eight months after the loan had been approved, I was reviewing my finances. I wondered, 'How come we haven't heard anything on that Barron loan? Tom hasn't been around since he got the money. I have no idea whether it's been paid off or not. I better call the bank.'

As it turned out, the loan officer was about to phone me. Not only did the bank records show that the loan's principal was still outstanding, they also indicated that Tom hadn't paid any interest in over four months.

I got off the phone to call Tom. Instead of reaching him, I was connected to a recording informing me that Mr Barron could no longer be reached at this number. He had left New York and had also left my favourite entrepreneur holding the bag.

We conducted a search. I found an old telephone book that listed the number for his house in New Jersey. We did reach a party there. They informed us that they had just recently bought the home from Mr Barron, but that the former owner had not left any forwarding address or phone number. I contacted Harry Stokes and his partner. They didn't know where Tom was either.

Getting back to the bank, I explained that Barron could not be found. I asked them to conduct their own investigation. With their resources, they could scour many of the nation's banks. If they found an account bearing Barron's name, we'd know where he was. Their explorations couldn't turn up a single clue.

As cosignatory, I was on that hook for the full amount of the loan plus any interest due. However, the bank couldn't press me for the funds until they had conducted a search, 'with due diligence'. They had to exhaust every avenue in trying to find Tom Barron.

A short while after this incident came to light, my son Tory entered the Harvard Business School. One holiday he came home lugging a poster that had been up in school. It read:

TOM BARRON
AMERICA'S TOP VENTURE CAPITALIST
WILL BE
ADDRESSING
THE ENTREPRENEURIAL CLASS
OF THE
HARVARD BUSINESS SCHOOL

Tory, knowing nothing about the loan, innocently asked, 'This is a fellow you knew, isn't it Dad?' I said, 'You're damned right I knew him! He stuck me! When was he up there?' It had only been the previous week.

I called the Harvard Business School. They didn't have Barron's address. He had conducted his business with them over the phone. They gave me a number. When I called, the phone was answered by a person who claimed never to have heard of Tom Barron. Welcome to the 'twilight zone'.

A couple of months go by. One morning, I am reading a copy of a business magazine. It contains an article entitled something like 'America's number-one venture capitalist is riding high'. Guess who the article was about? Bingo! It was an interview with the enigmatic Mr Barron. The article showcased all the marvellous deals Barron had engineered.

The publisher of the magazine happened to be a friend of mine. I got in touch with him and asked how I could reach Barron. He checked with the fellow who wrote the story. Another false lead. Apparently, Barron had made all the arrangements for the article by phone. He had sent the magazine a packet of autobiographical material bearing no return address. The actual interview took place in the magazine's New York office. I had seen this film before. Claude Rains plays a wacky scientist. He enters an English inn dressed in bandages. Whenever he wants to indulge in a little bit of mayhem, he whips off the gauze and vanishes into thin air. I was chasing the Invisible Man!

He didn't even give us the luxury of a few clues. In the interview, he mentioned several companies he had funded or brought public. When you called information for their phone numbers, you discovered they were non-existent.

These dead-ends both frustrated and tantalized me. I was determined to find this guy. Finally, we got a lead from a most unexpected source. I came home one evening to find my wife Ellen reading a circular. It invited Ellen to be profiled in a new book spotlighting female entrepreneurs. The book's author? Yes, it was the Invisible Man himself. This cheeky s.o.b. had the nerve to ask my wife for an interview!

The request listed some of Mr Barron's previous tomes. You've seen these sort of books. They all have titles like *How To Make Your First Three Million Before the Age of Eight*. His books were published by some company in California. I immediately called the publisher and asked for Tom Barron. The phone was hung up. When I called back, no one answered.

While my quest was going on, the bank was dunning me for payment on my guarantee. Interest had pushed the loan up to $27,000. I took the circular and the accompanying letter to the bank and reminded them that they were obliged to try to find Barron before coming to me. 'Your man is somewhere in Marin County,' I said. 'Go get him.'

Believe it or not, the bank finds him. It demands immediate satisfaction. Barron pays them all the interest due, but not a penny of principal. The bank then calls me and says, 'Mr Barron is contesting the loan. He claims he's made principal payments that we haven't recorded.' How's that for a stall? Of course, the bank sees through this ruse. They know if Barron had given them a penny he would have a cancelled cheque and the bank would have the transaction in its files. Despite the transparency of this ploy, the bank was now forced to dredge up its records, send copies of payment to Barron, and wait for him to reply. It started to look as if this thing would never end.

Six months of correspondence between the bank and Barron begin. The interest starts to pile up again. Finally, the bank decides to sue Barron.

I went to a meeting in England thinking the bank had finally got a handle on this thing. I had intended to be gone for a

month. An emergency put a crimp in my plans and forced me
to return home early. The matter was serious enough for me
to take the Concorde for the return flight. As I got on board
the plane, I saw Tom Barron and his wife already seated. I
suddenly felt like a benign version of the policeman in *Crime
and Punishment*.

I'm sitting in the back of the jet, completely out of their view.
I don't do a thing during the flight. After landing, I go up to
him as he's waiting for his luggage. We talk. I ask, 'Tom, what
the hell is going on with this loan?' He gives me the same story
he's been giving the bank. He's paid most of it, but the records
are in error. I told him what he could do with that fine tale,
and then I said, 'Tom, just pay what you owe. When you
walked out on the bank, you walked out on me. We've been
friends. Don't cheat a friend.' I grabbed my luggage and left.

Calling the bank on the following day, I told them Barron
was in town and apparently quite solvent. His wife was draped
in mink and they had flown in on the Concorde. They thanked
me and said they'd get right on it. The result? I got a notice
from the loan officer only a few months ago. Barron's company
had gone bankrupt. Over twenty million dollars of investors'
funds had floated up to the ozone. There was even talk that
charges of fraud would be brought against my former buddy.
The bank did not want to stand in what had become a long
queue of outraged creditors. They had completed their due
diligence. I had to pay back the loan.

I was taken in by Mr Barron. He gave every appearance of
being a man worthy of trust and respect. I thought he was an
entrepreneur. I was wrong. Don't make the same mistake.
Ninety-nine per cent of the people you'll meet in business will
be honest. Just be aware of the exceptions.

You may now be asking yourself, how can I protect my interests
and my ideas? Your concepts – no matter how innovative
– aren't worth anything unless they give birth to a tangible
enterprise. In order to sell the venture or to acquire the capital
needed to launch it, you'll have to share the idea with others.

Document every move you make! Whenever you frame the idea in a letter, send it via registered mail and be sure to have copies sent to your lawyer and/or business manager.

Learn from the experience of Mike Shanley. Shanley had created a national promotion that seemed perfect for a certain large American corporation that we will call the Omnipotent Corporation. He brought the idea to its marketing team. Omnipotent looked it over for about a month, and then rejected it, writing, 'Though this is a fine idea, we just can't see doing anything like this at this time.' Since the idea was tailored for Omnipotent and was inappropriate for any other sponsor, Shanley put it in his turn-down file and forgot about it. Six months later, he's watching TV. An Omnipotent commercial comes on, singing the praises of its latest national promotion. It's the very idea Shanley had proposed. They are even using the name he had suggested.

As soon as he recovered from the shock, Shanley called his lawyer. Mike had documented his idea. The initial proposal and all subsequent correspondence had been sent with a return receipt requested. In addition, he had held on to the letter of rejection. Armed with this evidence, his attorney approached Omnipotent and came away with a fat settlement for his client. Mike had been wise. Without documentation, he wouldn't have collected a dime.

There are other methods of protection. Some of them – like taping your business conversations – invade grey areas of legality and should not be done. They may support your case, but could also be inadmissible in a court of law. Why take chances? Invest a few dollars in a good attorney and have him outline the various precautions you can take. It will save you a lot of headaches.

One other thing you should remember. The four episodes described in this chapter all had at least one thing in common: the central charades were spun of the flimsiest gossamer. You often won't be fooled unless you allow yourself to be fooled. Always remember that all that glitters is just glitter. Then you'll take time to find the true gold. For example, if I had looked behind the Barron facade, and demanded tangible collateral, this tale would have had a different ending. No matter, I guess it could have been worse. I lost over $20,000 but I came away a wiser man. As for Mr Barron, I have no idea what has happened to him. Perhaps he's off somewhere with Madame Destazia. Writing an opera.

Your reputation: more precious than gold

Those people who refused to play their entrepreneurial hand according to Hoyle forgot a very important tenet. For the entrepreneur, nothing is more valuable than his good reputation. Without one, you'll be hard pressed to do business for very long. It is your coin of the realm! A good reputation can help open the doors to investment capital, and will make your profit or service more desirable to the public. It will also allow you to sleep soundly at night. Never underestimate its worth.

When we first started writing *Going For It!*, we hired a service run by a Mr Goodpromise to transcribe the hours of tape that eventually comprised its text. The chap we engaged seemed to have his act together. He promised to transform tape into finished copy within three days. His rates were competitive, his offices seemed to be in order, and his work samples looked outstanding.

At first, he delivered as promised. The results were dazzling. As the job wore on, however, the copy deteriorated. Whole sections of dialogue were missing. Typos, some of them terribly confusing, increased. Instead of taking three days, the turn-around time had gone to a week. The problems, were an annoyance, but we managed to cope. We were still right on target for our deadline and seemed to have neither the time nor the need to find a replacement.

Unfortunately, as we reached the final chapters, things got worse. We dropped off a pair of cassettes. After two weeks, the work still wasn't finished. We phoned Goodpromise twice a day, demanding to know when the copy would be ready. Each time, Goodpromise vowed we would have it in our hands by the next day. All that next day would bring was another rash of excuses. We finally were forced to pay Mr Goodpromise a surprise visit. When we arrived we found the reason for his delinquent service. Goodpromise, for reasons best known to himself, had let go of most of his staff. He was now doing all the work – ours and others – on his own. Though he had sworn our copy was 'eighty to ninety per cent done,' we discovered that it had hardly been touched.

We did the only thing we could. He was paid for what little had been finished, and the cassettes were taken out of his hands. Given to another service, the job was completed in less than three days. The incident gave us a few nervous moments, but we did meet our deadline.

Two years pass. Mr Goodpromise reads that we are about to embark on a second literary adventure. He calls me and proceeds to paint a stunning vista. He first apologized for all that had happened the last time we employed him. He explained, 'I've streamlined our operation. We've got a full staff now and we're completely computerized. You have to come down to the office and see all the technology we have. The place looks like the Houston Command Center.' It was an invitation we declined.

We had no intention of repeating a prior mistake. I have no idea why Mr Goodpromise failed us during our last encounter. Perhaps he had hit a financial blip and had been forced to lay off staff. Those things happen. If he had come to us at the time and explained his situation, we could have worked something out. We had been that pleased with his earlier work. Instead, he fabricated excuses and very nearly did serious damage to the project. There is no way we're going to trust him with another large job. The shiny new computers and the enlarged staff don't mean a thing. If potential clients are not convinced you can deliver, you're not going to get their business.

By the way, this can work two ways. If you as the client are less than professional in your behaviour, you'll have a hard time getting skilled craftsmen to work for you. Let me give you an example. A fellow you met in chapter three, Ted Barnes, owns a copy-writing service. Having seen his work, I can tell you it's first rate. The text is clear, crisp, and Teddy never misses a deadline.

He was commissioned by a large marketing outfit to write the copy for a 32-page pamphlet explaining the rules of basket-ball. It was not a large job. Most of the publication would be devoted to illustrations. However, it did come with a tight deadline. No problem. This sort of rush job was Teddy's speciality.

Barnes and his top sportswriter, Chris Zachry, started work-ing on the manuscript. As each section was done, it was sent to the marketing agency's promotions manager. Each day, this manager would call, praising the copy. Then she would ask for some changes. Drastic changes. Teddy would spend half the night making the alterations. He would fax the new text to the agency by the following morning. That afternoon, he would listen in astonishment as the promotions manager would once again congratulate him on a great job, and then ask him to switch back to the original text. It became painfully clear that this woman had no idea what she wanted.

Somehow, Teddy got the project done on time. Four days after the deadline, he received a call from the promotions manager. She said, 'Mr Barnes, I was about to send you a cheque, but we have a problem. One of my staff members has reviewed your manuscript and says it is filled with errors. Since it has already been sent to the sponsoring client and has been put to press, there is nothing we can do about it. We are not going to pay your fee until after the pamphlet has been distributed. If no one complains about false information, we will send you a cheque.'

Errors? The first thing Teddy wanted to know was 'Who on earth reviewed this thing?' He put his argument thus: 'The rules and records covered in the text are pretty basic and I double-checked all the material. You know, I have to warn you about something. Lots of amateurs think they know a lot about basketball when they really don't know a thing. It wouldn't surprise me if the person who looked the pamphlet over doesn't know what he's talking about. In fact, I would bet on it.' Ted wasn't being arrogant. It was not as if he thought he was incapable of making a mistake. However, he felt he was on pretty sure ground. The fellow who wrote the pamphlet, Mr Zachry, had covered basketball for over twenty-five years. Hiring him to turn out a pamphlet on the game was like hiring Field Marshal Montgomery to write on North Africa during World War Two.

Ted sent his copy of the manuscript to a friend who covered sports for a major New York newspaper. The reporter reviewed it and couldn't find a single factual mistake. Barnes again phoned the promotions manager and challenged her claims. During the discussion, it was learned that the supposed mistakes were spotted by a nineteen-year-old office boy of dubious sports background.

Ted demanded he get paid immediately. The promotions manager refused. When he called to complain to her superior, he was told, 'I'm sorry but it's her decision to make. I have to back my people up in situations like this.' Teddy was forced to accept her terms. Though the fantasy had occurred to him, he couldn't very well go to her office and force her to write a cheque at gunpoint. Eight weeks passed. One afternoon, Ted received another call from the promotions manager. She said, 'Mr Barnes, I have that cheque for you. Thank you so much for doing such a terrific job. The client and his vendors are all very pleased.' She went on to say how she looked forward to working with him again. Amazing! Teddy thought he was dealing with a blooming Jekyll and Hyde. It was as if the earlier accusations questioning competence had never been made.

Shortly after this, that promotions manager offered Teddy another assignment. He turned her down. Ted later told me, 'The money was pretty good, but I didn't need it that badly. It just wasn't worth the headaches. If they ever replace her, perhaps I'll work for them again. But I'm not touching another job from them as long as she is there.' I can't blame him. That promotions manager blew it. First, her early flip-flops were unprofessional. In administering a project, especially one that has to be done in a hurry, clarity is a must. Second, she should have called Ted the moment she sensed there might be a problem with the copy. This would have given him the opportunity to either allay her fears or make the necessary corrections. Finally, you should never be too quick to accept the word of a neophyte over a hired professional. If that office boy was indeed so knowledgeable, why wasn't he hired to do the pamphlet? This manager came across as an amateur. Too bad. Her behaviour has, at least temporarily, cost her company the services of a crackerjack copywriter.

A person like that promotions manager can cast a foul light on her entire company. It doesn't matter that she might be an exception in what might be an otherwise first-rate crew. Unless its members are given a chance to prove otherwise, they are going to be tainted.

Be aware that this form of guilt by association can adhere to you in a number of ways. One of the first products to be sold in our retail shops was a telephone. The phones shown to us as samples seemed to be a top-quality item. However, after they were delivered, we soon discovered the manufacturer had let us down. Customers started bringing the phones back and we soon had a small list of complaints. I tested a few of the instruments and discovered that their grumblings had been well-founded.

Remington acted quickly. It didn't wait for any more returns. Recalling every phone, we gave each customer a refund and an apology. There was no alternative way to handle it. Remington could not afford to have a shoddy product in the stores. We couldn't allow one dud's failure to reflect on our basic line. Without this philosophy, we risked having consumers think, 'Remington? Yeah, I bought that dreadful phone from them. I'm not going to get stuck again. If their phone was that bad, how good can their shavers be?' The entrepreneur who doesn't do everything he can to stop that sort of customer reflection before it starts is committing corporate suicide.

This concern for your venture's image must be shared by your partners, co-workers and employees. In the moments when they are dealing with a customer or an account, they are the company. It doesn't matter what position they hold. The larger your organization, the more crucial this becomes. When I first took over Remington, I inherited Paul Saltzman as credit manager. This gentleman's life has not been gentle. He had lived in Germany and had felt the lash of Nazi atrocities. He was married and had a college-aged son. That boy was the source of his greatest pride.

We experienced a rapid growth during those first two years. As a leveraged-buyout company, it was critical for us to keep a steady cash flow. We needed our accounts to pay their bills on time. In this regard, Paul was a godsend. You couldn't hope to find a more diligent fellow. A reserved, pipe-smoking gentleman, he seemed to charm our accounts into meeting their obligations. At least, that's what I thought.

The reality was somewhat different. Underneath the placid exterior, my credit manager was hiding a very low boiling point. Paul would lose his cool whenever he called on a delinquent account. It was almost as if the unpaid funds were coming out of his own pocket. As an entrepreneur, I would usually encourage such zeal in my employees. But this fellow was taking it to an extreme. He would imply that the customers were cheating him. If they disputed his allegation, Paul would rip into them with every foul word you could imagine. I mean he would curse up a blue haze.

This had apparently been going on for some time before we finally learned of it. Our sales manager had started to hear the first rumblings. In a typical exchange, he would call on a buyer and be told, 'You know our credit manager has asked me to tell you he's having a difficult time with Paul Saltzman. He can't believe the way this man talks to him.' The buyer would then usually continue by citing specific instances.

I was given a full report. When I asked Paul what was going on he said, 'Nothing. I'm just keeping pressure on them until we get the money.' I said, 'That's fine, Paul, but we don't want to antagonize these people. They're important to our success. When you call them be firm, but polite.' He said he would tone down his approach.

I didn't hear any complaints about Paul for about a month. Then one morning, the president of one of our accounts called me. He said, 'Mr Kiam, I know I'm one of your smaller customers and it is true we have fallen a bit behind in our payment schedule. But I don't think that's any reason to continue this campaign of verbal harassment. We will pay you soon. Now, when I told this to your credit manager, he found this most unacceptable. In fact, he responded with a stream of four-letter words that has left my ears buzzing. I like your company and your shaver. Think you're both doing a heckuva job. But if this gentleman continues to berate me or my people in this fashion, you can forget about doing business with us.' I apologized profusely to the fellow and then headed straight for Paul's office. I was accompanied by his immediate superior, the company controller.

I told him, 'Paul, we have problem. I can't have you abusing our customers. I don't care how much money they owe, this must stop.' I turned and left. As soon as I got back to the office, I took stock of the situation. The strange thing about this was that the outbursts never occurred anywhere else but on the phone. Saltzman's letters were models of business decorum, punctual and polite. In person, his demeanour bordered on shyness.

The furore suddenly died down. After several complaint-free months, it seemed as if Paul had a handle on his problem. Suddenly, tragedy struck. Paul's only son died. He was out for a while on compassionate leave. When he came back, his former behaviour resurfaced. In fact, it became more intense than ever.

We recognized the seriousness of the situation. I also understood that his personal trauma had to be exacerbating his condition. What could I do? With what he'd just gone through, I couldn't fire him. I gathered the sales managers and regional directors together and asked them to smooth things over with their accounts. They were to explain what our problem was and then ask our clients to bear with us.

This kept our accounts from bolting, but it didn't seem to help poor Paul. His haranguing became intolerable. We finally insisted that he seek psychiatric help with the company paying for his weekly sessions. That seemed to do the trick for a little while. Then the dam broke again and we were forced to let him go.

Sad. We had all the compassion in the world for him, but a company's reputation with its accounts was being jeopardized. That relationship was the lifeblood that supported several thousand jobs. We just couldn't allow it to be damaged any further.

Mr Saltzman was given a good reference. We said he was a hard-working, aggressive credit manager. I left out any mention of his erratic deportment. I just couldn't bring myself to badmouth this tortured fellow. He was in his mid-fifties. Finding a new position at that age would already be hard enough. Trying to do it after having left a company beneath a cloud would be damned near impossible.

Let me give you an example of how damaging an injured reputation can be for an entrepreneur. A good friend of mine is head of a Wall Street brokerage house. He had called me extolling the virtues of Norman, a chap with an exciting idea. He wanted to start a cable-TV network that would allow consumers to do their shopping at home. You would see the products and their prices on screen. After listing the choices' code numbers, you would use your credit cards to order the items by phone. These purchases would then be delivered to your door.

I met with Norman over lunch. I absolutely fell in love with his concept. Considering an investment in the venture, I did a background check on him. Norman had been the president of a cellular-phone company. That company had raised over five million dollars for its launch and promptly went broke. The alarm bells started ringing. I called the fellow who introduced us and said, 'The guy has a fabulous plan, but unless you can find out why his other venture failed so quickly, I'm not interested. There seem to be too many similarities between that phone company and his new business.'

It took a week to get the full story. Apparently, the phone company had an excellent product and an expert staff. It failed despite these virtues for one simple reason: Norman was a lousy administrator. He didn't know the first thing about running a company.

I went back to Norman and told him I would invest in his venture as long as he agreed to one proviso. He could not be the chief executive officer. He found my terms unacceptable. He insisted on heading the company. We parted. I can tell you that I was not surprised to learn later that he never was able to launch his idea. Several investors showed heavy interest until they got a close look at his background. Then they made the same demand as I did and received the same reply.

Norman could have overcome his stigma if he had been willing to compromise. No, he wouldn't have been the CEO. But if we had turned his dream into a success, his failing with the phone company would have been forgotten. He could have parlayed this triumph into other ventures. Instead, he was a man who couldn't get out of his own way. He tripped over his own ego.

This is not the first time I've seen this happen. Mack Lardner was a chap with a promising communications company. He took the enterprise public and raised $8 million. One year later, the company was bankrupt.

The blame rested with Lardner. For him, being a CEO meant first-class travel around the country, chauffeured limousines, exorbitant expense accounts, and plush offices befitting royalty. It was almost as if the business was an afterthought. Compounding this, Lardner just did not know how to run a business. When the company went under, tales of his extravagance surged through the industry. He is currently trying to launch a comeback. It's been a struggle. Though each one of his new ventures is attractive, no one will take a risk on them as long as he insists on being at their helm. Investors have told him this. He just doesn't seem to get the message.

This was not the case with Lyle Adams. Lyle had been a sales manager at Playtex. He was lured away from that position by a lucrative, two-year contract with the Revson company. One afternoon, he was called into Charles Revson's office just as the pact was about to expire.

Lyle felt he had done a pretty good job. He had just returned from a successful business trip and figured this meeting would be the opening of negotiations on a new agreement. It wasn't quite that. Mr Revson opened the discussion by asking, 'Lyle, how long have you been with us?'

'Two years.'

'I see. And what's the length of your contract?'

'Two years.'

'Uh-huh. Well, I guess your contract is about up, Lyle.'

That was the whole meeting. By the time Lyle got back to his office, his name was already being removed from the door. Revson never even told him why he was being dismissed. Now unemployed and middle-aged, Adams had a dickens of a time trying to find a position. Getting fired by a company at the end of your first contract is not the sort of thing that inspires confidence in a prospective employer.

Luckily, Mr Adams is nobody's fool. He realized that the chances of his getting work on an upper executive level were slim. He came up with an entrepreneurial solution. Adams called on a young, growing company. He took a position that offered a sizable pay cut and a backward step on the corporate ladder. None of that bothered him. Lyle Adams was an entrepreneur. He had confidence that, given a chance to perform, he would work his way back towards the top. His vibrant self-belief was rewarded. Mr Adams is once again ensconced in the top tier of a major corporation. Had he been too prideful to assess his situation honestly, he might never have recovered from the Revson firing.

I've seen a powerful example of this in my own company. A few years ago, I was introduced to a bright fellow who was in the midst of a private hell. He had been the executive vice-president of a company that had gone bankrupt. That company's failure was bad enough, but to compound the issue, its president was tried and convicted for engaging in illegal business practices. He was sent to prison.

The vice-president was as honest a man as you could want to meet. He wasn't charged with any crimes. When he claimed he had no idea what his superior had been up to, no one directly involved with the case doubted him.

Despite this and the chap's outstanding credentials, he was unable to find another job. Potential employers saw a shipwrecked enterprise, a CEO imprisoned for fraud, and they figured the number-two man had to be in on it no matter what the law believed. This fellow went almost a year without coming close to being hired. At fifty-four years old, things were looking mighty bleak.

I was convinced that this fellow would be an asset at Remington. I was curious about why he had stayed around while the cesspool built up around him. When I asked him for his version of what had happened he said: 'I was as surprised by what that man did as anybody. The chief financial officer reported directly to him, so I had no way of discovering what was going on with the company funds. If I had known sooner, I would have resigned. But I found out the same time as the banks. By then, his shenanigans were public knowledge. The company folded and I went with it. I didn't have a chance to get out with my skirts completely clean.' I checked his story out and was satisfied. The position I had for him was not as lofty as the one he had held. It paid only about 30 per cent of his previous salary. As executive vice-president, he had been running an entire company. Now he would be in charge of one small division.

He took the position and did one bang-up job. Not too long ago, he was offered a slot with a consulting firm at more than double what we were paying him. Because he was a realist, willing to start all over again, he is on the fast track back.

Contrast this with another acquaintance of mine. This fellow had been chairman of a good-sized organization. The company hit rough times and he eventually found himself out of a job. This failure haunts him whenever he applies for a top position. He refuses to prove himself all over again by accepting a lower level job. My misguided friend has been unemployed for over five years. He is unable to face the fact of his recent poor history.

The key point to remember is that the entrepreneur whose reputation has been sullied has to find a way to stay active. You might be the Fred Astaire of the business world, but in order to prove it to others you need a stage on which to dance. Don't worry about salary as long as it's enough to pay the bills. Coming back at a lesser job shows you've got some fortitude, that you're not a quitter. What sort of impression do you think my friend makes when he tells potential employers that he has been out of work for five years? Do you think they believe he's been on sabbatical writing a novel?

Re-entering the job market at a lower point gives you a chance to build up a record that will obscure any of the black marks that have fallen against you. It also allows you a peace of mind that will be an advantage when you are finally negotiating for a higher position. When that fellow I had hired was approached by the consulting firm, he didn't have to jump at their first offer. He already had a job. He was clear of debt and his current bills were being paid on time. He could now deal from strength. The position also kept his self-worth afloat, adding to his confidence.

If you are ever in a situation where you have to undo a tarnished image and are hunting for a position, use this fellow as a model. Put your pride in your rear pocket and opt for opportunity. Don't fuss over salary, perks, or titles. Do look to take on as much responsibility as you can. It will allow your performance to be easily measured and will let you strut your stuff for you employers. Most important of all, get the job!

Honest self-assessment can often help you avoid scenarios that are ripe for reputation gouging. George Lourie had started a leather goods company with several old cronies. One of his partners had a request. He wanted his 28-year-old son-in-law Carl brought in as executive sales manager. Apparently Carl had been a district sales manager for a leading brewery. George didn't think this young man was ready for such a large responsibility. He had never held a position this lofty before, and he was new to the business. George's partner wouldn't take no for an answer. He guaranteed the kid was up to the job and he promised to work overtime teaching him the ropes.

This might have worked out, except there was something neither George nor his partner understood. Carl thought much less of himself than his father-in-law did. He knew that he wasn't qualified for the title he was about to receive, but he was afraid of offending his in-law by turning it down. He reluctantly joined the company.

It didn't take very long for Carl to have his insecurities justified. Not knowing the business, he found himself unable to communicate with his salespeople. Most of them were an older bunch who had been raised in the leather business. They resented having to work under this upstart and they were not shy about displaying their animosity. Carl was not up to matching their little verbal broadsides. What little confidence he did have in himself began to deteriorate quickly. He started drinking.

Word gets around fast in any industry. Carl would show up loaded at sales meetings and appointments with accounts. He became known as the industry drunk. Scheduled to run a presentation for a mammoth client, he showed up so inebriated he had to desist after fifteen minutes. He turned the floor over to an assistant, stepped outside, and nearly passed out. Carl was fired the next day. I'm not sure what has happened to him. I do understand he's been unable to get any sort of executive sales job.

Just as a bad reputation is poison in business, a sterling one can give you a tremendous advantage. When I tried to come up with the financing for Remington, I had pretty good credit. I had borrowed money to start businesses before and had paid it back. Having worked for successful companies, I also had a pretty good resumé. Each one of them was known as much for its integrity as for its ability to produce a healthy profit margin. The ventures I had launched on my own had generally done well. This record did a great deal to make up for whatever funds I lacked. It showed I was a good financial risk and a business builder. Without it, I doubt the money for the Remington project would have been available.

Having told you all this, let me throw you a curve. There will be times when you will have to look past a reputation. Yes, you did read that. It's not a contradiction. Notice I said look past, not ignore. As an entrepreneur you might discover that the reason a person received a bad name in one company, might be the very thing that compels you to hire him. I've had this happen. I was looking for someone to run a Remington acquisition. Several candidates applied for the position. One fellow, Bruce Collier, stood out. He had worked as head of the retail department for a well-known conglomerate. We called it for a reference and the response couldn't have been more negative. His former boss wouldn't state it in direct terms, but he clearly implied we should stay away from Bruce. When I asked him why, he replied, 'Even though his record might not show it, he's a loose cannon. He was always questioning company policy, and proposing new ideas. He also worked too many hours. His co-workers hated him because he made them look bad. Nothing but a problem.' Hmm, a guy who bucks the status quo, thinks creatively, and works too hard? My kind of executive! I finished the conversation by making sure Bruce didn't have any serious vices or any recent burglaries on his record and then thanked the old fussbudget for his time. Then I called Bruce to offer him a job. I'm not sorry I did. From day one, he's been a tremendous asset to the company.

You all know the adage about sizing up a person by the company he keeps. That holds true in business. Ann Richards is the marketing director for an international fashion company. This firm has enjoyed a lofty reputation for quite some time. About a year ago, the founding executives sold the company.

The new owners had some peculiar ideas about running a business. Rather than continuing to build on what was already a prestigious foundation, they instituted a flock of cost-cutting measures. First they replaced many of their skilled craftsmen with less talented individuals who were willing to work at reduced wages. Then the efficient administrative staff, never an extravagance, was cut back. Finally, they became lax in their operations. Much of the company's merchandise is imported from Europe. Any fashion item entering the United States must carry its fibre content clearly labelled. It's the law. This company had become so negligent, 50 per cent of its imports often failed to show this required marking. All these items had to be reworked. By the time the merchandise was shipped, stores had been forced to cancel whole advertising campaigns. Ann would then be forced to chuck entire promotions and pricing plans into the wastepaper basket.

Clearly, her new bosses weren't interested in building their enterprise. They were looking to make a fast buck. As a result, the company is slowly sliding into decline. Ann is in her mid-twenties. This is her first upper echelon position and she savours her title. But she also knows she is now hooked up with a loser. When she asked me for advice, I told her to do her damndest to correct whatever problems she could, and to start looking for a new job. Leaving now, she goes out with a CV filled with positives. She will be able to say that she tried to make the best of a horrid mess, but that the situation was beyond her control. A marketing director can have little impact on corporate policy when the CEOs are such foul-ups. It's doubtful that any knowledgeable person will attach this company's eventual failure to her and her refusal to stay with this band of clowns will only enhance her record. However, she must move quickly. If she is still on board when the company hits its nadir, she will be tainted by the thick coating of the owner's mismanagement. It will be very hard to remove this particular smudge. In choosing a company to work for, always associate with winners. You'll learn more. If you go on to another position, you will be able to leverage off your

company's success. Employers want to hire those who have
been part of a triumph.

I'd like to end this chapter with one final example illustrating
the power of a good name. I had bought a company that
distributed industrial components through mail-order catalogues. It was called Pic Design. It had been running low on
capital for quite a while, and run far behind on deliveries. As
its credibility suffered, its volume fell off drastically. It was
finally on the edge of insolvency.

We grabbed it just as it was about to tip over. I thought the
basic company was sound and that an influx of cash would put
its workings in order. I also knew the enterprises badly needed
a new image. We decided to rename it 'Pic Design, a subsidiary
of Remington Technologies'. Nothing changed but the title.

Since the Remington turnaround, our company has become
known for its high standards. We are the shaver manufacturer
that exercises 100 per cent quality control. As you've seen,
we're also an organization that refuses to be associated with
shoddy products. Our money-back guarantees tell the public
that we stand behind our merchandise. It's a pledge of good
faith that has never been betrayed. By adding the Remington
monicker, we were letting the public know that we were standing behind Pic Design. Someone must like our history. In less
than fourteen months this nearly bankrupt company is back on
its feet. Business is already up by 25 per cent. Yes, we've
stablized the company's performance. Our customers now
know it's a reliable supplier. But we wouldn't have rebuilt
consumer confidence if the public hadn't been willing to give
Pic a second chance. We bought that confidence with the
Remington name. What kind of value can we put on that?

CHAPTER SIX

Entrepreneurship: more than just a business, a way of life

People often think of entrepreneurship as applying only to business. To them, it's nothing more than the art of building a successful enterprise or deal. This is a misapprehension. For me, entrepreneurship is a way of living. My bromide, 'Business is where you are', means we should keep our focus on the business at hand. No matter what the size of the store or company you are calling on, during the time you are there it is the most important account in the world. You are totally committed to it from the moment you walk into it until the moment you leave. You shouldn't rush through a shoddy presentation at a small drug store simply because you want to hurry off to pitch Harrods. This adage is just another way of underlining the importance of prioritizing. It is a philosophy that has helped me accomplish a good many things in business. It has also assisted in keeping my life from fraying at the ends.

The most important priorities in my life have been family, business, and tennis, in that order. There are even times when tennis creeps into the number two spot. A fourth priority would be the advancement of education. An educated society offers a higher standard of living for its people. So allot some time and financial support for educational organizations.

In terms of hours, business does demand the greater portion of my time. It has to. When I'm attending to it, the job commands my full concentration. Despite this commitment, I've always known that business isn't everything.

To some entrepreneurs that statement may seem like blasphemy. There's always been a stereotype about successful businessmen. Supposedly, the powerful CEO is so driven by ambition, his personal life is usually a shambles. The person at the top is often depicted as someone lacking compassion, a robot with a ledger for a heart. The film *Wall Street* with its Prince of Darkness, Gordon Gekko, reigning from the film's dark centre, certainly contributes to that caricature.

A great many people are now convinced that this sort of all-devouring android represents a business norm. However, in my opinion, the person who leaves life's real treasures by the wayside in some all-out assault on success, fame, and wealth is missing out on so much. I have been married to the same wonderful woman for over thirty years. We've raised a fine family. I couldn't be more proud of any of them. The happiness they've brought has taught me something and I'm here to tell you that *winning at the workplace is a shallow triumph if you're losing at home. Those who can maintain a healthy bottom line in both environments are achieving the greatest victory of all.* There is no reason why the entrepreneurial principles that engender success in business can't be applied to achieve a happier personal life.

Marriage and the entrepreneur

I was just looking at a copy of the magazine *Forbes*. It's the issue celebrating the *Forbes* 400, a listing of America's richest men. Looking through it I noticed that almost every one of them has been divorced. This is tragic. If a person is willing to put in the effort, I don't think this failure rate has to stand so high.

You should lay the foundation for a solid relationship as soon as things turn serious. Share your dreams with your prospective mate. More importantly, let him or her know the sacrifices those hopes demand. You are not going to be home at six for dinner every night. Social obligations will go unmet. Quiet, relaxing weekends are going to become less frequent. This might not seem shattering now, but after five or six episodes of missed dinners and cancelled invitations in a two-week period, the other half of a relationship might blow his or her cork. If the person you love is unable to cope with your lifestyle, it's best to find out before you make a deep commitment. If you can't work out a compromise, you will either have to cease being an entrepreneur or leave the relationship.

Ellen and I had to make adjustments after we married. Socially, she is much more outgoing than I. She has a lot of friends and would like to have them over for dinner. It is tough for us to entertain all that often with my schedule. She adapted to that. For my part, when she did plan a rare night with friends, I made sure I was available. Occasionally, we would be invited to a large function. I hate big parties. Who do you generally meet at these affairs? Someone you've never known before and will never see again. You have a light conversation about things of little if any interest. Bores me silly. When I do socialize, I prefer it to be at an intimate gathering. However, if we are asked to a large get-together, and it is something Ellen really wants to do, I go without complaint and do my best to make it a happy time. She pitches in by seeing that we don't get hooked into too many of these galas.

Here's a good example of compromise. Early in the writing of this book I found that the Christmas holidays were soon to be upon us. This is naturally a very important time of the selling season so my duties at Remington are heavier than usual. It is a Saturday afternoon. My wife and I would love to be finishing our Christmas shopping together. However, I have a deadline to meet and I've got to stay home writing this book. Ellen is disappointed, but she understands. She is once again in charge of buying gifts. Meanwhile, I'm working like mad to clear my calendar. Come Christmas eve, I don't want business or the book to encroach on our celebration. It's all a matter of give and take.

The entrepreneurial life is often a roller coaster. Your mate should be prepared for that. There is no reason why you shouldn't discuss your business with the one you love. Keep him or her informed about your losses, triumphs, and plans for the future. You want your loved one to be a partner in life. How long would you stay in a partnership in which you weren't allowed to know what the company was doing or to see the books?

A fellow recently told me his business's tale of woe. Sales were markedly down and he had to fire some of the people in his division. His own position was tenuous. I asked him if he had told any of this to his wife. He said, 'Oh, I never discuss business with her!' Is that fair? What on earth is going to happen if his enterprise falls apart? He should prepare her now. She needs to know and he is going to need her moral support.

I've always discussed my business with Ellen. It takes up so much of our life, I don't see how we could have avoided the subject. I value her cool head when I'm trying to come to a decision. I also need her support. Entrepreneurs often take on high risk endeavours. When they are in jeopardy you don't need a partner harping on how bad things are. You want someone who will see you through the dark days. This partner holds your hand, offers realistic counsel, and never loses faith in you. Depending on the severity of the situation, he or she might even pitch in to help in a more active manner.

For a time, Benrus went through a particularly rough period. The company was in trouble because we were undercapitalized. Orders were way down. I had to cut my salary in half. Ellen and I began to formulate a survival strategy. We started by making a list of personal cost-cutting measures. Our expenses would have to be rolled back if we were going to get through this. Thing were so grave, we were considering selling the house. I didn't want to have to take the kids out of school and this seemed the only way to raise their tuition while meeting our other bills. Having had a long run of success, it was all very traumatic.

One night during this horrible time, I woke up to find my wife in the bathroom sitting on the edge of the tub. She was working away with a pad and pencil. I asked what she was doing. She explained, 'A woman I know teaches dance. She's about to retire and close her school. I think I could take it over from her. I'm making a list of friends whose children might want to attend.'

Oh, did my heart want to burst! Ellen wasn't wasting energy, fretting over our predicament. She was ready to do whatever she could to help make ends meet. We righted the Benrus situation and that school never did get opened. However, on Ellen's next birthday, I gave her a gift from the heart: a pair of dancing slippers. It was my tribute to her for being such a rock. Throughout that entire bleak time, she never lost confidence in me. How can you lose with someone like that beside you? If I ever entertained any self-doubts, I could call on her strength. Then the spring would again jump into my step and I'd be hungry to find another Everest to leap over.

Entrepreneurs are often on the move and that can present a whole new set of problems to a relationship. I've seen marriages in which an enterprise forces the spouses to live in separate universes. A man or woman, climbing to the top in an industry, is flying off around the world. They have friends in New Zealand and China. They can quote the tariffs and duties in Kenya. Their spouses are lucky if they occasionally visit another state. They don't know anything about the international marketplace or the best restaurants in Tokyo. These people are at home in some little town trying to balance the family budget while raising the children. They might be involved in a small business. Their only contact with a foreign land occurs when they receive the local travel agency's annual calendar.

If they don't find a way to bridge the differences in their lives, they are going to have a problem. After a few years of this, the globe-trotter and spouse both look up and say, 'We're growing apart.' The next thing you know, they are spending time with marriage counsellors or, in the most tragic of circumstances, filing papers for divorce.

You can help avoid this by bringing your partner into your realm. When you get home from a trip, share as much of your experience as possible. Bring back literature, pictures, and anything else that will give your mate a sense of the country or city you've just visited. Don't spare any details; take time to present a full view. When you're away you should phone daily. To hell with the expense. Let the other person know they are still a vital part of your life's fabric.

I recently saw one marriage flounder because the husband never bothered to call home. Whether he was in the office or off on a trip, he just couldn't pick up the phone to see what or how his wife was doing. The guy just didn't think it was important. This behaviour was symptomatic of a generally uncaring attitude towards his wife. It wasn't that he didn't love her. He did. He was just too caught up with his business to be sensitive to her needs. When his spouse started to talk about divorce, he suddenly realized he hadn't been giving her enough attention. It was too late.

If you do have to travel and you have the opportunity, you should take your mate with you. Especially on the more exotic trips. I always try to have Ellen accompany me on certain travels. This does two things. First, you and your mate get to spend time with each other on an adventure. Second, your partner gets a taste of what your life is like on the road. That is not inconsequential. I know many wives whose husbands spend a lot of time in various lands. They are stuck at home tending to the mundane demands of daily living. Having never been on the road with their husbands, they create fantasies. They think, 'That guy is in London. He's probably eating at the best restaurant and schmoozing with exciting people. What am I doing tonight? I'm trying to convince Bobby to eat all of his spinach. Then I have to go over his homework. And of course the cleaning has to be done. I'm going to be exhausted. I'd love to sleep late, but I have to get up early tomorrow to drive the kids to school. Meanwhile, that guy is across the Atlantic having a hell of a time! The rat!'

It does happen. I've seen resentments fester over this very issue. These can be avoided. If you take your spouse with you on a trip, he or she will find that this view bears little semblance to reality. With a schedule that is anything like mine they will first experience the delight of waiting for your baggage and then plodding through customs during the wee hours. Then they will see you reaching your hotel at 2 a.m., getting up four or five hours later for that first meeting of the morning, and working all day long. No chichi friends. No fancy restaurants. If you can eat at all, you do it on the run. You have to take care of business. When you get back to the hotel, you're so exhausted, you can barely open your room door, much less trip the light fantastic in some fashionable disco. You plop into bed and swiftly drift into the land of sweet nod. If you're lucky, you had enough energy to get undressed before making that well deserved excursion.

How's that for a jolt of reality? When your spouse gets a dose of it, the envy and resentments will cease. They will realize they are in a partnership. You both have jobs to do and one is not necessarily more pleasant or exciting than the other. Only the locales are different.

The dynamism of your whirlwind pace might have another benefit. It could inspire a mate to get involved in a business of their own. I can't think of a better prescription for a happy marriage. It doesn't have to be a huge enterprise. A small mail-order business or some other cottage industry can provide more than enough challenge and excitement. With it in place, you both feel fulfilled. Your conversations are spiced by tales of triumph, disappointment, worry, and hope.

Ellen and I have been involved in several ventures together. She is currently running the Friendship Collection. We constantly talk over business. She has always had a keen interest in whatever I am doing. I give her accomplishments the same attention. In fact, I am more tickled by her successes than by anything I could possibly do. Our common interest and participation in businesses enhances an already solid rapport. It adds a little more sizzle and glue to the marriage.

Because entrepreneurs often live and work on the edge, humour is vital to the success of any relationship. I don't believe we have had a major fight in our marriage. There are two reasons for that. First, we don't bottle things up. If something is burning us, we let off steam before exploding. It's another case of 'Business is where you are.' If expressing your dissatisfaction is the business of the moment, deal with it then and there. Second, we both have a sense of humour. Neither one of us is afraid to laugh at ourselves.

This last quality certainly came in handy when I made a change in my commercials. The first Remington ads featured me in a suit behind a desk. Then I decided to be a bit more daring. Since no one actually shaves while wearing a jacket and tie, I appeared in a commercial wearing my bathrobe in a bathroom setting.

When Ellen got a gander at this ad, I thought she would brain me. Oh did she left off steam that night. You would have thought the living room was a sauna. She said, 'How could you, a distinguished businessman, appear on TV in a bathrobe? Have you seen any other CEOs or politicians prancing about dressed like that? What kind of image are you creating?' She really let me have it. You would have thought I had bared my buns in *Oh! Calcutta*.

Despite her worries, the commercials did quite well. However, we did get some letters claiming the ads were still not quite realistic enough. These writers pointed out that most people don't even wear bathrobes when they shave. I took an informal poll and found out they were right. What was I going to do now? I wanted a commercial with as realistic an ambience as possible. I was an entrepreneur always ready to break new ground. I decided to shuck the robe.

I shot a commercial with one towel wrapped around my middle and another draped around my neck. I made sure the top towel covered at least half of my manly chest. I didn't think the world was ready for a full exposure.

I neglected to tell Ellen about this development. Gee, I don't know why. I guess I forgot. I also told the rest of my employees that if they should talk to her, they should forget also. I knew the secrecy wouldn't last for very long. You didn't have to be the head of M15 to figure out that you can't carry out a covert operation under the glare of a national ad campaign.

One night we were watching the evening news. They cut to the commercials. What entrepreneur was brought into our living room via the miracle of the airwaves? Yes, it was Mr Kiam himself, half-nude from the waist up, extolling the virtues of the microscreen shaver. People across America were salivating. I was sinking in my chair. Knowing that the reckoning was near, all I could do was stare at the set. I didn't dare look at Ellen.

The commercial was a thirty-second spot. It seemed to run for two hours. When it ended, Ellen didn't say a word. The news continued. Again nothing. We watched the bulletin to its conclusion and still I didn't hear a peep.

I'm thunderstruck. I finally worked up the gumption to ask, 'Honey did you notice the new ad during the news?' She had. When I asked her what she thought of it, she said – and this really rocked me – she liked it! I said, 'Ellen, I just don't understand this. When I switched from a suit to a bathrobe, you blew your cork. Now I'm in nothing but two towels, and you're not angry at all. How come?' She replied, 'Because it won't be on for very long?' When I asked why she thought that, she answered, 'We both know that commercials are supposed to sell products, right? Well nobody is ever going to buy a shaver from a guy with a body like that!' The next sound you heard was that of a time bomb being defused by laughter.

We are family

If you're blessed with kids, I know it can be hard to find an equitable balance between work and family. Most things worth having never come easy. But I believe your task will be much simpler if you apply your entrepreneurial creativeness to your domestic life.

For instance, Ellen and I have three children, Lisa, Tory, and Robin. When they were growing up I didn't have as much time to spend with them as I would have liked. I was often on the road from Monday to Friday. Because we considered it important, we gave the weekend to the kids. They picked out our activities. Whatever they wanted to do – go ice skating, visit the zoo, take in a movie – became the marching orders for the day. One ritual we performed almost weekly was our Saturday morning soccer game. My son and our dog would play against my daughters and me. Ellen and I also took time to teach them how to ride bikes, how to swim, and eventually how to water ski. Unlike some dads, I couldn't give them little pieces of me every night. But those big chunks of father they got on the weekends made up for it. It created a bond.

On those occasions when I was able to come home at night, it was often very late. The kids would be ready for bed. With the help of a friend, I was able to steal some precious moments with them. The friend was a fellow named Squeemy the Rabbit.

Squeemy was my creation. On the way home, I would construct adventures for this eccentric hare. Squeemy was a spy in one of the tales. Needing a disguise, he covered himself in pink toothpaste. Everything went along fine for him until he walked in front of an open fire hydrant. The splashing water washed away his disguise. Now he had to escape before he was found out. Not exactly the Brothers Grimm. These were simple stories that amused the children just as they were going to sleep and gave me an opportunity to interact with them.

I don't think the children ever resented my absences. Part of the reason for that was communication. As soon as they were able to understand, they were told why Dad had to go away so often. We didn't make the demands of my position a mystery for them. When you're breaking your back to make an enterprise go it's going to cut into your time with family. Isn't your family one of the main reasons you're making that sacrifice? It's an act of love and you shouldn't be afraid to let your children know that.

I also eventually discussed the various projects I was working on with the children. If I had a success, I shared it with them. If one of my plans went bust, they found that out too. That was especially important. I didn't want them to think I walked on water. I wanted them to know that though I had tried and failed, I was going to keep trying. They learned that you don't allow a setback to unravel your dreams. You mustn't be an icon to your children. If they know you are not superhuman, that you understand failure, it will be so much easier for them to approach you when they are troubled by a mistake. They will know it's not the end of the world. There is nothing lonelier than a worried child who feels he or she has no one who understands their distress.

When our kids had a problem – schoolwork, peer-group pressure – we gave them our undivided attention. Business is where you are, and your family is your most sacred business. When I hear about communication gaps, I have to shake my head. You both talk, you both listen. Really listen! If one of your children is telling you about the difficulty she is having with maths, don't be thinking about tomorrow's meeting or have your nose buried in the *Wall Street Journal*. They need your focus. No matter what your successes enable you to bestow upon your children, the most important thing they can receive is yourself. Give it completely.

In some cases you might even be able to allow your children to participate in your venture. When Ellen and I started the Italian jewellery business, eight-year-old Lisa was our 'chief shipping clerk'. We ran the company from our home. Since I worked during the day, most of the business was tended to at night. Ellen and I would price and label the items on the living room floor. Lisa would pack the jewellery, then weigh the boxes for postage. She became a part of the business.

This was especially exciting for her because she was doing something none of her friends had ever done. It was also another chance to spend time with Ellen and me. As a by-product, Lisa developed a natural business acumen. When she had only a small number of boxes to pack, she would say, 'I guess the company isn't doing so well this week.' We'd then tell her why we were sending out fewer orders. She gradually got the gist of what went into running a venture. As I think you'll see in a later chapter, we planted an entrepreneurial seed back then, one that is still growing.

I also made it a point to time my own vacations from work with the kids' holiday from school. We would go away as a family. When the children started to play tennis, we spent most of our vacation time going to their tournaments. On weekends we took them to their matches. The entire family shared in the exhilaration of victory and the disappointment of defeat. We eventually began to play with and against each other. That sport became a marvellous mode of communication for us. Tory and I got so involved with it, we became a nationally ranked father–son combination.

You can watch a relationship evolve when you and your son or daughter participate in a competition. When Tory and I first started playing, I was the better athlete. I had to compensate for the weaknesses in his game. After his sixteenth birthday, his game started to soar. We became equals on the court. Time spent preparing for and participating in matches became quality time. You are both committed to a common goal and a common excellence. You have one more thing to discuss over the dinner table. As you learn to adapt to each other as players, you adjust to each other as people. I can think of few things that can promote togetherness between parents and children more than the sheer joy of playing a game.

The amount of interest you show in your children tells them how important they are. Any person who doesn't believe in himself isn't going to be much of an entrepreneur. An entrepreneur takes risks, is decisive, and is not afraid to call attention to himself and his work. This demands a high degree of confidence. The entrepreneur understands this and knows the value of a positive self-image.

Your children may have no interest in business. However, life is an entrepreneurial venture, the largest game of all. I've seen so many melancholy adults, trapped in existences that will never measure up to their adolescent dreams. These are people blessed with innate talent, even genius, but lacking the confidence to express it.

Imagine if Pavarotti were afraid to sing or Evelyn Waugh too fearful to write. Forget the loss to ourselves and think instead of the private hell in which these suddenly pathetic individuals would be forced to wander while haunted by their smirking, elusive muse. Could there be any greater pain? If so, I wouldn't want to know it.

Considering these tragic scenarios, a failed salesman comes to mind. At initial glance, you would think this fellow had it all. Good looks, a quick mind, and what seemed like admirable poise. Would you believe none of these attributes could help carry him through a presentation? Whenever he called on a customer, particularly a large one, his muscles would tighten, his voice would rise an octave, and a torrent of damning perspiration would sweep over his body. As the physical symptoms of this anxiety attack heightened, he would blank out whole sections of his proposal.

Everyone thought these occurrences were merely a manifestation of the jitters suffered by many rookie salespeople. They assumed they would vanish after a week or two of comforting experience and a few sales. The condition only worsened. The fellow resigned after only six weeks on the job.

In private conversation, we later got an idea why this chap was so insecure. Apparently, he had a domineering father. Throughout his childhood, nothing the son did could ever please his dad. High grades in school, a certain prowess in athletics, and an excellent moral character failed to make an impression. The young man lost sight of his value because he had never had it affirmed by the most important figure in his life. As a salesman, each customer he called on became the father he could never please. His best efforts – outstanding performances too, I might add – had always met with rejection. The pain inflicted by this particular cruelty was so crushing it crippled the young fellow's attempts to succeed. The violent physical reactions were insulating him from another disappointment. He had, after all, touched excellence so often, only to come away with fingers burnt by paternal indifference.

We have to give our children love and encouragement. One

without the other is nothing more than a brightly wrapped empty box. We always made it a point to let Lisa, Tory, and Robin know we had the utmost confidence in them. When Lisa had the idea to publish a newsletter centering on preschool education, we didn't tell her the idea was too risky or that she lacked the necessary experience. We urged her to run with her dream. If she wanted our advice, we were there for her, but we didn't stand over her shoulder monitoring her ups and downs. We were content to root like crazy from the sidelines unless we were called into the game.

Robin was working in sales and marketing for the Friendship Collection when she was approached by a medium-sized cosmetics company. It offered her the position of marketing manager. This was an impressive entry position. She would report directly to the company's vice-president and would be in charge of her own product lines. The job gave her a chance to participate in sales and product development and couldn't help but broaden her business experience. Having worked for Friendship and for a prestigious New York department store, she was already used to seeing things from the perspective of the retailer. Now she would look through the eyes of the manufacturer. We hated to lose her; she had been a valued employee. But Ellen and I both encourage our children to make their own decisions. We also knew this was an opportunity she couldn't pass up.

Unfortunately, three weeks after she joined the company, the vice-president in charge of marketing quit. His resignation left Robin and a second young lady, both relatively inexperienced, to develop the company's marketing strategy. As a result of their company's lack of organization, they were also required to solve problems outside of the marketing realm. Late shipments, mismarked items and other glitches were all brought to Robin's attention. She and her associate weren't given either help or guidance. They were left on their own.

It soon became apparent that both girls had been put in a position that required long hours and astute financial acumen. Robin was working twelve hours a day, six days a week in order to solve the problems and develop viable programmes. Although she enjoyed the challenge, it was gradually wearing her down. The company never got around to replacing the marketing director. As each week passed, Robin felt a bit more overwhelmed. She soon realized she needed a greater knowledge of accounting and finance in order to meet the demands of her position. She could not get this training while on the job. There just wasn't any time.

Robin took a pragmatic look at her situation. She was working for a disorganized enterprise. Its problems often seemed endless. In seven months, it had been unable to hire a new marketing director. Left on her own, she had no one to teach her the ropes. She also recognized that she needed a better grounding in finance and accounting. Weighing these facts, she made an entrepreneurial decision. Robin left her position. She was looking past the short-term illusion of job security. I am proud to say she took a long-term step and went back to school. Enrolling in a curriculum that includes financial planning and basic accounting, she is turning her weaknesses into strengths. She will resume her career as a more well-rounded and knowledgeable individual. By returning to university, Robin is giving herself the ammunition to achieve excellence. She's going for it.

When it came time for Tory to choose a high school, I had a preference. Tory was not very keen on my choice. We didn't argue the point and I didn't pull rank, ordering him to like it or lump it. Instead, we calmly discussed our differences. Tory wanted to stay in a local high school because of its outstanding tennis programme. The school team was about to be upgraded by the arrival of young John McEnroe, already a known star on the tennis circuit. The institution had high academic standards, so I had no quarrel with that and I knew Tory – as he pointed out in our conversation – had aspirations to become a tennis pro. After listening to the cool and reasoned explanation for his choice, I supported it.

I'm not just taking time here to commit the crime of many parents: bragging about one's children. I'm simply trying to point out the power of a lifetime of encouragement. A great athlete, now retired, had become a coach. He gained a reputation as an outstanding trainer of young players. When asked his secret, he replied, 'Simple. I teach them the fundamentals. If they have the reflexes, they can execute the basics. Then I tell them how great they are. It's amazing. If you keep telling a person how great they are, eventually they start to believe it.'

Call it positive thinking or anything else you like, we let our kids know that the only things they couldn't achieve were the things they didn't try. I don't want anyone to think I'm presenting the Kiams as a model and I wouldn't attempt to give specific advice on how to raise a family. By comparison, running a business is a much easier task. You want to lend guidance, give advice, and, when necessary, enforce some discipline. But to that mix add a heaping cupful of independence. Let your children know that all limitations are self-imposed. You're an entrepreneur. You want your enterprise to be manned by dynamic go-getters and risk-takers. You shouldn't want anything less for your family. I often say a new venture is like a baby that has to be nurtured. Well, your young children really are your babies and they're more important than any profit and loss sheet. We mustn't ever lose sight of that.

Choosing the family business

If you run your own company or business, your child might someday opt to join you in it. As long as it is their own, unpressured choice, I heartily endorse the decision. It is also one that should not be made lightly. There are easier things in this world than having mum or dad as a boss.

Tory took quite a while before deciding to join Remington on a full-time basis. During the summers he would work for our New York sales representative. Carrying a briefcase full of brochures, he would call on accounts – mostly drugstores – and try to persuade them to beef up their Remington lines. He wasn't walking out of stores with $10,000 orders; he was lucky to sell one or two shavers to each account.

After graduating from Harvard University, he was hired as a financial analyst by the brokerage house Drexel Burnham. He learned a good deal in the two years he spent there, but somewhere along the line he decided that Remington could be an exciting opportunity. However, his career with us nearly ended before it began.

He had accompanied me on a book tour of Australia. I received an unusual amount of publicity during the sojourn. It seemed everywhere I turned, someone either had a microphone or a camera stuck in my face. It was a circus of non-stop interviews for newspapers, magazines, television, and radio. People were actually asking me for my autograph. It was great fun, but we hardly had a moment to ourselves. Tory found the scene a bit overwhelming. They didn't teach you to be prepared for this sort of commotion in business school. Midway through a visit to Melbourne, my son excused himself and took off on a walkabout near the Great Barrier Reef. He said he needed to clear his head.

We agreed to meet on Bora-Bora. Away from the cameras and questions, Tory was able to share his thoughts with me. He was troubled. He said, 'I don't know how I feel about all this publicity and your obligations to the media. I don't know that I want to run around making speeches. If this is what Remington is going to be, I'm not sure I want it. Dad, you're a pretty hard act to follow.' I told him I could understand how that might appear to be the case, but that a lot of his perception was an illusion. I explained, 'This isn't a normal situation. It's a fluke created largely by the TV commercials and *Going For It!* This stuff has very little to do with our business. It's just icing on our cake. The real business of Remington is a lot of slogging away, doing the nuts and bolts work to build up the company.'

He was still a bit shaken. He wondered if joining Remington would be the correct move. Tory was particularly concerned about his identity. Throughout the tour, Tory thought everyone looked at him as being 'Victor's boy'. They didn't know anything about him and they didn't seem to care who he really was. He felt they had pigeonholed him. That irked him. He didn't want to go through life thought of solely as 'Son of Kiam'. I can't blame him. It sounded like some sort of damned monster movie. He wanted to be his own individual, not an addendum.

I said, 'You have an opportunity here that is available to few people. It might not be the company for you. Who can say? But I think it would be foolish to walk away from it without giving it a try. You're a young man. A year is not a long time at your age. If at the end of the year, you're not satisfied with the company or you feel your identity is still threatened, go off and do your own thing. I'll support any decision you make. And if you decide you don't even want to test this opportunity for a year, I'll support that too.'

I wanted him to join us. But, just as he had the right to choose his own high school, I had to let him choose his own business life. It doesn't matter how much you encourage a child's independence or boost their self-confidence, all that talk is just talk, nothing more, unless you allow them to stand on their own when it comes to crunch time.

Tory decided to come on board. As a parent, you are always looking for common interests to be shared with your kids. When that interest happens to be your enterprise, an entity that has become so much a part of your being, you have built the ultimate bridge over the so-called generation gaps. You are going to partake jointly in the marrow of life, participating in its triumphs and disappointments.

Be aware, though, that this can entail certain difficulties. You should do everything you can to avoid the appearance of nepotism in the treatment of your child. This can be done in a variety of ways.

I make a conscious effort to keep our Remington relationship on a businesslike level. When Tory enters the office, he ceases to be a son. He's another valued Remington employee treated the same as everyone else. In fact, I bend over backwards not to make it easier for him. For example, his pay scale is much lower than it should be. I probably shouldn't say that. In a later chapter, I'm going to discuss getting a raise. Armed with that information and this admission, he might come at me for a few more quid. I wish him luck. I keep his salary down, because I don't want anyone to think he's riding into work on a gravy train. Teamwork has been such a vital element of the Remington success. All it would take is a dose of jealousy to dent the spirit we have created in the company.

A charge of nepotism would have a similar effect. Tory came up with an entrepreneurial solution to head off any such claims. In business school, Tory had been taught the importance of learning everything you could about any company that employed you. He was also told that executives should build a rapport with the other employees.

Knowing these principles had succeeded at Remington, he decided to implement them in another, rather creative way. When Tory joined the company, he didn't come in as part of management. He started as a factory worker and held various positions on the work floor. He helped run the machines that manufacture our blades and sat on the assembly line. He put in time in every section of the factory. His pay cheque and hours matched those of his fellow workers.

At the end of half a year, he knew more about the actual manufacture and shipping of our shavers than I did. Tory learned so much, not just about Remington but the people who make it work. I doubt anyone appreciates the job they do more than he does. For their part, the factory people found that here was a young man who wanted to achieve his own success, who was willing to pay some dues. There was no animosity when we moved him into a junior executive position. He has been with us for two years and has become quite an asset. If he wants to, he might even be president of the company someday.

But like any entrepreneur, he'll have to earn it.

*

A shaggy dog story

I have found that even the small traumas of your daily domestic life can often be ironed out with some entrepreneurial creativity. For instance back when I was still with Playtex, we bought a dog for the kids, a Shetland sheepdog we christened Omar. He became a fourth child. Everywhere we went, Omar went. We took him to Central Park and let him play games with the children. One morning, they were tossing a ball to him in a large field on 79th street. I was talking to a friend of mine. The only other person around was a sallow man with a small whippet.

At some point, the kids' shouting pulled us out of our conversation. I looked over to see what was wrong. Omar had disappeared. He had gone running after the ball, turned behind a bush, and hadn't returned. Omar was well trained. He would usually appear at the call of his name. Scattering about the field, we shouted in all directions. We even got in a cab and called for him throughout the park, but it was no use. If Omar could hear us, he wasn't answering.

We didn't drop our search. I had each of the children cover a different block on the way home. Though highly unlikely, it was possible that Omar might have started back without us and got lost. We asked passers-by if they had seen him. No luck.

We called the ASPCA and gave its officials Omar's description. That night, the family was worried sick. Neither Ellen nor I could get to sleep. As I lay awake, I thought, 'This dog means so much to us, I have to approach this the same way I would go after a prized account. I've got to put everything I have into finding Omar.' The next day, I went to Playtex and told my boss I was taking a week off to find my dog. He looked at me as if four screws had just dropped off my head. I told him, 'Sure, I know it sounds crazy, but I've got to do it.'

I then immediately went to Young and Rubicam, our company's ad agency. I told an executive, 'I want to run an ad campaign to find my dog. Anything you can do to get me on

TV, radio, or into the newspapers is fine with me. I'll do anything.' We took out ads in every New York newspaper, advertising a $500 reward for the return of Omar. No questions asked.

The ads ran on a Tuesday morning. That evening, I got a call from a private detective who said he was an expert in finding lost people and animals. He thought he might have some ideas on how to find Omar. We arranged to meet.

This fellow was like someone out of a Raymond Chandler novel. He showed up with a snap-brim hat, ill-fitting trench coat, and he talked out of the side of his mouth. Throughout our interview, he kept cleaning his nails. With a stiletto. He told me, 'There have been a lot of dog-nappings in your area. The dogs are sold in an illegal show in Pennsylvania. They are then used for medical experiments. I'll check into those. In the meantime, I would suggest we hire a crew of kids to put notices concerning Omar in the lobby of every buidling from 59th to 96th street. Make sure the notices include a good, clear picture of the dog.'

I did as he asked. I also got a list of all the veterinarians and animal hospitals in the tri-state area, that is, in New York, New Jersey and Connecticut. I sent Omar's picture to each one of them along with a letter asking if anyone had brought in such a dog. We followed up every possibility. When someone mentioned that cab drivers often pick up stray dogs, we put our next ad in the taxi news.

Young and Rubicam got me on a local TV show called *New York, New York*. I went on the air to make an appeal. Prior to my appearance, the show featured a guest who had baked the world's largest pizza. I was sitting next to it off-camera. The fumes from the onions and peppers wafted about me. It was so intense my eyes began to water. By the time the interview started, I had tears cascading down my cheeks. It sure gave my appeal an emotional quality. New York just opened its heart. I was deluged with suggestions and clues. Unfortunately, none of the respondents had Omar. We followed all their leads though. One woman said she thought she saw Omar in a vacant lot in the Bronx. We scurried up there and spent the better part of an hour searching. Nothing.

We got the police involved. They told us that dog-napping rings often operated around the park. These crooks would use a small dog as a decoy for other pooches. Oh no. I thought about that sallow-faced man with the whippet.

Omar's disappearance occurred while Harry Stokes and I were trying to prevent the Riklis takeover of Playtex. At the upcoming weekend I would have to attend a crucial meeting which had been fixed with the owners of the Schlitz Brewery. This was the meeting which I chronicled in chapter two. There was no getting around it, so with what little time I had left, I hurriedly made arrangements with the police to set a trap. We would rent a dog, have Ellen and the cops go to the park on Saturday, and attempt to decoy any would-be dog-nappers into making a move. Ellen would keep me abreast of the progress by phone.

She called me Saturday evening. The plan couldn't have been a bigger dud. First, the rental agency misunderstood my instructions. I wanted a medium-sized dog of excellent pedigree, a pooch that looked as though it would sport a heavy price tag. I wanted a dog that the thieves would find irresistible. The agency sent us a six-foot-long Great Dane. You should have seen this animal. He had teeth that made the shark in *Jaws* look as if he were all gums. An armed Al Capone, accompanied by his entire mob, wouldn't have tried to steal this dog. Even the police were terrified of him.

It was too late to get a replacement. The Dane was brought to the park in a squad car. Lights were flashing. Sirens were screaming. If there had been any dog-nappers about, you can bet that display would have scared them off. Naturally, this thin charade didn't turn up a thing. When I heard the details, it nearly put me at my wit's end. I thought, 'What are we going to do now?'

We concluded our meeting with Schlitz that evening. Having returned to the hotel, I started to pack for my trip home. I wanted to get back and continue the search for Omar. Just as

I finished with my suitcase, the phone rang. It was Ellen. She said, 'He's back! We have Omar back!' I could scarcely believe it. In the last series of ads, she had raised the reward to $1000. Someone saw the ad and called to report he had the dog. He had been driving near the park on that Saturday morning. Omar had been prancing about in the streets, and this driver nearly hit him. After checking to see he was okay, he waited for someone to claim him, but nobody came. Omar never wore his leash and collar while playing, so he wasn't carrying any ID. Concerned for the dog's safety, the good fellow took him home.

Flying back to New York, I didn't care if the Schlitz deal came through or not. I was ecstatic to have Omar back. I doubt we would have if we hadn't made his return a priority. The episode proves something I've always believed: you can achieve anything, in business or out, with the application of entrepreneurial initiative. Think about it. What were the odds or retrieving a dog lost in a city as large as New York? A lot of people would have given up after our first couple of attempts. Who could blame them? But we got Omar back, because we refused to allow any alternative. I've run a few companies and have made a couple of acquisitions. My wife still thinks the effort I put behind getting Omar back is the most impressive entrepreneurial feat of my career.

Don't do business with friends

A happy domestic life does extend beyond the realm of family. You want to build lasting friendships. You can protect these relationships by keeping your social and business lives separate. This one isn't written in stone. Sometimes you can't avoid doing business with friends. If your lifelong buddy wants you to be a partner in the idea of the century, it would be foolish to reject him out of hand. Just be wary. I've seen many a friendship done in by a deal.

Damage can sometimes be done by the most well meaning

of arrangements. In 1961, Ellen and I met another couple while on vacation. We played bridge with them and went out on a couple of dinner dates. They were a lot of fun. The husband's name was Joe Pagan and he was the head of an advertising agency.

Some time after we had returned home, Mr Pagan called me. We exchanged the usual pleasantries and then he asked if I could come to his office on the following morning. He wasn't specific, but he did say he wanted to discuss an interesting proposal. My calendar was clear until the afternoon, so I agreed to see him.

I didn't have a clue as to what his agenda was going to be. Midway through the meeting, I was even more puzzled. He kept talking around things. Finally, he started to approach the subject at hand. He said, 'Vic, you have a very attractive wife.' I thanked him. Then he continued, 'But she's not as young as she used to be.' That didn't sit too well with me. I bristled, 'None of us are, Joe. What are you getting at?'

He stood up and took on a professional air. Putting his fingers beneath his lapels, he said, 'You were in the cosmetics business. As you probably know the maturation process takes its toll. As you get older, your face starts to take on some lines. Often they can make you look older than you really are.' I replied, 'Yes, yes, I know that Joe. *Now what on earth are you getting at?*'

His words came out in a rush. His agency was representing a cosmetics company. It was coming out with an astringent guaranteed to tighten the skin and reduce the lines in a person's face. The agency needed a model to do a high-brow TV commercial. It was going to be used during a gala to celebrate the opening of the Lincoln Center and would be seen nationally. Pagan thought Ellen would be a perfect choice to star in the commercial. He said, 'I can't call her and go into that spiel about aging and wrinkles, but you could. I promise you, if she does the spot, she'll get paid a handsome fee.'

Ellen had been a model before we got married. I thought she might be interested in Pagan's proposal. I had a dickens of a time, though, trying to figure out how to broach it to her. I waited until breakfast the following morning. I opened by saying, 'Honey, you look sensational.' She thanked me. Then I said, 'You know both of us are getting along in years and . . .' She cut me off with such a look. I was treading on unsteady ground now. 'What's that supposed to mean?' I replied, 'Nothing. It's just that you have this great maturity now. You have this look of experience. You know, your face isn't young and innocent any more. You're a mature woman with all the attractiveness that goes with that.'

As vistas go, I had the feeling this one was drowning me in my own paint. She asked me what on earth all this drivel meant. I told her about my conversation with Pagan. When I first described the product, her eyes began to narrow. She thought I was suggesting that she needed it. I calmed her and said, 'No, I love the way you look. Wouldn't change it for the world. It's just that they are doing a commercial for the Lincoln Center opening and want you to star in it. It will run all over the country. If it's a hit, you can make a small fortune in residuals. And, it's bound to be fun.'

Ellen wasn't having any. I asked her not to make up her mind so quickly. Joe didn't need an answer until the following afternoon. There wasn't any reason why she couldn't sleep on it. 'Besides,' I told her, 'you don't have to commit to anything over the phone. You can go to the agency and see what they have planned. If you don't like what they have in mind, you don't have to go through with it.'

I don't know if my remark made any difference, but by that evening she had decided to give it a whirl. She and Joe arranged to meet. When she gets down to his office she discovers she isn't the only woman competing for the role. The room is crowded with professional models and actresses. This placed the idea in a whole new perspective. Here was a job Ellen had been reluctant to take, but the sight of all those competitors stoked her fires. Now she was hell-bent to get the part! When my wife sets her mind on something, she invariably finds a way to achieve it. By the end of the day, she was cast in the ad.

They shot the commercial the following evening. After make-up, she was photographed for a series of 'after' shots. Six hours into the shooting, with the lines deepening from exhaustion, they took the 'before' pictures. The filming ended at four in the morning. Bone-tired and *sans* make-up, Ellen was asked to sit through a few more shots before leaving. And I said this would be fun!

We joined some friends for the commercial's debut. They set up the TV in the kitchen, put out a buffet, and waited with us for the big moment. It was one of the first ads of the evening. Ellen, the picture of elegance, comes out of Lincoln Center with her 'husband' and bumps into an old girlfriend. The other woman is deliberately frumpy looking. The girlfriend takes Ellen aside and says, 'We were in the same class in high school, but you look so much younger than I do. What's your secret?' Ellen then tells her about the wonders of this miracle cosmetic. The friend replies, 'Oh boy, I can't wait to get it so I can look as good as you.' Then both women rejoin their husbands and move off at the fade. We all thought Ellen did a terrific job and she was pleased with the way it came off. All we had to do now was sit back and wait for the residuals to start flowing our way.

About a week and a half after the commercial airs, I get a call from one of Ellen's best friends. I asked how she was doing and she said, 'I'm fine, but I'm not sure if Ellen's going to be. Have you seen this morning's *New York Times*?' When I told her I hadn't she sighed, 'You better see it before she does. Turn to page twenty-three.' When I did, I nearly had a heart attack. There was a full page ad underneath the headline, 'Now you can have a facelift without surgery!' Ellen was featured in the accompanying photos. They had the 'after' shot in which she looked like a film star. For the 'before' photo, they used the final shots taken at four in the morning. They even doctored the prints, deepening the lines to make her look as awful as possible. Ellen joined me just after I had looked at the photos. I'm trying to figure out a diplomatic way to break this to her, but there isn't any. Handing her the paper, I said, 'You're going to see this sometime. It might as well be now.'

She was embarrassed by what they had done to the photo and how they had used both it and her. I wasn't ashamed; I was furious. If Pagan had been there I would have thrown him out the window just to see how high he bounced. That was my first reaction. After cooling off, I thought there might be a better way to handle this. I asked Ellen to bring me her contract. It contained a release for the TV commercial. It did not, however, say anything about a print ad. Pagan and his agency were in trouble.

I called Joe and said, 'For God's sakes, how could you run those photos without Ellen's permission! You've got to pull those ads!' He said it was already out of his hands. Only the client could halt the campaign. I started screaming so hard I nearly swallowed the telephone. Pagan tried to soothe me. He offered to call the client, explain the 'mistake', and have the advertising lifted.

Joe got back to me that afternoon. He meekly explained that the programme had been launched nationally and had become a juggernaut with its own life. There was no way to stop it. I screamed, 'Oh yes? Well here's something else you won't be able to stop. I'm going to sue your butt and your client's.' Pagan replied, 'Don't do that Vic. Ellen's going to do very well with this commercial and . . .' Refusing to let him finish, I yelled, 'We don't give a damn about that. You signed an agreement and you violated it. Now take care of this or you can see me in court.'

I hung up on him. That evening, I told Ellen about our conversation, promising that we would sue if something wasn't worked out. She was just as upset as I was, but she didn't want to take Pagan to court. When I asked her why, she said, 'He's our friend.' I explained, 'Honey, we can't look at it that way. He made a business deal and went back on it. This thing is going to run everywhere now. If he was our friend, he should have looked out for you.' Despite my reasoning, Ellen wouldn't be dissuaded.

A month later, her mother, abroad on vacation, sent us a European fashion magazine. The ad was running over there. Faced with this fresh upset, I asked her to at least speak to our lawyer to see if there was any way to end this thing. She did. He told her that a lawsuit was her only recourse and repeated my view that it shouldn't be looked upon as a personal vendetta. He added, 'As a businessman, I'm sure Mr Pagan will understand.' Even with his assurances, Ellen still wouldn't press the suit. That incident occurred over twenty-five years ago. We never did sue. However, I haven't spoken to Joe Pagan since that last phone call. I see him at parties and just turn my back on him. I don't believe I'd have the same violent reaction if this had been just another business deal. Yes, I would have become hot, but in time I would have forgotten about it. But this was a 'friend'. When a friend pulls something like this, the hurt is lethal. Good will and trust are drained from the relationship. Not too many deals are worth this risk.

The proper fit

Many people seem to think they have to make their lifestyle fit their entrepreneurial venture. It isn't always so. Depending on your priorities, you can make it work the other way around.

Fred Nichols was a chap who had a big hand in our getting the original financing for the Remington turnaround. After the purchase, he joined the company as its treasurer. I enjoyed Freddy. He was easy-going, considerate of others, and a top professional. Each evening, before going home, he would drop by the office. We'd discuss the company over cups of coffee. Sometimes he'd stay an hour, sometimes only five minutes. The amount of time was unimportant. What mattered was the feeling I got for Freddy. Here was a fellow who genuinely cared about the company and what we were trying to accomplish. Having been through the early struggle to purchase Remington, he treated it as if it was his own. He was committed to its success.

One afternoon, Freddy asked if he could see me on an important matter. We went into my office and poured ourselves our ritual coffee. He sat in his chair for minutes without saying a word. Then I noticed his eyes were watering. When I asked him what was wrong, he still couldn't get any phrases out. He was choking with emotion. I told him to relax. Finally, his story gushed forward. Having been divorced, he was about to remarry. His bride-to-be had three children. Freddy had three kids of his own. She was a practising midwife and had to work odd hours. As you know, babies usually pick the most unpredictable times to enter the world. When she was on a call, someone had to be home with the children.

A friend of Freddy's owned a company that manufactured boat-in-a-bottle kits. These kits were bought by hobbyists who used them to build bottled replicas of the *Mayflower*, the *King George V* and other famous ships. It was a small venture run mostly through mail order. This friend was now about to retire and had offered to sell his business to Freddy.

It was perfect for him. The whole enterprise could be run out of his home and was an answer to all of his problems. Despite this, he was torn. He didn't want to leave the company.

I was also being pulled in two directions. I didn't want to lose Freddy. He had been a valuable right arm. But I also knew he had found an ideal situation. I told him, 'Buddy, you have been one hell of a man here. You've given me quite a void to fill. That's all right. This is your shot. I know you'll make it go. If by any chance it doesn't work out, you'll always have a home here.' We hugged each other and then we both cried.

I'm happy to say, he had a big success. He bought a big rambling house in a small town in Maine. His workshop is on the top floor and his bride is the local midwife. He is not in the fast lane. The needs of his loved one put some limitations on his business options. Yet, he is as much an entrepreneur as when he was playing for higher stakes with Remington. More of one. Now he's building his own business. He's faced with the same decisions that I or any other CEO have to make, only on a smaller scale. Most importantly, Freddy is a man with his priorities in order. He wanted a happy home life. He also wanted to have a success in business. Freddy is the ultimate entrepreneur. He got both.

Always the entrepreneur

The entrepreneurial spirit should enliven every waking minute. I know a businessman who is involved in several successful ventures. Whenever he goes to a restaurant he tries to choose at least one dish, even if it's just an appetizer, that he has never tasted before. When he and his wife celebrate each other's birthdays, they invariably go out to eat. They always pick a place featuring an exotic cuisine.

On his last vacation he hiked along a river to its source, scaled mountain cliffs, flew kites at midnight, attended his first opera and even went skinny-dipping in a mountain gorge. The water was about forty degrees. Brrrr! That will get your blood moving in the morning. Didn't faze this fellow. He's always trying to experience new things. On my own vacation two years ago, I stoked coal on a barge going down the Mississippi. When I first went to Japan, I couldn't leave without trying their legendary Kobe beef marinated in beer. What was the point of these exercises? Adventure. At heart every entrepreneur is Indiana Jones.

When we talk about an entrepreneur, we're talking about a swashbuckler who sops up huge portions of life with gusto. This person can approach his or her life away from the office with the same energy, creativity and enthusiasm they bring to their enterprise. This should be easy for the entrepreneur. He or she is a doer, an activist who refuses to be a passive victim to bogeyman Fate. Throughout this chapter, domestic obstacles and problems were often overcome by the application of a little entrepreneurial initiative. Do you want to spend more time with your family? Create time. You've just seen that it can be done. If you are willing to go the extra mile – and all entrepreneurs are – you will negotiate the compromises that bring bliss to relationships. You have the power to make life work. You don't have to settle for a shining business record, but a damaged home life. You can make your lifestyle fit your business, and vice versa.

My friends, you can have it all!

Going for it around the world: the global entrepreneur

If your enterprise grows large enough, you might be able to expand into the international marketplace. With all the complexities of world-wide trading, I wouldn't want to attempt to give anyone specific advice in this chapter. To really help you, I would have to know the complete background of your particular business. However, I would at least like to paint the broad strokes by sharing some of my own globe-trotting adventures.

A lesson learned in Panama

The entrepreneur looking to perform on the global stage has to be ready for just about anything. Back in the sixties, as president of Benrus, I was approached by a gentleman who wanted to distribute our watches in South America. I checked out the man's credentials and came away impressed. He was South America's largest distributor of Seikos and did a great deal of business with a major US electronics company. Checking with both companies, we found they had enjoyed a long and happy relationship with him. Further investigation revealed that he enjoyed excellent credit.

I was going to meet this fellow in his native Colon, Panama and show him a full range of our samples. This trip would be combined with a rare vacation. The plan was to spend time in

Nassau with my family and a few friends, and then fly into Colon for my get-together with the distributor.

Arriving in Nassau, I naturally had to pass through customs. The inspectors looked through my package containing the seventy-two boxed samples and suggested the watches be placed in bond. They explained that this would allow me to avoid paying a duty on the samples. I could place the samples in their care while I was in Nassau, and then pick them up before leaving for Miami *en route* to Panama.

I took their advice. The container holding the boxed watches was wrapped in impressive steel bands, defying even a modern Houdini to break into the package without disrupting the seal.

When I came to pick up my goods, it looked as if everything was going to go according to plan. I received the samples out of bond, took off for Miami, landed safely, and then caught an Air Mexico flight to Panama City. Once there, I was met on schedule by the distributor's driver and whisked off to Colon. The samples case, still bound in steel, had been placed next to me in the back seat.

Arriving at my hotel, I had dinner with my host and arranged to meet him at his office the next morning. The opening negotiations went without a hitch. The distributor wanted our product and he thought the opening prices mentioned were quite reasonable. I was now ready to apply the *coup de grâce* with a mesmerizing presentation of our samples.

Reaching into my display box, I held up the watch case so that its contents could be seen only by him, and then slowly opened the top lid. This was a deliberate tension builder. I wanted him to savour the magnificence of this miracle of modern timekeeping. My host's eyes fixed on the case's contents and his eyes widened. There, I thought, I've really made an impression. Before I could get through patting myself on the back, the distributor did an odd thing. He started laughing. I didn't see the humour of my presentation until I turned the case around to face me. There, in the indentation that should have held my sample was a gorgeous, perfectly rounded rock!

I was dumbfounded. Ploughing through the rest of the cases,

we discovered that all the samples had been similarly displaced. Someone had lifted the watches. Whoever it was, they had been farsighted enough to realize the package would be weighed as it passed through customs. The stones were obviously meant to substitute for the lost weight of the samples. Pretty clever, but it turned out that I had something of a last laugh on the unknown perpetrators. Those watch samples had been nothing more than empty cases. They lacked the innards needed to keep time.

The thieves' presumed discomfiture gave me little solace. I left Colon without an order. I was able, however, to arrange to meet with the sympathetic distributor during his next trip to the States. It was at that meeting that we eventually came to an agreement.

I learned two valuable lessons during that adventure. One was not to trust bureaucracies. As an entrepreneur, I should have known that. If I hadn't placed all my faith in those steel bands or the customs officer's official seals, I could have uncovered the loss of the samples immediately. I was also taught the error of false confidence. No matter how strong your presentations have been in the past, you must be sure to review every aspect of it before each new airing. Had I bothered to check my case on the evening prior to the meeting, I would have spared myself some embarrassment.

A most amazing alchemy

When selling internationally, you'll sometimes discover that a product unable to find a market in one country, can be successfully introduced in another. The air purifier we discussed in an earlier chapter was one example of this. My adventures with a popcorn maker provide further evidence.

Remington hadn't planned to manufacture popcorn machines. The fact is we fell into the business on the wildest fluke. One afternoon, the managing director of our English company received a call from the American embassy's commercial attaché. This fellow was phoning to see if we made popcorn makers. When told we didn't the chap sighed and said, 'Oh, that's too bad. The Department of Agriculture and the Popcorn Institute of the United States are trying to promote the world-wide sale of popcorn. We have a surplus of corn back home. If we don't unload it soon, the grain will start rotting in the silos. We thought it would be a good idea to introduce a top quality popcorn-maker in the UK in order to increase the demand for corn. Someone suggested Remington as a possible manufac-turer. Your products are well known in this country and they have excellent distribution. We thought it would be perfect if you would launch the programme on an exclusive basis.' When I heard about the conversation, I knew the fellow had not called to ask a question. He could have found out if we manufactured popcorn-makers without phoning our managing director. I got the clear impression we were being invited into a new business.

We were interested in learning more about the project. A meeting was set up at our embassy in London. The director and I represented Remington. The attaché was joined by mem-bers of the Popcorn Institute, an American association dedi-cated to increasing the international sale of popcorn.

During our discussion, it was made clear that Remington was being brought quite an opportunity. The PCI representatives told us that they had garnered popcorn orders from the major food stores in the United Kingdom. A mammoth promotional campaign was already approved and in place. All it needed was the additional marketing support of a top quality popcorn maker. The PCI was willing to spend over a quarter of a million dollars on a UK test market for the popper. It would put up additional promotional dollars if that experiment proved successful. They also produced statistics bolstering their conten-tion that the machines would find a warm welcome in England. At the time, high-fibre foods – and you would have to place popcorn in that category – were enjoying excellent sales in the UK. The medical industry had apparently released a number of reports praising the effects of a high-fibre diet. England had also always been a large consumer of commercially produced popcorn, albeit this version was often covered with caramel or some other sweetener. We thought it was a pretty good bet that Britons would like a chance to make their own popcorn at home.

These facts and the promise of substantial advertising support were too much to ignore. If Remington could successfully open the market in England, it could then move on to the rest of Europe. My goodness, we had the chance to become the emperors of popcorn! With a possibility like that staring us in the face we had no choice but to agree to manufacture and distribute a popcorn machine.

Having researched the market prior to our gathering, we had already determined that a hot-air popper would be the route to follow. It didn't use oil in the cooking process. This meant the corn came out less greasy and was lower in calories. A lab study had also shown that the hot-air machine could pop more kernels in less time than other models. We actually had a fellow pop corn on every type of machine available. After it was done, he would record the number of unpopped kernels for comparison. The hot-air popper always came out on top.

Remington had one other advantage in this enterprise. By studying the many popcorn machines on the market, our engineers were able to design a superior model by integrating the best features of the other brands. In a short time we manufactured 40,000 machines that met our high company standards.

Since popcorn is really an American product, everyone agreed it was appropriate for this new popper to make its debut during a press reception at the American embassy. We had Glyn Christian, the well-known British TV chef, handle the cooking. What an amazing fellow. No one would have dreamed he could create so many recipes featuring popcorn. We served popcorn with sauteed mushrooms, popcorn with Italian spices, Cajun popcorn, popcorn with exotic cheeses melted over it. We must have fed forty varieties to over 400 people including international dignitaries and the press. They couldn't get enough of the stuff and their insatiable appetites were ample proof that the party had been an unqualified smash.

I hardly had time to munch a morsel. Most of my afternoon was spent with TV reporters seeking interviews. That was fine with me. I wasn't there to eat. Getting exposure for the corn and the popper was the whole purpose of the gathering. One reporter from the BBC expressed some scepticism over our party's success. Confronting me on camera, he said, 'The people here are gorging themselves, but most of them travel a great deal and have been exposed to this style of popcorn before. I wonder if you can sell your popcorn to the average Brit.'

My reply was a good five minutes on the miraculous benefits of popcorn and the Remington popper. I also pointed out that popcorn was so delicious, it didn't need the sweet coatings that distinguished much of England's popcorn. All it needed was just a pinch of salt and possibly a bit of butter.

When I was done, the reporter said, 'Since you believe in your machine's popcorn so strongly, let's see if you can sell it to the man or woman on the street. Where are you bound for after the reception?' I told him we were spending the next three days in Manchester. He replied, 'Super! Find a spare hour or two and we'll send a crew up there. We'll pick an outside location and film you trying to sell your popcorn.'

There was a challenge I was ready to accept. I always feel that if I believe in a product, I can sell it. I thought our machines produced the best homemade popcorn you could buy. With my experience as a salesman, I was certain I could convince a few British citizens to try this luscious treat.

Three days after the reception, the BBC man arrived at my hotel. He brought a pushcart laden with my machines and a chef's outfit to be worn by me. I was told that the cameras would keep filming until I had made a sale. He then escorted me to a location that had already been picked by his crew. It was the Manchester spot known as the 'Shambles'. I had never seen so many derelicts in one place. Most of them were either scrounging cigarettes, sleeping off a drinking session or getting one underway. There were liquor bottles strewn all over the place. It wasn't quite the test-market site I had had in mind. It just didn't appear as if it could yield the proper demographics.

Decked out in my apron and cook's hat, I pushed my fancy little cart to the nearest corner. My four popcorn makers were cooking away. I knew I couldn't possibly sell any popcorn to the derelicts. It was unlikely they would have the 20p needed for the purchase. So I was forced to go after pedestrians as they passed through the Shambles. This was not easy. No one wanted to linger in this place for very long. I found myself in a series of foot races, trying to catch up to anyone who remotely resembled a potential customer. I ran up to one prosperous-looking bloke and said, 'Would you like to try some great popcorn, cooked American style with salt and butter? Only 20p!' He wouldn't look at either me or the popcorn. Instead, he just brushed by, nearly knocking the bag from my hand. A few moments later, I got the attention of a young woman. She wasn't any more receptive to my pitch than that first fellow. For the next fifteen minutes, no matter what I tried, I couldn't make a sale.

Finally, I came across a nanny accompanied by a little girl. Having had no success dealing with adults, I decided to capture the youth market. I placed a few kernels in the child's hand and encouraged her to try them.

Before she could place one in her mouth, her nanny slapped them from her hand, and yelled, 'You mustn't ever take sweets from strange men!' I must say that last comment made me a bit huffy. I replied, 'Madam, this outfit might look silly to you, but I can assure you that I am not strange and this is not candy. It is American popcorn. It's much better for this girl than any sweet. Here, try some yourself.'

The nanny accepted a small handful. After tasting it, she turned to the child and said, 'Yes, all right my dear. You may have some.' The little girl grabbed a few kernels and placed them in her mouth. I could feel the tension rising. Was she going to like the popcorn? Would she beg nanny to buy her some? I couldn't take any chances. I wasn't merely trying to sell a bag of popcorn; I was defending the honour of God, country, Remington, and the Popcorn Institute of America! I had to get this order! As soon as she started chewing, I began painting a vista, saying, 'There now, isn't that wonderful? So delicious and healthful! I bet you've never tasted anything as good!'

To be quite frank, the child didn't look pleased with this culinary experience. She appeared to be chomping on a wad of styrofoam and kept making the most extraordinary faces. I was afraid she was going to spit my delectable creation into the camera lens. Working fast, I turned my attention to the nanny. I was pretty sure she had enjoyed her little sample. I asked, 'Wouldn't you like to take a bag of this healthy snack home with you?' She eyed me suspiciously and asked, 'How much is it?' I'm an entrepreneur. I had already discovered that the product wasn't moving at 20p, so I came up with an instant marketing ploy. A one-time only, half-price sale. I offered her a bag for 10p.

I can't tell you how grateful I was when this lovely woman handed over the money. I had finally sold a bag! It gave me the same satisfying jolt I had received when I sold my first account as a young salesman with Lever Brothers. The cameras moved in to record the historic transaction. I looked into the lens and said, 'As you can see, while it might take a little time, Britons will love this popcorn once they give it a chance.'

In the midst of my triumphant words, a derelict approached the cart. He was a battered fellow, wearing a dilapidated overcoat and sporting a number of fresh scabs on his forehead. I couldn't tell if he had been in a fight or had just fallen down. His eyes were bloodshot, his face dirty with week-old stubble. When he opened his mouth to speak, his breath nearly blinded me. Grabbing my sleeve he said, 'I'm hungry, could you give me some of that stuff you're making?'

How could I refuse? With the cameras still rolling, I handed him a bag. He stuffed his cheeks with a fistful of popcorn and commenced chewing. Unfortunately, he had no teeth. As he put the popcorn in the right side of his mouth, the half-gnawed, slimy white bits would drool out on the left. It was one of the most disgusting sights I had ever seen.

The piece was part of that evening's news. Wouldn't you

know it, they showed my big sale, but they ended the story with the shot of the hobo spouting corn. I held my head and thought, 'Great, just the thing people want to see after dinner. That picture is going to sell a lot of machines.'

As it turned out, the popper was about to have greater worries than this humorous news story. A month after leaving England, I received a telex from my managing director. It read, 'The popcorn programme is in trouble. Please phone.'

I reached him that afternoon. He said, 'I received a call from the attaché at the embassy. There has been a drought in your American regions and there is no longer any excess corn to sell. The Agriculture Department and the Popcorn Institute are pulling out of our agreement.'

This meant Remington was stuck with 40,000 popcorn makers and no promotional support. Our entire marketing strategy depended on that government-financed advertising and the mammoth influx of American popcorn into the British market. Boy, I'll say the popcorn programme was in trouble. When I asked my director how we could salvage something out of this debacle, he replied, 'Why don't we buy popcorn from an American company and give it away with our machines? We can build a promotion around that.'

That sounded like as good an idea as any. We purchased a truckload of popcorn from Orville Redenbacker and hired women to demonstrate our machines across England. Without the advantage of any advertising, we managed to unload about 30,000 of the poppers – at cost. We didn't make a single penny from their sale. In fact, we were actually operating at a loss. The cost of the popcorn and the demonstrators cut into our margin and there were still 10,000 machines sitting in our Bridgeport factory. We couldn't sell them in the US. They weren't equipped with the proper voltage. Frankly, we didn't know what to do with them.

A few months after this episode, our Middle-Eastern distributor was visiting our plant. Passing through the lab, he noticed one of the machines. The guys in the lab had been using it to make popcorn during their lunch break. The distributor was taken with the gizmo and asked for a demonstration. After watching it go through its paces, he asked if the machine could be adapted to cook other foods.

That was a good question. We'd never thought about it. When we asked him what, specifically, he had in mind he explained that everybody in the Middle East ate nuts during their Sabbath. Hosts had continually to heat up these treats in the oven whenever guests arrived. This roasting was time consuming and involved the use of messy oils. Our distributor thought the hot-air machine might offer his countrymen a more trouble-free cooking alternative.

After careful examination, our engineers found that the machine could be easily adapted at a low cost. We just had to add a minor attachment and a nut tray. This done, the transformed corn poppers were then shipped to the Middle East as nut roasters. The result? Not only did we sell our remaining inventory at a profit, we ended up with a new business. The Remington roaster is still being manufactured in, and sold throughout, the Middle East. It is a very popular item. This should show you that a product that is a dud in one country can be a winner in another. It also proves that a good entrepreneur is not just someone who can turn a lemon into lemonade. On occasion, he can make peanut butter out of popcorn!

Sir Clive and the C5

Sometimes even a bit of global manoeuvring cannot turn the most worthy lemon into lemonade. About two and a half years ago, I was visiting the UK on business. While there, several of us happened to attend an exhibition at Earls Court. A model greeted us in the building's lobby. She stood next to the C5, an electric mini-car manufactured by Sinclair Vehicles, and was passing out leaflets extolling the vehicle's virtues.

The car is actually an electric tricycle, built low to the ground, and able to carry only one driver-passenger. It has a single front wheel with two more in the rear and a steering bar that's positioned beneath your legs. I thought that it could serve as a wonderful transport over short distances. For instance, my wife and I have an apartment in Florida that we use as a vacation hideaway. It is located on a development that is barely four miles long. That mini-car looked like it would be the ideal leisure vehicle for travelling within that complex. I could drive it whenever I went to the nearby tennis court or had to pick up a newspaper. That would free our regular car for Ellen's use. She could take it whenever and to wherever she wanted and not have to be concerned about dropping me off or picking me up.

We asked the model what she could tell us about the car. All she could do was hand me a pamphlet. She didn't know what kind of mileage it did or how often the battery had to be recharged. She didn't even know where or how the thing could be purchased. This was an egregious error on the part of her company. You should never allow anybody to present or demonstrate your product unless they are thoroughly schooled in its use and benefits. You want them to know the item as well, if not better, than you do.

I asked some of the chaps connected with our English company to find out where I could buy the C5. Locating the distributor, they had a car shipped to our factory in Bridgeport. I was like a child on Christmas morning when it arrived. I couldn't wait to tool around in it. A quick spin to the local grocery store convinced me that the C5 had been a sound purchase. I wasn't alone in this assessment. Almost everyone who saw the mini-car wanted to buy one. As I was soon to find out, this was not a reaction shared by consumers across the Atlantic.

Sir Clive Sinclair, the C5's inventor, was having a devil of a time trying to sell his cars in England. His company had been marketing this battery-powered vehicle as an alternative to gas gulping automobiles. Ads showed the C5 making its rounds through urban traffic.

This was a mistake. Several factors militated against the C5 being able to replace more traditional vehicles. For one, the car could only do about twenty miles an hour, so it wasn't practical for highway use. In addition, it was built so low that a flag had to be attached to a high pole connected to the car's rear. This served as a warning to other vehicles. Without it, drivers might not be aware that your car was in front of them. They could easily run over you before realizing what they had done. Knowing that the flag was the only thing standing between you and disaster did little for your peace of mind. Of course, this flag also offered no protection if a car in front of you suddenly stopped short. Your C5 could slide beneath the larger vehicle, possibly causing injury. Finally, the car's body was made of a light but durable plastic. This lack of bulk could make a driver, used to the armour of metal automobiles, feel particularly vulnerable.

The British press crucified Sir Clive for manufacturing a product that lacked a practical use. Admitting it was not a replacement for conventional vehicles, Sir Clive defended the C5 as an important first step towards the manufacture of a truly all-purpose electric car. This hardly silenced his critics in the media. One ran a picture showing the C5 attempting to fight through city traffic wedged between two lorries. It was not an inspiring sight. In fact, it was downright frightening. It gave the impression that the mini-car and its driver were about to be crushed by the two elephantine vehicles.

I was in England at the height of the bad publicity. Though I had never met Sir Clive, I knew of him as an innovative leader in the computer and electronics industries. I felt it took a lot of guts to come out with a product this innovative and wanted to phone him with some encouragement. One entrepreneur to another. It seemed a good time to let him know that he had at least one very satisfied customer.

Sir Clive wasn't in to take my call. I left a message explaining who I was and congratulating him for making such a fine product. Two hours later, one of his officers phoned me. After thanking me for the unsolicited praise, he asked if he could meet with me that evening.

He arrived at my hotel accompanied by a small delegation of Sinclair executives. They didn't waste much time getting to the marrow of their purpose. They had hardly removed their coats when one of them asked if Remington would like to help their company market the C5. I told them it was a possibility we could explore. Sold in the US as a leisure vehicle rather than an urban auto, the C5 would not have to endure the ridicule it had suffered in England. I suggested that this fresh start could make all the difference in its acceptance by consumers. Buoyed by my response, the executive arranged for Sir Clive to meet with me at our Connecticut factory. That encounter resulted in an agreement allowing Remington to distribute the C5 in the US. The mini-car would be sold in community developments such as the one I visited in Florida, and on college campuses. We thought the vehicle would have an appeal to students. The cars would also be offered to some select retailers.

The first shipment from England brought us about 1,000 C5s. 150 of them were used in a southwestern test market. Sold at various prices, we found the mini-car received its most favourable response when retailed at $400. A higher price hampered sales significantly; anything under that made it an unprofitable venture.

Sir Clive had agreed to sell us each C5 for $250. Even with the cost of shipping, this left us with an adequate margin for advertising and fair profit. Unfortunately, the value of the American dollar began to erode rapidly just around this time. Our analysts projected that this sudden free fall could find us paying $350 for each C5. Such a slim margin would leave us little breathing room.

Though the increased price would multiply our risk, we were still ready to leap into the market. We had that much belief in the venture. Then our insurance company squelched the deal. They had issued us a policy for the test market at a relatively low cost. Insuring a nationwide retail launch, however, was going to require a more extravagant plan.

The insurance company thought the vehicle would pose a

high risk if used on the open highway. There wasn't anything we could do to allay these fears. Therefore, when the company agreed to issue us a policy, protecting us from liability, it was for a princely annual premium of $500,000.

We just could not cover that. It had already been established that the C5 could not be sold to retailers for more than $400. Such a high premium would have wreaked havoc with our margins. What a predicament. We could have sold a lot of C5s without making a penny of profit! Unable to negotiate a lower rate with the insurance company, I had to call Sir Clive and tell him our deal was off.

Being an entrepreneur, Sinclair was not about to accept failure easily. He came back to us with another plan. Apparently, an Israeli company had recently expressed interest in manufacturing, distributing, and exporting the C5. Sir Clive had convinced them they could build the car for $250, returning us to the original profit margin. An Israeli insurance company had already offered to underwrite a policy at rates that would not be ruinous.

After meeting with representatives for all sides, we drew up a trilateral agreement. The Israeli company would manufacture the car, Remington would distribute it in the US and Canada, and Sir Clive's company would receive a royalty for each C5 sold. It was further stipulated that the car had to be manufactured for $250 or less. Any rise in price, unless first approved by Remington, would immediately void the contract.

When it came time to sign the document, Sir Clive could not get the price limitation into the contract. The Israelis didn't want to be on the hook if their costs became dramatically inflated. I could understand their hesitancy. No one wants to be locked into a potential loss. But without that guarantee, Remington could not risk the deal either. It's a shame. Properly marketed, I think the C5 is a splendid product. It's too bad its story couldn't have had the same happy ending as the popcorn maker.

*

Know your market

If you are able to do business in a foreign country, you should realize that each nation can have its own peculiarities when it comes to doing business. Learning what the nuances might be in advance can help you avoid some unusual pitfalls.

For example, suppose you had been in the American watch business in the sixties and seventies and had wished to compete for government or military contracts. Benrus had been involved with several of these open bids. We found you had to do more than just tender the lowest bid or offer the best quality. Federal officials required that you buy a certain brand of jewel to be used in your watch movements. If you didn't, your offer wouldn't receive any consideration.

An American Indian tribe mined the mandatory stones. Their products were called Turtle Mountain Jewels. I'm sure the law demanding their use was well-intentioned. Unfortunately, the jewels had one minor flaw: they didn't work. They were the wrong shape and tended to crack rather easily. If you inserted them in a movement, there was no way you could guarantee how long they would keep the thing running. You also couldn't vouch for the watch's accuracy.

Luckily for us, the government contract only stipulated that we had to buy the jewels. It didn't mention anything about using them. Benrus would purchase the appropriate number of Turtle Mountain Jewels for each of our watches. If we had a contract for 10,000 watches, each requiring seventeen jewels, we ordered 170,000 gems. Then we would place them in storage, and use better quality stones. At one point, we had over two million gems locked in a warehouse. We tried to use them on some of our Wells jewellery, but they just weren't good enough. They ended up as fodder for our disposal. It used to break our hearts to see such waste, but this was the price of doing business while handicapped by a well-intentioned, misguided policy.

Knowing the special needs of a country can help inform many a decision. When I first took over Remington, we were looking to cut all the fat out of our operation. Anything that could save the company money and perk up its cash flow was examined. One of the first things to catch our eye was a shaver that operated on a dry-cell battery. It hardly seemed practical. This model had the same power and cutting efficiency as our more convenient Remington rechargeable. However, after eight to ten weeks of regular shaving, the batteries would have to be replaced. It didn't sound terribly economical to me, and looked like something Remington could live without.

I was ready to put this item on the list of possible cuts, when two things grabbed my attention. First, the shaver was sold almost exclusively in the UK. Second, this battery-powered Remington accounted for over 25 per cent of our English shaver sales!

It's always been very important for us to keep a strong profile in the British Isles. I wasn't about to kill a product that was enjoying such a great success over there. Curious to discover the reason for this extraordinary, isolated performance, I called my English managing director. He explained that bathrooms in many older, British dwellings do not have electric outlets. A man tackling his beard after his morning bath or shower had no place to plug in his shaver. Using an extension cord to reach a socket outside of the bathroom was too much of a bother. If we took away the convenience of the dry-cell shaver, our customers would probably either jump to a competitor or go back to shaving with a blade. Those possibilities made up my mind. We continued manufacturing the battery-powered Remington and eventually offered it in our catalogues to our American customers. They've been buying it as a back-up shaver to be used on long trips or outdoor outings where an electrical outlet might be hard to find.

Often the quality standards for products vary from country to country. The Friendship Company was importing a large number of jade items from China. At least, we thought they were jade. The invoices said they were jade. The Chinese customs officers didn't dispute this claim. Every country we shipped them to accepted them as jade. Every country, that is, except Great Britain. The UK has a higher standard. After we brought these items into the country, British authorities claimed they didn't qualify for jade classification in the UK. We showed them our bills and duty slips but couldn't persuade them to abandon this stand. Hit with a $10,000 fine, we were ordered to call our jewellery 'carved Chinese stone'. We had a fabulous jade elephant that had been racking up tremendous sales throughout England. As soon as we rechristened it, the numbers took a nosedive.

Chinese silver gave us another problem. The Oriental version of sterling and what the English regarded as sterling were apparently two different metals. Friendship was not allowed to advertise any of our earrings, bracelets, necklaces, or other silver items as sterling in the UK. Again, this dented our sales. We tried to persuade the Chinese manufacturers to adapt to the British system of standards, but they wouldn't consider it. We were trapped between two conflicting perspectives.

I couldn't fault either side. The English authorities weren't about to lower their high standards for anybody. On the other hand, in China we were dealing with a country that had got along rather nicely as a closed society for more than sixty years. As far as the Chinese were concerned, they knew what jade was. They had been using it to produce breathtaking *objet d'art* when our ancestors were huddling in caves. They couldn't see any reason why they should acquiesce to what they felt were the wacky requests of some uneducated Westerners. If we had only known the difficulty the contrasting views would cause, we wouldn't have allowed ourselves to get stuck in the middle. We would probably never have attempted to bring the products into Britain. It just wasn't worth the hassle.

Your advertising can be restricted by the laws of certain nations. Though I speak French, I wasn't allowed to use my own voice for Remington TV ads airing in French Canada. You had to be a member of the Union des Artistes in order to do commercial voice-overs. I could appear in the ads, but my voice would have to be dubbed. The law was very strict about this. The authorities had even gone so far as to dub the voice of Catherine Deneuve in her Chanel commercial. This despite the fact that the actress's native language is French!

In order to comply with their regulations, I offered to become a dues-paying union member. We were informed that union membership was closed. My commercials couldn't run unless we allowed somebody else's words to be placed in my mouth. Stonewalled at every bureaucratic turn, we reluctantly complied.

The dubbed spots had been running for almost two years when I gave an interview to the Montreal *Gazette*. Most of the questions centred around an economic analysis of Quebec. At one point the reporter asked what it was like for an American to do business in French Canada. He also wondered if I would ever open a Remington factory in one of the provinces.

I responded that while I enjoyed the French-Canadian people, I found the climate for business most inhospitable. When the reporter asked why, I replied, 'I do my own commercials in my own voice because we have found it heightens the realism. We tested dubbing in languages other than English when we first took the spots aboard. It was so much less effective. Seeing this silver-haired gent speaking their language flawlessly and with the proper accent made people doubt I was the American who had actually bought this company. They thought I was an actor from their own country. When they hear my voice speaking their language less than perfectly, there isn't any confusion. I'm obviously a Yank with enough confidence in his product to put his name, money and reputation on the line. That's the whole thrust of our ads. Your government and its union regulations are destroying the image we are trying to portray.'

The article ran that weekend. Less than a month later the union called inviting me to become a member. I've been using my own voice in French Canada ever since. I guess that says something about the power of the press and the power of entrepreneurial perseverance. I just wouldn't let the issue die.

Remington encountered a similar problem about three years

ago. I had already done a German commercial and had hoped
to run it in both West Germany and Austria. The German
government had no objections, but the Austrians balked.
Apparently most of the commercials that ran in Austria were
made in Germany by Germans. Native Austrian performing
artists weren't fond of this arrangement. It cut into their own
employment. In response to their difficulty, the Austrian
government passed a law identical to the one we had found in
French Canada. Only native voices could be heard in commercials shown in Austria. Citing this restriction, the authorities
refused to air our spots.

Attempting to resolve the problem, I flew into Austria to
meet with the proper officials. I made the same argument I had
in Canada. A slickly made commercial featuring a Victor Kiam
speaking flawless Austrian would undermine the integrity of
our spots. They countered by saying my demand would deprive
an Austrian announcer of his employment. I sympathized with
their position but could not accept it. I would even have agreed
to a version of the Turtle Mountain solution, paying an Austrian
actor his usual fees if they would just let me use my own voice.
They would not change their minds.

I wasn't going to give up until I had made my case before
the country's highest authority. Telling the officials that their
insistence would render my commercials useless, I asked to
speak to the director-general of the Austrian Television
Authority.

We met the next day. The fellow in charge was a pleasant
man. We discussed the shaver and chatted about the general
state of Austrian TV. After a few minutes of this, I bore down
on the purpose of my visit. I said, 'I doubt you're aware of it,
but the law you have forbidding me to speak in my own
commercials is both oppressive and discriminatory. Forgive me
for speaking so harshly, but that's my honest view.'

The director-general thought I was overreacting. He couldn't
believe that dubbing my voice could cause us any real harm.
I replied, 'I can understand your scepticism, but this tenet
eliminates opportunities for certain entrepreneurs. Remington

is a comparatively small company. The electric-shaver manufacturers I compete with are international juggernauts. They are
impersonal monoliths; their commercials don't rely on a personal message.'

I then proceeded to lay out the history of our commercials,
how they demonstrated that the little guy has a chance to fulfil
his own dream. I further explained that Remington had a
reputation for honesty in advertising. I was the only one who
could tell my story because it was *my* story. If an announcer
did it, the public just wouldn't buy it.

The director-general hummed and hawed a bit and finally
said, 'But Mr Kiam, we have this rule. I can't change it just
for you.' Mr Director-General, I thought, welcome to the
wonderful world of entrepreneurship. I told him, 'I don't want
you to change the rule; it's a good law if it protects your citizens'
chances for employment. Augment it. Make an exception for
those people who own companies and would like to make their
case before the public. How many of us are in that position? I
doubt the amendment I'm suggesting will have anything but an
imperceptible impact on the television artists' industry.'

He agreed that my case had some merit and offered to bring
it up at a meeting the following week. Shortly after that gathering, the rule was amended and we were able to go on the air
as originally planned. If I had accepted the first no, gone along
with the status quo, we would never have been able to use my
voice. In that case, I doubt we would have run the commercials
at all.

Brought to you by the BBC

I love British television. It's so much more freewheeling than
the TV I've become used to in my own country. For instance,
on one British show I was asked to be part of an 'expert'
panel. The evening's topic centred around the legalization of
prostitution. I'm still not sure why they picked me for that
particular subject. It wasn't clear whether they wanted me

to discuss the possibilities of money-back guarantees or to determine the industry's Intangible Balance Sheet. I would guess that each of the prostitutes who appeared on the show did have a USP.

The *Ruby Wax Show* certainly gave me a jolt. I was one of her first guests. Ruby's approach to hosting was, shall we say, unorthodox. In preparation for my own appearance, I had made it a point to catch her act. It was the craziest show I had ever seen!

On the evening I tuned in, her studio audience included a 500 pound man dressed as a woman. He was one of the less eccentric people in attendance. Ruby's guest that night was the American actress Katherine Helmond. Sometime during their discussion, Ms Helmond mentioned that she was friendly with a certain British celebrity. That woman's name escapes me now. Apparently Ms Helmond was going to meet this luminary after the show.

Ruby asked, 'You're seeing her tonight? Do you know where she is now?' Katherine replied that the woman was probably dining at a well-known London nightspot. The next thing you know, Ruby races from her chair, commandeers her camera crew into a car, and takes off. She was going to try to get a live, impromptu interview with this unsuspecting star.

The cameras continued to roll as she pulled up to the nightclub. A bouncer tried to block her entry, but Ruby was an entrepreneur. She was not going to be deterred. Pushing him out of the way, she stormed through the door, made her way to the star's table and announced, 'Hello, I'm Ruby Wax and we are on television right now.' The celebrity looked stunned. She screamed, 'Oh my God!' and leaped to the sanctuary of the ladies' loo.

Ruby took after her like a heat-seeking missile. Yanking her reluctant cameraman, she charged into the bathroom and headed straight for the star's stall. Restaurant employees ended up having literally to drag her out of the ladies' room. I couldn't stop laughing, but Ellen started to have some second thoughts about my upcoming appearance. She wondered if it was a good idea for me to go on such a wacky show. I can tell you right now there is nothing like this on American TV.

I considered her concerns but decided to do the show anyway. After all, I'm an entrepreneur, a risk-taker, right? I got to the studio and was disappointed to find that there weren't any 500 pound transvestites waiting to enliven my audience. Instead, I got a fellow dressed in nothing but a G-string and tattooed from head to toe in tiger stripes.

They had scheduled me as the evening's second guest. Dressed in a bathrobe and clenching a long cigarette holder between my teeth, I was supposed to run through my commercials in several different languages. Then we were going to talk about the various Remington products. I showed her the VicVac and demonstrated how it worked. Then I pulled out the Fuzz Away, a new product used to shave bobbles off your clothes.

Ruby was enthralled with this item. I was about to show it off when she said, 'Let me try it!' Taking it from my hand, she turned her back to the audience, hiked up her dress, and peered between her legs. Then she bolted back up, turned to her audience and announced, 'No, the fuzz is still there, folks!' Oh, if I hadn't been howling so hard I would have died from enbarrassment. I couldn't believe she had said that. Pulling such a stunt would have earned her a week's suspension on an American network. It didn't bother me though. However, if I'm ever on her show again, I'll be sure to leave the Fuzz Away home.

Doing business in the Land of the Rising Yen

I've always been impressed with the industriousness of the Japanese people. For them, doing the very best job they can is a matter of honour. With Japan moving to the forefront of the global marketplace, you can see how this attitude has paid huge dividends.

Remington has had its own company in Japan for the better

part of this decade. Before entering the Japanese market, we sought the help of a consultant, an expert on trade in that area. Ninety-nine per cent of the time, I won't use consultants. I've always maintained that they are like castrated bulls. They can't perform; all they can do is advise. However, in this case, we needed someone familiar with the territory to draw up a market profile. His research convinced us that we could create a niche for ourselves in Japan. With that information in hand, I went over and paved the way for our entry. If you're thinking of entering a foreign market you can also use a consultant or trade organization to help with your research. But once the facts and figures are in, you have to go to that country and handle your own negotiations. You can't allow a consultant to run with that ball. No one can sell your company, product, or idea better than you. No consultant or advisor can know your business or your competition as well as you.

Our initial foray into the country came as part of a joint venture with a Japanese company. Fifty per cent of our board of directors were Americans representing Remington. The remaining half was made up of our Japanese partners. Having worked closely with its people, I have come to know the nation well. In a time of huge US trade deficits, we are one of the few products made in America and sold in Japan. To succeed over there, you have to be more than just a good businessperson. You have to understand the people, and be able to adapt to their culture and its nuances.

For instance, my Japanese managing director and I once called on the buyer for one of Japan's largest department stores. This was at a time when Remington was first trying to open up Japan. It was crucial that we had a big success with this initial test of the market. I wanted to make a sale to every store we called on. Netting this large account would certainly give our programme a terrific opening boost.

The buyer, let's call him Mr Tanka, greeted both of us warmly. He asked me how my flight from the States had gone and how long I was going to be in his country. My managing director, Hank Saitoh, served as translator for both of us so there was no communication gap. A few minutes after our arrival, Tanka's secretary brought in rice cakes and tea. Everything seemed to be going splendidly.

When the buyer asked what he could do for me, I told him we were launching our shaver with a mammoth market test. It was going to be backed by a national advertising campaign, with heavy concentration on television. Mr Tanka was shown product samples, along with graphs and charts describing our entire promotion. I thought it looked like a first-class presentation. If I had been the buyer and this campaign had been brought to me, I would have leaped at the chance to put in an order.

When I finished, Mr Tanka was all smiles. He looked at me as if I were the Easter Bunny and Santa Claus all rolled into one. Speaking through Mr Saitoh, Tanka agreed that we had a wonderful programme. He asked some questions about pricing and congratulated us on the craftsmanship of our shavers. Then he bowed deeply. The meeting had ended.

I couldn't wait to ask Hank how large an order we could expect from this chap. As soon as we got out of the office, though, I sensed something was amiss. The polite smile had faded from my director's face. I said, 'Hank, what on earth are you looking so glum about? I don't think I've ever had a better meeting with a buyer.' Shaking his head, Saitoh said, 'That may be, Vic. But we didn't get the order.' I couldn't believe it. I asked, 'Are you sure? That just can't be. What did Tanka say?'

Hank explained that it wasn't important what Tanka said, it was what he didn't say that underscored our failure. He hadn't given us the name of his wholesaler. The significance of this was lost on me until Hank explained how the Japanese system works. Unlike stores in the US and Europe, Japanese shops have no room to carry any inventory. Space is at a premium in this overcrowded country. So wholesalers will hold a store's merchandise and use it to stock each retailer two or three times weekly. These wholesalers are the only route into the retail market. Without an introduction from a buyer, a manufacturer cannot do business with a wholesaler. This means he has no way of getting his product into the consumers' hands.

Was Mr American Entrepreneur about to accept this rejection with Oriental detachment? I should say not! I suggested we go over Mr Tanka's head and speak directly to the merchandise manager. Yes, it was the Gray's drugstores strategy all over again. Hank kiboshed that bright idea. He said, 'That would never fly. No matter how delicately you handled the buyer's boss, things just aren't done that way in Japan.' From the grave tone in his voice, I knew this was a status quo I could not undo. However, the situation was not hopeless. Hank had hatched his own entrepreneurial plan.

He made an appointment for us with the branch manager of our bank in Tokyo. Hank explained our predicament to this fellow who promptly called the manager of the store's bank. We didn't get an immediate solution. Instead, we were told to wait in an adjoining office while the two bank officials worked on our problem. Some ninety minutes later, our bank manager came in with good news. His colleague had just called back. We were to meet with the store's president at nine o'clock on the following morning.

This meeting was held at an office located about a mile from the store. I gave the president the same presentation I had given his buyer. When I concluded, there was more bowing and smiling before we left. As we made our way to the elevators, I must admit I was more confused than ever. That must have showed. Laughing, Hank looked at me and said, 'Don't worry, Victor. We got the order.' I asked if this meant the president had proffered the wholesaler's name. Hank shook his head and replied, 'No. But we have permission to see the buyer again at two o'clock this afternoon. Only he can make the final decision.' Terrific. This was the same guy who had turned us down only yesterday. I wondered why should things be any different twenty-four hours later.

Hank assured me everything would be all right. That afternoon, we kept our appointment with Mr Tanka. I suddenly felt like I was participating in a Noh drama. Both Tanka and his secretary acted as if they had never laid eyes on us before. Everything happened just as it had the previous day. The first thing Tanka asked me was how my flight to Japan had been and how long I intended to stay. The secretary once again brought in rice cakes and tea. And then he asked what he could do for us.

I made my presentation as if it were for the first time. He asked the same questions about pricing. When we were finished, we bowed and made our way out of the office. As soon as we got clear of that room Hank said, 'I told you everything was fine. We got the name of his wholesaler.' We were in business! I later asked Hank why the transaction had taken such a circuitous route. He explained that we couldn't have seen the store president without going through the banks. We needed the introduction. I had understood that, but I couldn't see any difference between my going to the merchandise manager, as I had first suggested, or our speaking to the store president. As I would find out, there was a very big difference. It was all a question of face. Obviously, the store president had interceded on Remington's behalf. But having us repeat the presentation allowed Tanka to create the illusion that the order was his decision and that he hadn't been influenced by his superior. This allowed us to make our sale while Tanka retained his honour. To Orientals, nothing is more important. The entrepreneur who forgets this won't do much business in Japan.

He should also know that the Japanese are an intensely loyal people. Remington's operations in Japan are now in the black. In our first few years over there, however, we had quite a struggle. We were getting murdered by the strong dollar. The company lost over half a million dollars in our first year.

Six months into the following year, that trend continued. I began looking at cost-cutting measures to ensure our survival. Eventually, I had to consider our payroll.

Mr Osaka, our company president, had come to us with a financial background. We no longer had much financial business to worry about and Hank Saitoh was actually running the company's day-to-day operations. It appeared as if Mr Osaka, who was costing us over $75,000 a year, was expendable.

Since he would be taking on added responsibilities, Hank was the first one to learn of my decision. He suggested holding a board meeting before taking action. That was fine with me. I must admit my mind was pretty well made up, but I knew the move would require board approval. I was hoping our Japanese partners wouldn't oppose the dismissal too strenuously.

We met the following day. The board consisted of six members: myself, two other Americans, and three Japanese. One of these was Mr Osaka. He sat there while I made the case for his dismissal. That was awkward. I felt like Lucretia Borgia discussing a choice of poisons with her intended victim.

I tried to handle it as best I could. I praised Mr Osaka for his past performance – easy to do since he was a fine executive – but explained that circumstances necessitated his removal. When I was finished, the three Japanese directors talked amongst themselves in their native language. It seemed like a calm, reasoned discussion. I thought they were helping Mr Osaka come to terms with the inevitable. Therefore, I was somewhat surprised when Hank Saitoh asked if we could adjourn the meeting until the following day. Hoping to keep things as harmonious as possible, our American contingent agreed.

We met the next morning. Hank Saitoh opened things up by announcing, 'We have taken your points under advisement and agree that we must cut back on spending. We have had a discussion with the company staff. They have volunteered to take a ten per cent pay cut so that Mr Osaka can remain as president. Mr Osaka, Mr Morita, and I will also decrease our salaries by the same percentage.' I almost fell out of my chair! I said, 'If that's OK with you, that's more than fine with me. I wasn't happy about having to let Mr Osaka go in the first place. I'm glad you came up with this most entrepreneurial answer to our problem.'

Does that story tell you something about the Japanese? It taught me that they operate as a team. When one person in the company is having difficulty, it becomes a joint problem. No wonder there doesn't seem to be an obstacle they can't overcome.

*

I'd like to finish this chapter with a little story that might provide some further insight into the Japanese businessman's philosophy. I was dining in a Tokyo restaurant with several prominent Japanese executives. They were showing me quite a time. They honoured me with a seat at the head of the table and saw to it that our waiter tended to my every need. When it came time to order our meal, they all recommended that I join them in enjoying a great Japanese delicacy. How could I refuse such gracious hosts?

The dish was brought out and placed before us. I wasn't certain what it was, but it seemed to be some sort of fish. As I started to eat my portion, I noticed that everyone at our table was watching me with rapt attention. I chewed a morsel, swallowed, and smiled my approval. It was a succulent dish. They didn't say a word. They just kept looking at me. After several moments of this, they finally heaped the fish on their own plates and started to dig in.

I asked one of my hosts why everyone had been staring. Had I committed some sort of culinary offence? Was I supposed to lead everyone in a Japanese version of grace before indulging my palate? He assured me I had done nothing wrong. Hardly able to hold back a grin, he explained. 'You see Victor, this is a very special fish. Only a select few chefs in our country are licensed to prepare it.' When I asked why that was, he continued: 'Because it is blowfish. It contains a powerful poison that must be extracted before cooking. If this is not done properly, just a few bites can be injurious, even fatal. My colleagues were just checking to see if you would survive before they partook of their own meal.' Oh my lord! I guess I should have been offended. Instead, I was impressed. I figured 'No wonder this country is doing so well. These Japanese are even entrepreneurial about dinner.' After all, in essence they were trying to measure the chef's intangible asset: his ability to remove the toxin from the blowfish. They just happened to be using me as their balance sheet!

Brainstorming

I'd like you to come into my office. Don't worry. You're not about to be called on the carpet. I just thought we'd lean back, throw our feet up on the desk, and do some brainstorming. We'll share some ideas on elements of entrepreneurship. We won't worry about a formal structure. Let's just free-associate and talk about any topic that jumps into our heads.

Getting a raise

Some time ago, Senator Edward Kennedy was trying to capture the Democratic Party's presidential nomination. During an interview with newsman Roger Mudd, he was asked why he wanted the country's top post. He couldn't answer the question. It's not just that he couldn't find the right words; he couldn't find any words at all. It made it seem as if he either didn't have any concrete motivation for competing for the office or that his reasons were too trivial to share with the public. You can imagine how this went over with the nation's voters. They figured, 'If he can't make a better case for himself than this, why should I give him my vote?' Almost immediately after the interview, the Kennedy campaign went into a tailspin from which it never recovered.

Senator Kennedy had committed the same blunder made by thousands of employees every year. He had asked for a raise – in this case a job promotion – but couldn't show his employers, the voters, why he deserved it.

I've seen this happen countless times. A person calls on his boss and says, 'I've been here for a year and I think I should have my salary increased.' You ask them how they have earned the pay hike, and they give you an answer as substantial as the senator's. I don't understand it. If you were selling a car to someone, what would you do? Go up to a potential customer and say, 'Buy this car because I want to sell it.' No, you would paint a vista detailing every attractive aspect of the vehicle. You'd talk about the great mileage it offered, safety features, its affordable price and all the other items that turn on the consumer.

Whenever you make a presentation, you go in armed with facts, figures, charts, graphs and anything else that will support you. In both instances, you come as prepared as possible. If you're looking to get a pay rise from your employer, you should bolster your request with the same thoroughness.

As a first step, take the time to make your case on paper. Document everything you have done for the company over a specific period of time. Be honest with yourself. A list peppered with hyperbole won't withstand the slimmest executive gust. One overstated item can cast doubts on your entire paper's credibility. You can guard against this by drawing up a private comparison between yourself and a fellow employee in a similar position. See how you stack up against this person. Are you producing a measurable amount more for the company? Remember, this is a *private* comparison. This list is for your eyes only and shouldn't be used in your actual presentation. Its only purpose is to provide you with a perspective.

Once you've established that you have indeed made a substantial contribution, put together an outline for your employer. No matter how much you've done, don't overload your boss with paper. The emphasis should be on the quality of your performance, not the quantity of print you can produce. One or two pages should be enough. It should look something like this:

Memo to: Mr Boss
RE: Past Year's performance of Mr E. M. Ployee, Director of Promotions

Over the past year at Boss and Sons, Mr Ployee has created the following programmes:

1. *The International Submarine Band Memorial Dinner*: an event that opened up forty new accounts for this company and attracted nationwide news coverage.

2. *The World Cup Sweepstakes*: a promotion that boosted our sales 33 per cent during its six-week run. It was so successful we already have a variation of this idea in place for next year.

3. *The Krazy Widget Giveaway*: a premium promotion of a new product. We gave away one Krazy Widget sample with each purchase of a container of Hammond's Miracle Hair Restorer. An enormous hit – it increased sales by 40 per cent and provided the base for the successful launching of our Krazy Widget bracelets.

In addition, through a judicious use of vendors, Mr Ployee has managed to bring in our ongoing promotions at 20 per cent below their usual cost, saving this company over $100,000. Even with these savings, the company's past high standards were maintained and in some areas surpassed. Looking at the near future, Mr Ployee has already arranged to have Krazy Widget featured as a November cover story for *Nuts and Bolts Magazine* (circulation: 3,000,000 national, 8,000,000 worldwide) and has a commitment from Sylvester Stallone to feature Hammond's Miracle Hair Restorer prominently in his upcoming film *Rocky V: Rocky Meets Frankenstein* (February release date).

In closing, I would like to point out that, over the last year, Mr Ployee has represented the company in several community service and charitable projects including the Cancer Fund, and the Annual Community Christmas drive. In December, he received the company's annual safety award for officially suggesting the installation of a safety net beneath the tightrope in the corporate gymnasium. He has been with the company for three years and receives a base salary of $40,000. Based on his performance, he would like his remuneration re-evaluated.

What have you done with this summary? You have cast a brilliant spotlight on your achievements and have drawn a vista bright with future promise. With this document drawn up, make an appointment with your boss and present it to him at that meeting. Bring two copies so you can both go over your claims together. You have now given him something tangible to wrestle with. If you went in without proof, and said, 'Mr B., I think I've done a lot for our company over this last year and would like to discuss a raise,' he could dismiss you simply by saying, 'Really? Well I don't agree with you. Your raise is denied.'

He can't easily dismiss that piece of paper. He might dispute some of your claims, in which case you would reach into your briefcase and bring out any records you have to support them. Remember, you're going to come with all your cannons loaded. By the time your meeting is over you will have obtained one of three things: a raise, an understandable refusal ('Yes, you're doing great, and I know you're not aware of this, but the company is about to have some rocky times.'), or a clue that you might want to seek employment elsewhere. The off-hand refusal, without reason, means your good efforts are unappreciated and might mean they will be forever under-valued.

Common sense should tell you the proper time to request a raise or a promotion. If you or your department recently made a blunder, you're not going to call on your boss no matter how good a year you've otherwise had. He could use that recent failure to undermine all your other accomplishments. If your meeting is about to begin and he seems to be in a bad mood, make an excuse and cancel. Reschedule for what you hope will be a more opportune time.

Whatever you do, don't look for a pay increase or a pro-motion when you know the company is going through some difficulty. That advice might seem so obvious as to be unnecess-ary, but I've known employees who used these critical moments to attempt a form of blackmail.

When I was chairman and president of Benrus, we were constantly up against the problems caused by undercapitaliz-ation. Things got particularly dicey just prior to a Christmas sales period. Needing additional capital to buy goods for that busy time, we were forced to re-do our loan agreement. The fellow negotiating the terms for us was one of my key execu-tives. The banks were playing hardball, but he was giving as well as he was getting. I was confident his efforts would reap the money and the conditions we needed.

In the midst of these dealings, he came to my office to discuss his progress. After filling me in, he floored me by saying, 'I think the company would be better off if you didn't spread yourself out so thin. You should divvy up your responsibilities. Why don't you continue as chairman, and put me in as president of the company?'

Nothing else he said was specific. There wasn't even the hint of a threat uttered, but I got the clear inference that if I didn't agree to the change and the accompanying raise in pay, that our loan agreement would be in jeopardy. Without that capital, Benrus could very well go under.

Now this fellow knew our backs were against the wall and he was almost certain that he was the only person in the company – at that particular time, anyway – who could handle these negotiations.

He was right on that score. Anyone else in the company would have been out of his element. I wouldn't have felt completely confident taking over the discussions; I had been too busy with the marketing side of the business to give it my full attention and it really wasn't my area of expertise. I couldn't hire a financial professional to replace him. It could have taken weeks to find someone. That new person would have had to spend several gruelling days steeping himself in the company background. Once he was finished, he would have had to start the negotiations at ground zero.

What on earth could I do? Benrus couldn't afford that kind of delay; we needed a commitment for the money as quickly as possible. I also knew that firing one of Benrus's high-ranking officers at such a crucial juncture in the negotiations wouldn't be the best way to hold the bank's confidence. This fellow had every right to believe he was indispensable. He had entered my office with a loaded gun and had drawn a bead on my heart.

I was tempted to accede to his wishes, but I knew that wasn't any way to run a business. What sort of entrepreneur would I be if I bent with every threat that walked through the door? Putting on a jaunty air, I called his bluff. I told him that if he was unhappy with his present position and was unable to complete the negotiations, I would be happy to step in for him.

Thank God, he backed down. The loan agreement went through in time. As soon as it did, this fellow's importance to the company dropped considerably. Unable to trust him, I grew to depend on him less and less. He never got close to the position he craved and left Benrus shortly after this episode.

I'm going to let you in on a little secret, something he didn't know. I thought his idea of separating the two top spots in the corporation did in fact have some merit. Indeed, I had been toying with that very idea for a good while. I wasn't quite sure if it was the thing to do. I was still wrestling with the decision when he came to my office. Had he approached me at a less critical time, I would have given the matter serious consideration. He would have been one of my top candidates for the presidency. An able man, he possessed many of the qualities I look for in a top executive. These didn't count for anything once he tried to cut the legs out from under me and Benrus. I suddenly saw him as a selfish, grasping individual, ready to threaten the company's welfare to advance his own cause.

Thinking he could make good with this gambit also showed poor judgement. It was the sort of faux pas that leaves an indelible stain on your record. There was no way he could ever hold another high position in one of my companies. If your company is ever in a tough spot and your particular talents place you in an advantageous position, don't commit a similar error. Cast your self-interest aside and grab an oar with the rest of your colleagues. Then row for all you're worth. Once out in calmer seas, you'll find an appreciative employer ready to grant you your well-earned reward.

Keeping the spirit alive

I'm often asked how can you keep the entrepreneurial spirit alive within the corporate framework. I think you do it, first, by hiring people possessing the same zest for hard work as you, and then by challenging their talents.

For instance, Remington's chief financial officer used to accompany me on my trips to our Japanese company. He would analyze their operations and their cash flow, do all the usual fiscal chores. About a year and a half ago, I found my schedule no longer permitted my frequent visits to the Orient. Wishing to keep open a clear line of communication, I called my financial officer in and said, 'John, instead of having Hank Saitoh report to me, I'm going to have him deal with you from now on. You've seen the business over there and understand how it works. You are now responsible for the entire operation – the marketing, advertising and all the rest of it – not just the financial end. You'll give me regular reports and we'll discuss the business's progress. If any questions or problems arise, you can come to me at any time. But the direction for the company will flow through you.' I had shifted the responsibility from me to him, while keeping my hand in via the reporting process.

In most companies, the CFO wouldn't even be considered for a position of this sort. People would take one look at his present position and assume that he wasn't qualified to run a company's entire operation. As an entrepreneur, you have to look past the stereotype created by titles and see the worth of the employee.

We try to prevent the corporate tendency towards pigeon-

holing by encouraging all our Remington executives to familiar-
ize themselves with management areas outside their usual
realm. A marketing executive at Remington is going to have
more than just a passing interest in the manufacturing end of
our corporation. When you're a growing enterprise, you want
your management to be flexible enough to adapt to the demands
of an always-growing, ever-evolving business. This means your
company is prepared to face just about anything. It also adds
a generous helping of spice to your corporate life.

Clear goals and incentives can also set off some entrepreneurial sparks. We have a chap who handled all our company
forecasts. He had never headed up his own product division. I
made him product manager for our pool alarms. Along with
the increased responsibility, we also gave him 10 per cent of the
profits from that business. Operating a mini company within
the Remington framework, he experiences fully the thrills and
disappointments of guiding an entrepreneurial venture. He gets
a taste of everything I go through. It makes him a tremendous
asset. With a personal stake in the enterprise, he's more committed than ever to our success.

He's not alone in our company. As a matter of fact, every
Remington employee shares in an incentive programme. They
know they are working for more than just a pay cheque. If the
company does well, they are going to do well. Consequently,
they are constantly thinking of Remington's welfare and creating methods to improve our products. This takes place on
every level of the company. Remington has become more than
just a job, it's a vital part of their lives.

The atmosphere this creates is electrifying. When you walk
through our doors, you can sense that you're looking at more
than just a group of employees pulling themselves through
another day. You're looking at a company of highly motivated
entrepreneurs. Has it made a difference? You be the judge.
We were recently named one of the '100 Best Companies to
Work For in America'. At the end of last year, for the first
time since 1952, Remington became America's number-one
manufacturer of men's electric shavers. This from a company

that was teetering on the edge of extinction when we took it over. I'd say that's a pretty good endorsement of our product, our people, and our approach.

A cure for growing pains

More than anything else, entrepreneurs running small businesses often ask me how to raise capital in order to expand. If you're looking to branch out, I assume your enterprise must be doing well. As you already know, I've always been a great believer in leveraging one's intangible assets. One of these intangible assets is your success.

Suppose you had a thriving book store and wanted to open another in a different section of town. As the owner of a proven enterprise, you can approach venture capitalists or private investors and offer them equity in your new store. Equity investors are looking for a high return on their money; they are willing to take some risks. Show them what you've done. Your glowing bottom line gives eloquent testimony to your managerial abilities. Draw up a plan detailing how you will have an even greater success. Then sell them a piece of your dream. When your business keeps prospering, these happy investors will be a continual source of cash for any possible future expansions. If you take this approach, try to hold on to at least 51 per cent of the enterprises. This will allow you to maintain a controlling interest in the business.

Any time your business grows, you are going to be faced with a number of decisions. For example, a gentleman from Surrey recently wrote asking if he should turn his lucrative part-time business into a full-time enterprise. I've often suggested that the budding entrepreneur should launch an initial venture as a part-time affair. It's an excellent test of your idea's viability, yet it allows you still to have the security of a regular pay cheque.

Once this test has worked out, as his apparently had, you've taken the first step to entrepreneurial freedom. You must now estimate how much capital and cash is needed to take the business full time. Don't scrimp with the numbers! Cash is always king. When you don't have it, it's awfully hard to get. Call in an accountant, someone versed in the ways of small businesses, and have him help you with your figures. Be careful to add 25 per cent to your final budget to cover any unforeseen glitches. With this figure in hand, estimate your weekly return from a full time enterprise. If it is enough money to support you, take care of your overhead, and cover your start-up debt, then I heartily recommend your taking the full plunge.

A graphic design company owned by two young men in London faced another kind of decision when their business started to boom. With this increase, the administrative duties – ordering couriers, billing, handling the daily mail, and answering the phones – were demanding much of these gentlemen's time. They needed an administrator who would tend to these duties, freeing the owners to place their full attention on their work.

Their chief concerns centred around cost. They wondered what would be the more cost-effective move, hiring an experienced pro, who could jump into the job immediately, or a junior trainee. The less experienced employee would work at a lower salary, but would require a good deal of training.

As entrepreneurs, they had only one choice. They had to hire the best person they could find. There is nothing wrong with hiring trainees to work within your company. However an administrator in a service business usually holds a key position. If the company's performance starts to lag because of late deliveries or other tasks that have not been carried out efficiently, a reputation can be severely damaged. Since the administrator is often a liaison between company and account, he or she should be someone able to speak the technical language of the customer. You mustn't place your company in the hands of an amateur. In a situation like this, the established pro is worth the extra investment.

Having decided to spend an extra few bob, the designers wondered how they could soften the impact on their overhead.

Such an expense would have to be at least partially passed on to their customers. Nobody likes a price escalation. However, when they are necessary they should be presented in as straightforward a manner as possible.

I suggested the two men broach the additional costs while presenting contracts to their clients. They could list their usual charges and add a 5 to 10 per cent surcharge, depending on the job and the administrator's salary. This would be identified as an administrative fee. As long as the billing is reasonable and the firm maintains its high standards, the customers shouldn't raise a squawk. No one, after all, expects you to lose money while providing your service.

One of the more unusual growth 'problems' brought to my attention in recent years came from a dear lady in Sussex. She owned a small cattery. From 1986 to 1987, her turnover had more than doubled. She had advertised in the past, but, to use her own words, 'business grew too quickly, forcing me to stop.' Of course, when she ceased using the ads, business fell off. She was about to revive her ad campaign when she wrote to me, asking what percentage of her annual turnover should be allotted for advertising.

With apologies, I told her she was asking the wrong question. She already knew how much money to spend. Obviously her past advertising campaigns had been smashing successes. Why not repeat that formula? When I worked at Playtex, and someone wanted to tinker with a proven, winning product or promotion, one of my bosses had a stock response, 'If it ain't broke, don't fix it!' Business knocking down her door! Why, I can't think of an entrepreneur who wouldn't love to have this woman's difficulty. Placed in her position, if your business had increased dramatically with your last batch of ads, there is no earthly reason why you wouldn't do again exactly what you had done previously – but with the added advantage that the first bit of advertising has already acted for you as a wonderful test of the market. If business had improved by only a trickle, you would make changes. You might even discontinue the ads; a campaign that can't at least pay for itself with increased business is a campaign to abandon. On the other hand, if your ads generated a strong positive response, such as this woman received, you would be advised to make an entrepreneurial investment and enlarge your facilities before purchasing any more ads. *The person who takes the fullest advantage of success is the person who plans for it.*

You want to be able to accommodate that wonderful increase in business. Don't turn it away! In this case, the question you should be asking yourself is how much can I afford for expansion? You can estimate that figure easily enough. Just forecast how much your business will improve if you go back to your former advertising budget. Then enlarge your facility accordingly. Remember, a great success often brings along a bagful of new choices and responsibilities, from increasing a capital investment to hiring more employees to moving to a larger location. If you believe in yourself and the success of your venture, you have to be ready to grow with your business. You have to keep going for it!

Get off the air!

Because I appear in the Remington commercials, I often get calls or letters from entrepreneurs who are appearing in their own ads. They ask me about everything from how their copy should be written to how they can hire a good film crew. I offer them what little advice I can. I also warn them of the perils of starring in a commercial. Once your visage is flashed throughout thousands – and sometimes millions – of homes, your life undergoes a radical change. Like it or not, you become a celebrity. More than that, you become so firmly associated with your product, the two of you become indivisible in the customer's mind. From that point on, your public behaviour will cast a direct reflection on your enterprise. Do you think that doesn't carry a heavy responsibility? As a fellow who can't even think about leaving his home while carrying a hint of five o'clock shadow, I can tell you it's no picnic.

A personal disgrace brought to the public's attention can destroy an ad campaign, and, if not properly handled, ruin your business. The best evidence of this was brought to me not too long ago. A bank president had been doing his own TV commercials. They featured this rather staid, sombre individual, talking about how secure your accounts would be in his venerable institution. In the commercial's closing moments, he looked into the camera, his slate-grey eyes dispensing waves of integrity, and said, 'You can sleep at night as long as you know I'm here watching your account. Your money is safe with me.' Not bad. His pitch had a warm, personal approach. It was almost as good as, 'I liked it so much, I bought the company!'

The commercial ran for about six months and had received a lot of favourable comments. I had never met this gentleman, but one afternoon I received a phone call from one of his representatives. This young woman introduced herself and asked, 'Mr Kiam are you at all familiar with Mr Jones's commercial?' I said I was. She said, 'Well, based on the latest news, what do you think he should do?' I had to ask her to back up a bit. I wasn't aware that there was any news concerning her boss. She apologized and explained that the story had apparently not gone national yet. If it had I would have discovered that Mr Jones had been arrested on the previous night for driving while intoxicated. He had apparently been zig-zagging his car all over the road. The police stopped him and had him submit to a breathalyser test. He didn't pass. In fact, I'm afraid it sounded as if he didn't come close.

I told her I could see where the adverse publicity could be a problem and I was about to offer some advice. I was thinking that he might be able to get through this mess if he called a press conference, admitted he made a mistake, and then set up a fund to help educate youngsters on the perils of drunk driving. A compassionate public can be awfully forgiving when a man does his penance in full view. Perhaps this fellow could make some lemonade out of this lemon. It would certainly make for a safer drink than what he had been imbibing.

As I started to offer this sage advice, his employee said, 'I'm afraid the drunk-driving charge is only one of his problems. You see, after he flunked the test, state law required the police to do a thorough search of his car. When they got to the trunk, they found his arsenal.' His arsenal! Yes, that's what the woman said. It seems this fellow was caught with an unlicensed cache of armaments including a couple of .50 calibre machine guns, an automatic rifle and about thirty pistols. I imagine he kept his anti-aircraft gun home because it wouldn't fit in the trunk. Well, at least his commercials were truthful. Your money really was safe with him as long as he didn't run out of bullets. He had enough weaponry to hold off Colonel Gaddafi, Rambo, the Ned Kelly gang, and the entire Iranian army singlehanded.

After taking in the whole tale, I said, 'I can't give him much advice on this one, but I will tell you what I would do if I were in his position. Get off the air! And do it as soon as possible. Yank the commercial you already have on, and reshoot a new one without this gentleman. You can't have him announcing "Your money is safe with me" when he is being touted through-out the media as the drunk with an arsenal large enough to raid Fort Knox. I don't think it will go down very well with the public.'

I added that, in time, he might be able to return as the company spokesman. In our Warholian world, where every-body seems to achieve their fifteen minutes of notoriety, people tend to forget scandals such as this in about a year. If Mr Jones could forge a semblance of a reasonable excuse for his behaviour and get off with a quiet fine and reprimand, he might even be back sooner. But as long as he was a hot item, he was going to have to distance himself from the bank so far as the public was concerned.

As you can see, appearing in your ads can be a two-edged sword. Yes, there is a certain amount of ego gratification when people recognize you on the street. On the other hand, you are no longer just you. The individual has merged with the company or product. You have to think twice before you do anything out of the ordinary in public. It's almost like being a political figure. Any taint on the person will attach itself to the office. Anything that publicly injures you is going to harm your enterprise.

Turn it around

The entrepreneur launching a first venture is going to encounter a number of disappointments and unforeseen problems. You mustn't let them stop you! It's a rare business that doesn't have its share of problems. Greet these downward turns with your best face. They are nothing more than opportunities to exercise your entrepreneurial ingenuity.

In *Going For It!*, I introduced readers to my favourite barber, Jack. He's been cutting hair for years. At first he was employed by someone else, but, after a while, he had an urge to open a shop of his own. Finding what he thought was a prime location, he struck a deal with his landlord, a prominent New York hotel. They agreed that if he made his New York shop a success, he could open similar shops in the chain's other hotels across the United States.

This seemed like quite an opportunity. Jack walked around the hotel while it was still under construction and was mesmerized by its sheer size. At any one time, it would house over 2000 people. Jack would be its exclusive barber. Of course, the hotel's promise made the deal especially enticing. In one small leap, the barber could go from shop owner to franchise CEO.

The chasm that had to be cleared, however, turned out to be a mite wider than Jack originally figured. Jack worked as hard as he could to build his business, but he hadn't figured on a few obstacles. Though the hotel had a prestigious name, and offered magnificent service, it did a transient business. Visitors rarely stayed for more than two or three days and often had their hair cut before coming to town. Businessmen staying at the hotel would come to his shop only for a shoeshine. Those chairs were always full. But the shoeshining profits hardly made a dent in his overhead. Being inside the hotel and unable to advertise his presence on the street, he attracted virtually no walk-in business.

Jack's shop is large and the already high rent has been raised four times since the business opened. Anticipating a huge clientele, he was certain he could meet those gargantuan rates. When his bottom line failed to live up to his projections, Jack began to struggle. He was on his feet twelve hours a day, six days a week. Patches of snow began to swirl about his temples. Dark circles began to creep in under his eyes. After a year of barely making ends meet, no one would have blamed him if he had tossed in the towel. Jack is an outstanding barber, an artist with shears, and he had a small core of loyal customers. He could have found work at high wages with any shop in the city.

Jack, though, wants something more. He's an entrepreneur and he was not about to let his dream disintegrate without taking action. Rather than allow his problems to overcome him, he decided to attack them.

The first thing he had to do was broaden his client base. He had to increase his shop's profile. When it first opened, Jack's business had primarily catered to men. He began offering unisex styling in order to attract businesswomen on their lunch breaks. Brochures, outlining his full range of services, were printed and delivered to businesses in the area.

This increased his walk-in business. In an effort to catch the attention of the hotel's visitors, he persuaded management to enclose an advertising insert in each room's guest packet. That had a slight impact, but he was faced with the problem of timing. Most of these tourists and business travellers would still be getting their hair trimmed prior to their New York arrival.

Readjusting his thinking cap, Jack found another solution. He asked the hotel to provide its reservation list. A week to ten days before a guest was due to leave for New York, they would receive a coupon in the mail. It was an invitation from

Jack, asking them to experience the pleasures of a professional New York haircut at a 30 per cent discount. This promotion was such a success, he began to circulate the coupons, offering the same price break, to local business people. He would just drop by an office and leave a handful.

There haven't been any miracles, but business has gradually turned around since Jack implemented these ideas. Bills are being paid, salaries are being met, and the shop is keeping busy. Jack is going to make it because he won't allow himself to fail.

If a venture of yours is wobbly, there is no reason why you can't resurrect it as Jack did. All he really did was take stock of his business's assets and liabilities. His talent was the store's greatest asset. The shop's low profile was its greatest liability. By doing everything he could to erase that weakness, he was able to expose people to his store's strength: his skilled hands. Jack's actions have given his dream some fresh hope. Take a look at your own enterprise. Pinpoint the problems and ask yourself if you've done everything possible to overcome them. If you haven't, draw up a fresh strategy with an eye towards eliminating the liabilities. Be as wildly creative as you like. Then gird yourself, and jump back into the fray. The adventure is just about to begin.

Building on your USP

The owner of a ladies' hairdressing salon in Torquay wanted to increase his turnover. He had already considered stocking the reception area with a wide range of products to be sold to his customers. He wrote to me, asking what other measures could be taken.

As a general rule, no matter what your enterprise is, you must showcase your Unique Selling Proposition (the USP). Discovering your USP is simple. Just ask yourself what your business or product offers customers that places you apart from your competitors. If you don't come up with an answer, then you must create a USP. Do some research. Learn as much about your competition's operation as possible. Try to think of ways you can be different. These additions can come in the form of added services or new products. A longer schedule, offering your customers the advantage of more varied hours, can also help set you apart from the crowd. Whatever you choose, it should be something that makes your venture stand out to your customers in a positive manner.

For example, if you were this salon owner, you might offer a frequent-user coupon. If a customer were to receive a certain number of haircuts over a specified period of time, they would be entitled to get one free. You could also arrange for women to receive a credit for every new customer they introduce to the shop, say a free styling with every three new accounts. Gift certificates are another option. Customers could buy them as gifts for friends on birthdays and holidays.

If you wanted to increase your range of products as a way of beefing up your USP, you should look at new items that offer an easy fit to your general clientele. For instance, if you sold hunting rifles, you might augment the shop with a knife department or perhaps you would add a line of rugged outdoor wear. You wouldn't try selling antique jewellery or silk lingerie. What would be the point? Your existing traffic would probably have little immediate use for goods of this sort. People who did want to buy these things would be unlikely to come to your store to purchase them. Stay with what you do best.

For the salon owner, the choices are readily seen. Women who walk through his door are looking to enhance their beauty. Anything that helps them accomplish this task should be considered a potential salon product. Along with cosmetic items, you might offer jewellery, scarves, small portable hair dryers, or even Jane Fonda's home-exercise video. If the space permits, you might hire a reflexologist to offer soothing foot massages while your customers have their hair dried. Show some flair. Anything relating to your customer's obvious needs should be appropriate.

*

Breaking old habits

In Birmingham, there is a preventative maintenance company for computers. The company possess a solid core of highly satisfied customers and do a strong repeat business. As well as offering preventative maintenance they also repair machines. One of their biggest chores is trying to convince their potential customers that preventative medicine is better than a cure and far more cost effective. They needed a method to develop this market, particularly with larger companies, who were set in their ways and resistant to changing from the old 'fix it when it falls apart' concept. They wrote to me, just recently, asking for suggestions.

The company's problem isn't new. Entrepreneurs are often bucking against old ideas. There's nothing harder than trying to persuade people to change their habits. The best way to do it is to present them with evidence of past success. Even if you have only three or four clients who have already given you that opening chance, their satisfaction should be put to your advantage. If you were the owner of the Birmingham company, you would already have that band of pleased customers. Those who have followed your suggestions should be asked to provide written endorsements of your prevention service. Try to get as many endorsements as possible. Make sure they showcase how your prevention system is more economical than maintenance, allows your customers to give more reliable service, and any other virtues your service offers. Use these endorsements as part of an artfully drawn brochure, to be handed out to your more resistant customers whenever you make your presentation. That sort of approach should go a long way towards breaking the ice.

If you are just starting out and find no one will give you that all-important first break, do what some crazy American did when he bought a shaver company. It's awfully hard to wrench people from the archaic ritual of blade shaving. It is steeped in traditions handed down since the first human sacrifice. This bloke tried to break this savage habit by offering a money-back

guarantee to anyone who didn't find his electric shaver could
shave as close as a blade. That offer told consumers that this
fellow believed in his product so strongly, he was willing to
back it with a financial risk. I understand that since that guarantee was first issued, the shaver and company have done rather
nicely! It's not all that surprising. When you show that much
confidence in your service, product, or company, you'd be
amazed at how many people will be willing to give you a
chance.

David versus Goliath

A fellow with a small landscaping business wrote wanting to
know how he could keep up with his bigger competitors. They
apparently had more manpower, allowing them to cover an
immense amount of territory in less time than he ever could.
Due to their size, they could order materials in greater volume,
keeping their overheads down. This would enable them to keep
their prices below his.

Despite the obvious disadvantages weighing against this fellow, he had a chance to win this battle. I have found that small
entrepreneurs can compete successfully with larger companies.
To do so they must develop a powerful USP. Put in his shoes,
you would have to ask yourself, 'What can I do to make this
enterprise different from the rest?' You could, for example,
look at your competitors' working hours. When aren't they
available? Do they make house calls during the evening? If
they generally don't, that might be the time to be offering your
talents. You could also invest in an answering service and a
telephone bleeper. Then let your customers know that you are
available 24 hours a day.

Maintaining a high profile is most important. You might
perhaps have flyers printed (in other words, brochures touting
for business on spec), with which – along with your business
card – you flood the countryside. You should be very aggressive
about marketing your firm. Your flyers must highlight your

USP. Draw up a list comparing your company to your competitors. Once again, it's assets and liabilities time. Shore up your
liabilities as best you can, and then cast a cold eye at the other
fellow's negative column. These represent his vulnerable side.
They are the areas where you can outperform those larger
companies. You can come out on top. Just remember this
general rule: if you can't undercut the competition's prices,
don't worry. You can always overwhelm your potential customers with hard work and outstanding service.

The value of starting small

Part-time entrepreneurial inventors often wonder how to
turn their creations into a viable business. A gentleman from
Middlesex recently asked us how he could go about marketing
a patented device that fitted on to any standard spade. It
reportedly made digging an easier chore for the gardener.

We were not sent a sample, but since the product was
protected by patent, we presumed it had a USP. When you
have an invention that deserves your full confidence, you should
be willing to make an initial investment in the manufacture of
a small quantity. These should then be brought to a number of
appropriate local outlets. In this particular case, an inventor
could take them to hardware and gardening shops.

If the store owner finds your product attractive, you can
arrange for him to sell it at a specified price. You and the shop
owner would each get 50 per cent of the sale price on each item
sold. This will serve as your market test. If the product sells
well on this small scale, you can broaden your base by taking
it to other stores outside your area. Your success in the local
shops can be used to persuade others to carry the item. At this
point, you can sell it to them at a set wholesale price, allowing
them to mark it up at their own discretion for retail. If your
business continues to grow you could even offer it as a mail-
order item. A successful market test would also give you another
alternative. Armed with the results, you could take your proto-

types to a manufacturer of related products and try to persuade him to make and distribute the creation while paying a royalty to you.

Drawing the line

In a corporate structure, the entrepreneur has to cope with rejection. Highly creative, he will see a number of his concepts spurned merely because they go against the status quo. I've always said you should fight for your idea until your bosses have officially placed it in its grave. At Playtex, I fought like hell for the feminine deodorant to be placed in cosmetics but lost. Once it became clear that the boss's decision was final and the products were placed in the store, I went on to other business. You have to know when the bout is over. If you keep punching out in the name of lost causes, that dead body you are working over may turn out to be your own. This is especially true if you've been given ample opportunity to test your theories.

Let me give you an example. At Benrus, Robert Grim was a fellow in marketing who never took no for an answer. We would have a meeting and someone would report something like, 'The co-op [advertising bought with a retailer] for the product this year will represent 6 per cent of the purchase.' Bob would start pounding his fist and say, 'No, it should be double that amount. We'll be so much more successful if we spend more money on co-op ads.' Then he would outline his reasons.

As this fellow knew, we had a corporate policy that limited our co-op spending, most of which took place on a local level. We were more inclined to invest in national campaigns. However, I have always encouraged my employees to be entrepreneurial. Bob had a degree of flexibility with his budget. When he asked to test market his co-op increase for one key account, we gave him the OK.

The results came back and they were not in his favour. The

increased spending had had no impact at all on sales. Despite this, Bob wouldn't drop the idea. He kept bringing it up in meeting after meeting.

I would have admired his fortitude. But, having failed once already, it was incumbent upon Bob to present some compelling reasons for us to give him another crack. He didn't have any. He was just reiterating his now tired and disproven theories. After a good ten minutes of his haranguing, I would finally say, 'Bob, for god sakes, we've made that decision. You've nothing new to offer here so let's all go on to something else.' He'd still give me a fight!

Having to face this each time we had a meeting, I began to grow weary of this man's face, especially the part that played host to his mouth. I told his immediate superior that if there was any way he could exclude Bob from future meetings without disrupting the organization, he should do so. I just didn't want to be in the same room with him. If he hadn't been so good at the rest of his job, I probably would have fired him. As it was, his lack of judgement halted his corporate advancement.

The lesson here for entrepreneurs is simple. Bob was given an opportunity and it did not support his claims. At that point, you either have to come back with an improved version of your idea, or go along with your organization's thinking. The status quo isn't always wrong.

Not the shy and retiring type

I've often been asked how I feel about corporate policy providing for a mandatory retirement age. In *Duck Soup*, the Marx Brothers' zany political satire, Groucho sums up my thinking with the title of his anarchistic hymn, 'I'm Against It!'

Age is just a number. I know a score of young men who have been walking this planet for over seventy years. I also know a lot of elderly thirty-five year olds. Our company attorney just turned sixty-five. A few years ago, he came into my office and announced, 'I don't want to retire, provided I'm in good health,

until I'm seventy years old. Is that a problem?' I assured him
it wasn't. This guy has been with Remington for over thirty
years. His background and his knowledge are invaluable to us.
Why should I chuck it all away because of a date on a yellowed
birth certificate? As an entrepreneur, you don't allow yourself
to be swayed by appearances. You're open to everything;
nothing is ever mandatory. I just turned sixty. I get more done
now in a day than I did thirty years ago. Because of my
experience, I can not only work harder than many people half
my age, I can work smarter. I've learned the value of prioritizing
and can make every minute work for me in a way I never could
before.

I don't see any reason why I can't go on like this for five,
ten, or even twenty more years. I'm an entrepreneur. I don't
put limits on myself or the people who work for me. Why
should we stop? Did anyone tell Picasso to put away his brush
when he turned sixty-five? Should Sir Alec Guinness stop
learning his lines? An entrepreneur is an artist too. When he
or she can still hit those high notes, why should anyone care
about their age?

If the time comes that you voluntarily retire, your
entrepreneurial life doesn't necessarily have to end. If you've
left your enterprise or your position with a company owned
by someone else, I have to assume you've prepared yourself
financially. You have some sort of steady income either through
a pension plan or some other set-up. Financial pressures, for
the most part, are behind you. The children are grown-up and
have moved out. Don't you know how lucky you are? Your days
are completely your own. You can fish, see your grandchildren,
scale Mount Everest, or do any one of a thousand other things.
You can also track down new entrepreneurial horizons.

Take Bob Leeds. He was chairman of the board of Manhattan
Industries, one of the top 500 American companies included in
Fortune magazine's '*Fortune* 500' listing. He was a bright fellow,
who liked people and enjoyed working with them. Having
enjoyed some success, he wanted to give something back to
business and the community. Bob thought he might like to try

a hand at teaching. He did not have a masters degree in education. However, he did have an immense storehouse of business knowledge and an ability to communicate well.

Bob took on three part-time teaching jobs in colleges in the New York area. He loved it. The challenge of shaping young minds appealed to his entrepreneurial creativity. His performance was so impressive, he was offered a full-time position teaching marketing at the University of Southern Florida. This required an uprooting and an even more intense commitment. Free of any ties to a corporate job, Bob was able to grab hold of this opportunity with both hands. He is now the head of the MBA programme in that very university. Older entrepreneurs never die, and they certainly don't fade away. They just keep going for it.

The entrepreneur and charity

Successful entrepreneurs are often asked to render service to charitable organizations. This means more than just making a mere donation, it often entails giving a certain number of hours while fulfilling a role within the charity. For example, you might be asked to head up a community fund-raising drive or to take an active role on the board of directors. For those who assume this responsibility, a couple of words of advice.

Don't spread yourself thin amongst a number of charities. As we've said before, the entrepreneur can't be half-pregnant. You approach life with a high-powered, state-of-the-art rifle, not a shotgun. This doesn't mean you can't make financial contributions to other worthwhile causes. Write all the cheques you want. Just don't dabble with your time. Fully commit to one organization that works on something that catches your heart.

Once involved with the organization, be prepared to come up against some of the same archaic notions you've encountered in the corporate world. A non-profit organization is a corporate entity. In fact it generally has more than its fair share of bureaucratic stone-heads and lovers of the status quo. Any time these people are asked to do something differently, they don't see it as opportunity. They see only the risks.

It's hard to get around these attitudes. In business, if you have a product selling for $5.99 and it's a stable, consistent item, you know you're going to sell a certain, profitable percentage of that product at its current price. Let's say you want to improve your volume. You decide to slice the price to $4.99. Consumers love to see prices drop, so the item will be somewhat more attractive. However, there is a risk involved. If that cut doesn't increase business by an appreciable amount, you have a problem: a rise in volume, but a loss in profits. You can soften your risk with a market test. Selling the product at a reduced price in a small, select area will tell you if the change is worthwhile.

If a charity has run its annual fund-raising drive – its most visible product – the same way for many years, a sudden change offers the same risk you faced with your price cutting. However, the charity usually can't afford the luxury of a try-out. What can it do? Run a miniature test-drive and see if it works? It's very difficult. This risk of failure causes most charities, especially moderately successful ones, to loathe any attempt at serious innovation.

Because of this, I would advise that your involvement should not include membership of a board of directors. Unless you have retired you don't have the time, and the bureaucratic stonewalling of your creativity will prove to be too frustrating. Instead, lend your talents to an organization in an advisory capacity.

I'm not talking about consulting; I'm suggesting more of an activist's role. Find a problem that the charity has been unable to solve. None of their set ideas will have an impact here, because none of them have worked. Give the board a plan showing clearly how you can undo this puzzle. Then you take the responsibility to see that this single project is carried out.

For instance, in 1983 I was asked to head up a United Way drive in Fairfield, Connecticut. United Way is a conglomeration of major American charities which uses its resources to make a powerful, concerted effort on behalf of its member organizations. For years, the local group had been trying to reach an annual goal of $4 million dollars. They had yet to do it. When I came on board, I looked over all their past plans and budgets and came up with a few ideas of my own. Then I put a bit of pressure on myself – some extra motivation – by telling the board, 'We are going to reach our mark. There's no doubt about it. I hate failure and, to me, making only $3,950,000 would be a defeat. I didn't get involved with this thing to come home a loser.'

The plan I formulated was based on the current drive's intangible assets and liabilities. Examining these, I could see that the United Way's campaign material was very strong. An asset. However, it was almost exclusively national in scope. There was the liability. Nothing was prepared on a local basis other than a listing of regional institutions that benefited from the charity. The would-be town philanthropist can't relate to a national campaign. They have a hard time seeing the direct benefits of their good works and contributions. This was a shortcoming in need of swift correction.

I suggested the formation of a regional advertising fund. This money was used to buy time on radio stations and space in the local newspapers. We also spent two days filming at the eighteen agencies in our area that received contributions from the United Way. This film was used as part of our overall presentation.

As I had suspected, we found out that most of our corporate contributors knew little about the institutions they had helped support. We arranged for bus tours to take them to the YMCA, Goodwill Industries, Meals on Wheels, and other agencies. They got to see exactly how their money was working. It encouraged them to give more and to solicit contributions from others. We also made presentations to diverse town groups. By the time our drive, with its new emphasis, was over, we passed that four million mark with ease. Having a specific goal and the leeway to institute an untried strategy made this a most satisfying entrepreneurial venture.

Burnout

We've all heard about this. A hard-driving executive has been a mover and shaker with his company for over twenty years. One day, his secretary walks in to find him seated at his desk, staring blankly into space or reduced to a state of tears. He can't bring himself to lift a pen or read another report. A recent TV special showed executives in Japan whose burnout was so severe they had to be hospitalized. They didn't have the strength or motivation to get out of bed in the morning. Most of them looked as if they could barely keep their eyes open. Each of these men was a high-powered figure, holding a lofty position.

I hope this doesn't sound like notes from an ivory tower, but I've never experienced serious burnout and, what's more, I don't know any entrepreneurs who have. Oh, yes, I've worked myself into near-exhaustion, but a week's vacation with a few days of banging the ball around on the tennis court and I was as good as new.

You're probably wondering what my secret is. I can tell you I have not stumbled on to a fountain of youth or some magic elixir. Or maybe I have. From what I've seen and read, the executive who burns out is usually the corporate hack. This is a player who enters the corporate ballgame and moves up the ladder until the Peter Principle comes into play. He reaches his level of incompetence and has no place further to go.

You see these lost souls all the time. They trudge off to work in the morning, lugging a briefcase that threatens to anchor them in place, wearing vaguely uninterested looks on their forlorn faces. What started out as a great adventure twenty years ago has become just another mundane exercise in clock punching. They are not making time, they are marking time and there is no worse hell on earth. The walls of the office draw closer every day until they eventually squeeze all the remaining juice out of these prisoners. They don't wake up in the morning, ready to charge into battle. Alas, there are no longer any battles worth fighting. No wonder these people retreat into the safe folds of collapse.

Entrepreneurs should never be prone to this breakdown. These are people in love with what they are doing. Their ladder reaches up to the heavens and beyond. There is always another step to climb. They never rest on any one rung long enough to allow boredom to tighten its grip. They are pleased with their success, but are always hungry for more. When the day finally arrives when no new challenges seem ready to present themselves, they go out and find some. Or create them. Their vitality is as inviting to the demon burnout as a cross is to a vampire. They are too busy to be bitten.

I recently heard about a fellow, a head of a large corporation, who was asked by an interviewer if he ever thought about slowing down. He seemed to be on the go night and day, often getting only four hours of sleep per night. The reporter wanted to know if this demanding schedule, especially the lack of snooze time, might not lead to burnout. The CEO, a recent celebrant of his seventy-fifth birthday, said, 'No, I don't think so. I'm having too much fun for that to happen. Besides, I don't like to get too much sleep. I'm afraid I might miss something.' For him, work is no more taxing than breathing. That man has got to be an entrepreneur.

CHAPTER NINE

They keep going for it: entrepreneurs I have known

I'd like to introduce you to four people from rather diverse backgrounds. They do, however, have at least one thing in common. They are walking advertisements for the wonders of the entrepreneurial life. They have gone for it and won. So can you.

Lisa and the case of the undefined market

Sometimes an entrepreneur has a great idea, but can't find a ready market. Don't get discouraged. If your concept has any merit, your perseverance can bring it to reality. Let me give you an example that's especially close to home.

As you already know, my daughter Lisa got her first taste of the entrepreneurial life when she was eight years old and employed by our jewellery company. That entrepreneurial streak has stayed with her. Like all my children, she has always been enterprising, a self-starter, and someone who was not afraid to shake up the status quo. For instance while only a freshman in college, she started teaching learning-disabled youngsters. Enjoying this experience, she went out and set up a special teaching programme in an inner-city junior high school.

The students there were in dire need of guidance. The school suffered from a high drop-out rate and absenteeism was rampant. Many of the students who did attend classes with any regularity were just going through the motions. Fortunately they had a principal who cared. He would do anything to ignite his students. This good man allowed Lisa and some of her classmates to teach whatever courses interested them. For instance, a biology major would tutor these children in the basics of science. Small groups gathered to take advantage of these special classes. Just the fact that someone was showing an interest in them seemed to have a vivifying effect on the students. Strong relationships between teachers and students were gradually formed.

At first, Lisa's college refused to give any college credit to the students teaching these courses. No one had ever done anything like this before, and the school didn't quite know what to make of it. Lisa successfully argued that the students were doing field work in sociological studies, an assertion that won credit for the teachers and recognition for her programme.

Her argument was grounded in fact. Having taken a number of education courses, she had found a hard time reconciling what she had been taught and what actually took place in the classroom. Consequently, she went for her degree in urban studies and had approached her students from a sociological point of view.

She discovered, for example, that many of these children had trouble reading, not because they lacked the necessary intelligence, but because the schools had failed to teach them properly. They had been shunted from class to class with no one caring whether they could read or not. Schools just wanted to get them through the system and out as quickly as possible.

Lisa tackled this situation without any degree in education. That caused her, she says, to 'do a good deal of soul-searching. I did wonder if I had a right to teach, if there is such a thing, without a heavy background in education. I came to the conclusion that teaching was really a selling job. I had to sell my students on two things: reading and my love for learning. These kids were now too old to be handed a first-grade primer and asked to start all over again. Such material wouldn't hold their interest. Without a motivation to read, they would be a difficult lot to teach.'

Lisa found an entrepreneurial remedy for this problem. She took what she would call a 'language and experience' approach. 'We brought in material that was related to their everyday lives or that would capture their attention. Playboy cartoons for instance. The boys were very interested in those. We brought in examples of common signs like No Smoking or Yield. Job applications also went over very well with them and were something they had to be able to deal with. We made it a point to keep the structure rather open. We never insisted on tackling only the material we offered. Instead, we would ask them, "What would you like to read?" and then we'd read that.' This approach, born of the creativity of Lisa and her classmates, yielded gratifying results. Not only were the students' performances markedly improved by the programme, it also cemented Lisa's deep love for teaching.

This stayed with her even when she took a job as textbook editor at Harper & Row. One day, some people came to her with an idea for a book. It was, she says, to be 'focused on early childhood education. I thought it was a terrific idea, but I couldn't get my publisher to go for it. Harper & Row turned it down, claiming there was no such thing as the early-child market. When we argued that there was, they retorted that the market could not be defined.'

That company was not the only one to take this stance. The book industry as a whole was dubious about the prospects for this project's success. They quoted the same misgivings as Harper & Row. Despite this Lisa was undeterred. The proposal's authors had, she says, 'convinced me that there was a market out there. People who ran or worked in day-care centres or took care of children in other circumstances would form the core of the readership.'

That sounded good in theory, but you never launch a venture in theory alone. Before proceeding you need facts. You must do the homework that can tell you if your enterprise is worthwhile. Says Lisa, 'I started by calling Washington and asking how many day-care centres were located in the United States. They gave me some number like 64,000. Then I called California to see how many of those were in that state. I was told something like 63,000. Now that didn't make any sense. I started to see why it was so hard to define this market, but those high numbers convinced me more than ever that a readership did exist.'

Trying to nail down that elusive market, Lisa asked a friend, the editor of a small weekly newspaper in New York, for advice. He recommended that, rather than start with a book, she should consider the possibility of doing a newsletter. Distributed to day-care workers and teachers, it would help establish a mailing list, give a clear demography, and define the existing market. If the numbers were impressive, Lisa and the authors would have the ammunition to do all the books they wanted. The three of them brought in other writers to help them produce the publication.

They called their newsletter *First Teacher*. It featured articles for the teachers and activities that allowed teachers and children to interact. They had hoped to launch the premier issue at the annual National Association for the Education of Young Children convention in Atlanta. Timing proved to be a problem. Lisa recalls, 'By the time the first issue was ready for presentation, it was too late to secure a booth at the convention. We asked NYAC officials if they could distribute the newsletters, but they rejected that idea.'

Entrepreneurs aren't discouraged by closed doors. If they can't bang one down, they simply build another one. For Lisa this meant 'hiring some young boys to stand outside the convention centre and hand a free copy of *First Teacher* to everyone who went inside. We felt it was especially important to get it into the hands of those people who were presenting the various workshops that weekend. To meet that end, we somehow secured – I'm really not sure how – a list. It carried each of the presenter's names as well as their hotel address and their room number. Going to each one of their rooms, we shoved a copy of the newsletter beneath their door. It was something. We just wouldn't be denied. Even today, people still remember our campaign down there.'

That premier issue of *First Teacher* was good enough to attract 2000 initial subscribers. As the power of word of mouth exerted itself, the newsletter took off. Today, the sixteen-page publication is published eleven times a year. Its readership has grown to over 15,000 subscribers.

In addition, Lisa's editor chum turned out to be a seer. As soon as *First Teacher* established a viable market, Lisa was approached by an editor at Macmillan. 'She asked if we had thought about doing books! I said it was something we wanted to do, but we couldn't afford it yet. We didn't have the distribution of a big publisher. She replied, "Suppose we committed to buying 15,000 of your first run?" I allowed that that would certainly make a difference. With that order, we had finally entered the book market, which was of course our original goal.'

Lisa and the *First Teacher* crew have already brought out ten books and are exploring other vehicles involving child education. They have achieved this success because they had an idea they believed in and put all their energies behind its implementation. As it turned out, as with many entrepreneurs, they were pioneers. Entrepreneurs relish the unknown. They see its darkness as a thin disguise for a world ablaze with opportunity. Since the publication of *First Teacher*, the early-childhood-education field has flourished. Whereas conventions used to attract only fifty or sixty exhibitors some of them now feature over 6000. Publishers who had once been adamant about the industry's 'undefined market' are now leaping into it with books and newsletters of their own. *First Teacher* didn't cause this explosion by itself. But Lisa and her friends were among the first to point the way. Like all entrepreneurs and pioneers, they were activists. They didn't wait for someone to bring the market to them. They went out and virtually created it.

*

The power of the USP

I was so pleased when I heard this story. Mr Charles Caffarella is an advertising man in Massachusetts. His business, Caffarella Enterprises Inc., was doing well, but Charles knew it could do better. The question was how do you go about bringing your company to its full potential. Charles wasn't afraid of hard work; this fellow is a real go-getter. He would make any sacrifice necessary to make his venture go. However, he felt he needed some entrepreneurial guidance in setting up a success formula for the enterprise.

His mother made him a gift of *Going For It!* As Charles would later write, it was just the tool he had been looking for because he says, it 'explained *how* you made it to the top, step by step, move by move.' He not only read the book, he took notes and applied them to his business.

First, he analyzed his company on paper. This required the drafting of an Intangible Balance Sheet. What were his company's strengths and weaknesses? Mr Caffarella had a strong advertising background. People who used his service knew they were dealing with a first-rate professional. Charles sets high standards for himself, and demands the same of his employees. In what is essentially a personal-service business, this commitment to excellence is the most valuable strength your enterprise can have.

His agency's ability to act as an all-purpose company was another important plus. Besides advertising, Caffarella Enterprises offered related services such as public relations, direct response programmes, strategic planning, artwork and design, and recruitment. A potential client could have all his needs taken care of under one roof. If a customer was launching a large campaign – a promotion comprised of a wide range of elements – this sort of one-stop shopping was a blessing.

Offering a necessary service was another entry in the positive side of the ledger. As Charles had learned in graduate school, there were three fundamental parts to almost any business: finance, marketing, and operations. Charles felt that marketing buttressed the other two factors. He realized the financing had to be in place to start an enterprise and keep it going. The operations had to be professionally run. But, as he put it, 'If you don't have effective marketing, you won't have any finances to worry about and you won't be able to afford any operations.'

Looking over the plus side of the Balance Sheet, Charles knew he was in the right business. It was something he loved, was very good at, and fulfilled a need. Simply fulfilling a need, however, was not strong enough for Charles. He knew most of the agencies across the state could make that same claim. The one glaring weakness on Charles's IBS was the lack of a USP. What set his company apart from all the others?

The first thing he looked at was his office's location. Though Boston is a beautiful city, it's a tough place to call attention to yourself if you're an ad agency. The town is filled with competitors. It has its own version of New York's famed Madison Avenue. As an alternative office site, Charles decided to move twenty miles south to nearby Raynham, Massachusetts. Located between Boston and another large city, Providence, Rhode Island, it would allow Caffarella Enterprises to draw on both metropolises for clients. Charles's meticulous research also revealed that Raynham was a rapidly expanding area, booming with condominium developments and large industrial parks. There could hardly be a more perfect setting for an enterprise that also wanted to grow.

Separating himself from the crowd gave Charles the opportunity to stand out, but it wasn't enough of a USP. He needed something sexier, something that would capture his potential clients' collective imagination. He went back through *Going For It!* and reviewed the chapter on advertising. One anecdote stood out amongst all the rest. It was our story explaining how we had come to offer the Remington shaver with a money-back guarantee.

That guarantee had actually been inspired by a competitor's marketing campaign. In Britain, rivals of Remington had instituted a trade-in policy. You brought in your old shaver, they would give you £5 off your new one. The brand you returned did not necessarily have to be the brand of the company giving you the rebate. Not bad, but I thought we could go one better. We developed the no trade-in trade-in. If you liked our shaver, you kept it and continued to get the best shave you've ever had. If you didn't like the shaver, you returned it, trading it in for a refund. We did the same thing in America, touting our product as the one that 'shaves you close as a blade or your money back!'

This was really more than just a marketing programme. It was a public stand, attesting to my pride and confidence in the Remington shaver. That campaign was a big success and, I'm happy to say, we get returns from less than half of 1 per cent of all our customers.

Charles had the same confidence in his venture as I have in mine. To his company slogan, 'Advertising that Works,' he added one more word: 'Guaranteed!' Caffarella Enterprises would guarantee all of its labours. If a customer found that the cost of a Caffarella campaign exceeded the additional profits generated by that promotion, the agency would refund its 15 per cent commission.

You always want a USP that sings; this one belted out arias. Talk about standing out, nothing like this had ever been attempted in the industry. The press latched on to the marketing strategy and trumpeted the story throughout the state. Businesses flocked to Caffarella because they had no reason not to. They had nothing to lose!

This USP had two things going for it. First, it told the public that Caffarella Enterprises had high confidence in its ability to deliver. In essence, Charles was publicly declaring, 'This company can do the job. All we want is the chance to prove it.' Second, it put a benign pressure on Charles and his staff to outdo themselves. Once the policy was instituted, Charles knew that 'in order to make it work we *had* to be the best.' The agency redoubled its efforts to offer maximum service. It thoroughly researched – at a cost of considerable time and expense – each possible client until it had a clear picture of that business's needs. It then designed its programmes to address these specific areas.

This hard work paid off. Within weeks of launching the money-back guarantee, Caffarella Enterprises secured over $1 million in new clients. It has picked up virtually every new account it has pitched. With this recent 100 per cent closing ratio, Caffarella Enterprises is taking on some of the largest agencies in New England and winning! I bubble up whenever I hear someone has derived so much from my book. It's what the entrepreneurial experience is all about. You want to help others reap the same rewards you have. You want to help build a world of entrepreneurs.

A crowning achievement

Rolph McCollister is the closest thing you can have to American royalty. This young Louisiana entrepreneur has been so successful his home town has dubbed him, 'The King of Baton Rouge'. Despite the impressive title, Rolph wasn't born to the purple. Like any entrepreneur, he achieved his position by going for it.

He started out hoping to be the next Horace Rumpole. However, after two years of studying law at Louisiana State University, he decided legal briefs didn't hold enough excitement for him. Looking for alternatives, he was attracted to the newspaper business. His father, himself an attorney, had successfully run a small-town newspaper for a number of years and had been asked to start up another. It was to be called the *Enterprise*. Focusing on local news, sports, and other tidbits, it was given away free at groceries and on news-stands. Its advertising provided the paper with its profits. Rolph joined the *Enterprise* as a part-time ad salesman and worked his way up to advertising manager. He also augmented his school curriculum with journalism courses.

After joining the newspaper full time, he found this business didn't spark his engine either. This was not unusual.

Entrepreneurs set high standards for themselves and are not easily satisfied. The demands of the entrepreneurial life require you to choose an endeavour that inspires commitment both in your mind and your heart. Many entrepreneurs spend their first few years trying several different ventures until they find the proper fit.

Rolph discovered his in a most unlikely locale: a college basketball game. He remembers, 'LSU was in a tournament. The fans of the other school were very local in their support of their team. They kept yelling and waving Confederate flags. I thought those flags were especially impressive, because all we poor LSU fans had to wave were a dinky set of pom-poms. They didn't look like much. I thought it would be great to design an LSU flag. When I got back home, I drew up a prototype featuring the team symbol, a tiger. I had a sample made up, took it to school officials, and sold 5000 of them. I made about a dollar for every flag I sold.'

More important than the profit, Rolph got a tingle from actually selling a product he had created. The entrepreneur in him had come out. He suddenly realized, 'I wanted to be in business for myself. The newspaper job had been a good experience, but it had me doing the same thing day after day. Week after week I was pitching the same routine to the same accounts. In a town like ours where most of the print media advertising was locked up by the major dailies, there was only so much a tiny weekly could do. We had run out of room to grow.'

Rolph took the profits from the LSU pennant and invested them in himself. He set up a corporation called Sports Fans of America, designing flags for colleges all over the country. Eventually, he was selling his product to professional baseball and basketball teams. His business was skyrocketing.

He did, however, have one problem. Though he designed his products, he didn't have the facilities to manufacture them. This was done by a well-known company. Rolph had to buy his own flags from them, mark them up, and then sell them to concessionaires at the various sports stadiums. These con-

cessionaires were used to dealing directly with the manufacturer. In order to compete with that arrangement, Rolph had
to keep his profit margin slim. Though he was selling a lot of
flags, his bottom line was less than it should have been. Whenever you are involved with a new enterprise, you must weigh
its Risk-Reward Ratio. If it were a mathematical equation, the
Risk-Reward Ratio would look like this:

$$\frac{\text{possible financial benefits of your venture or idea}}{\text{time expended} + \text{money spent} + \text{reputation risked}} = \text{your decision}$$

With its low margins, Rolph's first enterprise wasn't giving him
the maximum return for his time and money. Recognizing its
shortcomings, this entrepreneur made the best of the situation.
He sold the rights of his various trademarked designs to a
manufacturer for a 5 per cent royalty. With the manufacturer
keeping his margins competitive, Rolph wasn't making any
more money than before; neither was he making much less.
However, he had done something most important: freed his
time and attention for another venture.

He decided to take another crack at the newspaper business.
The *Enterprise* had been floundering. Rolph was asked to revive
it as co-publisher. Unlike his last experience, he was coming
back to a challenge. His few years of running his own company
had taught him a good deal about marketing. Rolph felt he
could apply these lessons to a weekly tabloid and turn it into a
success. He recalls: 'The flags worked because they were a
unique item. I was filling a need with something that hadn't
previously existed. I wanted to accomplish two things with the
Enterprise right off the bat. First, I wanted to increase its
revenue by charging for it. If people wanted to read the paper,
they were going to have to pay for it. We built up a subscription
base of over 11,000, not bad for a small-town weekly. My
second goal was to put together a second publication that was

like the flags. It would have a strong USP. I wanted it to be something that had never been offered in this town before.'

Your USP does not have to be as innovative as the creation of the wheel. As Rolph McCollister so ably demonstrated, you can borrow a USP from another venture and adapt it to yours. He had noticed that a whole new journalistic industry had sprung up across the country. Newspapers touting local business news were doing very well, especially down South. No one had ever published one in Baton Rouge. Rolph thought his fellow citizens might be interested in such a newspaper. Looking to find out how they worked, he picked up forty of these publications and read each one of them. Rolph was then able, he says, 'to pick out the best elements of each and incorporate them into something I thought would appeal to Baton Rouge. I noticed that most of them concentrated on news concerning the local businessperson. People like reading about themselves and their neighbours and want to know how someone achieves a success. In a small town, a lot of diverse businesses impact on each other, so it was valuable to learn what other local companies were up to.'

McCollister's *Baton Rouge Business Report* made its debut in September 1982. This was a monthly tabloid devoted to local business news and personalities. It reported on everything from real-estate transactions to bankruptcies. If you wanted to know who sold what to whom in Baton Rouge, you bought his *Report*. The first issue was only fifty-six pages and it was an immediate money maker. People were starved for this kind of news. They just couldn't get enough of it. Now in its fourth year, the *Report* comprises over 148 pages. It has won thirteen national awards. What started out as a two-man operation – Rolph and his city editor from the *Enterprise* – currently has twenty-two employees on its payroll. Had this been Rolph's only success, his story would still be an unqualified triumph.

But there's more. Rolph McCollister is, after all, an entrepreneur. He's not content to cushion his behind with laurels. In chapter one, you saw how Remington parlayed its success by expanding into new, related territories. With his paper enjoying smashing sales, McCollister did the same thing.

We were a manufacturer of an electrical shaver, an electrical grooming product; in branching out, the first thing we got involved with was a hair and beard trimmer, a grooming appliance. McCollister's paper served as a pipeline for the Baton Rouge business community. It was a network strung together by the printed word. Rolph decided to expand that network by bringing its members face to face. This led him to the magazine's first spin-off: a business trade show.

Such an event would serve as a showcase for local businesses. For instance, computer companies would set up booths featuring their equipment. Demonstrators would show the public how these items worked. A printer might erect a booth displaying samples of his craftsmanship. A major medical facility, new to the world of marketing, could have its own information centre. The show would cater mostly to businesspeople, who were either hoping to attract new clients or find fresh sources for products and services. It would also appeal to the average citizen, curious to see the many wonders of our latest technology.

It was quite an idea. Of course the first thing Rolph needed to pull this off was funding. It's a common problem, the one I'm asked about most when I'm on the lecture circuit. How does a young – McCollister was less than thirty – entrepreneur raise the capital to launch his enterprise? McCollister gives us one good example and I think it can be applied to a lot of scenarios.

McCollister had a powerful asset on his Intangible Balance Sheet (IBS). The strong business ties he had built up through his publication. He used these to help find potential exhibitors for his trade show. Rolph had already reserved an auditorium for the event sixty days in advance. The cost was $2100 for the three-day show. His contract with the landlord stipulated that the rent had to be paid within thirty days of the show's scheduled opening. This gave Rolph about four weeks to raise the required capital.

Rolph did this through an advantageous structuring of his terms. He asked for an immediate down payment from his exhibitors. They put up a certain amount of money for each of their booths. The balance would be due two weeks later, fifteen full days before the landlord was to receive his money. When it came time to pay that rent, McCollister had already collected over $65,000. He hadn't borrowed a cent or used any of his own money. With this cash in hand, Rolph was able to pay for the hall, furnish it, pay salaries to a small staff, spend $20,000 on advertising, and still see a $13,000 profit. All this a month before he even opened the doors!

The show was a smash. The hall was packed throughout the event's run. Exit polls proved that it had managed to attract precisely the sort of crowd the exhibitors needed. Of those who attended, 92 per cent were involved in purchasing decisions for their company. They were either office managers, buyers, executive vice-presidents, or CEOs. Rolph couldn't have had a more suitable attendance-profile if he had handpicked each customer himself.

Rolph recalls that he was 'particularly impressed with the networking aspects of the show. An exhibitor would come up to me and say, "I've been trying to see so-and-so for months, and I never could get an appointment. Today, he happened to come by my booth, we started chatting and bingo! I'm supposed to see him next week!" I liked that because it was one of our major aims. We wanted to open up doors for people. That enhances the exhibition's value. One fellow made a contact that led to a $396,000 sale. That wasn't bad return for his investment, the $595 he had paid for booth space. Someone like that will be in every show we run for years.' Rolph's idea has grown since his first convention. From a medium-sized event it has become the Louisiana Business Expo, attracting over 3000 exhibitors.

McCollister has found a way to augment this success with another spin-off. Remember how the Remington warranty-card list led to our catalogues? We took something already in place and transformed it into another business. Rolph did the same thing with his Expo. Realizing he had all these businesspeople gathered at one site for a concentrated period of time, he offered business seminars. Executives would pay a fee to listen to experts wax poetic over the great business issues and problems of the day. The synergy produced by these two endeavours was enormous. The Expo fed the seminars and the seminars, in turn, fed the Expo. The result was an even greater success for McCollister.

With the shows and seminars booming, Rolph still kept his hand on the pulse of his monthly business report. A good lesson there. No matter how well you do with the offshoots of your venture, never forget that they are offshoots. The core business is your solid base. With all his success, Rolph did not let up. If anything he was even more aggressive in marketing his paper, doing everything he could to step up the *Report*'s already highly visible profile. An annual dinner was part of this programme. Hosted by the *Business Report*, it honoured a different national business figure each year. The first one saluted Stephen Forbes of *Forbes* magazine. His appearance made the dinner – and of course the hosting *Baton Rouge Business Report* – front-page news throughout the state.

From a simple beginning, Rolph McCollister's empire is growing. In addition to his *Business Report*, he publishes a directory for the Louisiana Chamber of Commerce, a similar publication for the Baton Rouge Chamber of Commerce, a Louisiana visitor's guide and – a direct offspring of his popular monthly publication – *The Real Estate Report*. Somehow, he has even found the time to launch a direct-mail business. Boy, I love this. He looked at his publication mailing list – *à la* Remington once again – and realized it had an attractive demographic profile. Many of his periodicals' readers were business people. They were movers and shakers looking to invest in themselves. Rolph put together a card pack that allowed sponsors to reach these people via the mails. Not only does this return a handsome profit, he is able to include his own projects in the package for no cost. He is making money and receiving free advertising to boot!

When I last spoke to Rolph, he had no intention of slowing down. He said, 'Every day there's a new opportunity if you're open to it. You can't let it pass you by. Right now, the oil-based economy of Louisiana has slowed. People are holding back. Some people are scared. Not me. I'm putting the pedal to the metal. By the time things start picking up, I'll have spread the gap between me and those naysayers who are standing still.'

This man can't lose. And neither can you if you adopt the same positive attitude. What I like most about Rolph is not what he has accomplished, but how he accomplished it. He did not buy a company. He did not patent some amazing technological innovation. Instead, he saw a vacuum and looked to find something to fill it. He adapted other entrepreneurial vehicles to fit his own needs. When he didn't have capital, he did not despair. He came up with a highly creative way to raise it. He saw possibility where others may have viewed liability. It's not surprising. After all, he is an entrepreneur and an entrepreneur is more than just a risk taker. He is a visionary. In the film *Butch Cassidy and the Sundance Kid*, Paul Newman's Butch says, 'I see visions while the rest of the world wears bifocals.' Butch probably didn't know it, but that could be a credo for the entrepreneur. Rolph McCollister can attest to that. The King of Baton Rouge has proven that opportunity is everywhere. To take advantage of it, all you have to do is be able to see it. Sharpen your eyes. Pick out your path to excellence and you'll be polishing a crown of your own.

A personal turnaround

I'm often asked, 'Are entrepreneurs born, or can they be made?' I might be mistaken, but I think anyone can be an entrepreneur. It doesn't matter what sort of background you come from. With the proper guidance and motivation, you can do more than just reach the stars. You can make them perform at your command.

Sean Lally is a young man living in New York City. Not too long ago, he was at one of life's junctures. He had spent four years in the restaurant business. It was a career that saw him gradually work his way up from junior waiter to apprentice chef.

He had accomplished this without formal culinary schooling. Obviously this was someone to watch, a fellow of intelligence, drive and ambition.

At some point, Sean says, he discovered that he really didn't love the restaurant business. 'I think a number of things soured me on it. For one, I had hit the ceiling where I worked. The next position up was master chef and I knew I wasn't going to get that spot any time soon. Also, I wanted to have greater control over my weekly pay cheque. My earnings were limited by what my employers could afford to pay me. No amount of hard work or sweat could change my reward by very much. I wanted to find something without these limitations. Of course, maybe I also just realized that cooking was terrific as a hobby – I still enjoy doing it at home – but it just wasn't what I wanted to do with the rest of my life.'

That was fine in theory, but in reality Sean had never worked in anything but the restaurant industry. He didn't have experience in any other field. When it came time to think about a new career path, he was at a loss. If I may indulge in what fellow author Norman Mailer describes as 'advertisements for myself', Sean was turned on to a new option when a relative gave him a copy of my favourite book.

He explains: '*Going For It!* attracted me to entrepreneurship and selling. I knew I was willing to put in the hours to build a success. Victor's book convinced me that having that sort of attitude was half the fight. The only drawback was my confidence. I had read how Mr Kiam said you had to have confidence in your idea, product or service and in yourself. If I was careful about choosing the right company to represent, the first part wouldn't be a problem. It was the second part of the equation that presented the difficulty. I didn't have any confidence in myself. I must say I liked Victor's remedy for that. In his book he said "If you don't have self-confidence, find some!" He then immediately went on to suggest a strategy for building your self-image. It revolved around drawing up a Personal Balance Sheet, reading books on positive thinking, taking courses, anything to spark your self-belief. I was willing to try that.'

Without realizing it, Sean had taken an important first step towards becoming an entrepreneur. He already found the first item to jot down on the liability side of his Personal Balance Sheet. Sean recognized a major shortcoming and was going to do his best to correct it. He took out several books on positive thinking and read them religiously. They were kept on a table near his bed. Right next to a copy of *Going For It!*

His lack of confidence was so severe at first, he cancelled several job interviews at the last minute. He recalls, 'I just couldn't face the challenge yet. I guess I wasn't ready. But I was determined to give sales a try. One day, I saw an ad for a door-to-door food service. It sold quality steaks, shrimps and other items to households and businesses. Perhaps it was my background in food or the positive thinking books I had read – I like to think it was fate – but I did call for an interview with that company and I did keep the appointment.

'At that meeting, the manager asked me questions about my background and asked for references. He said, "As long as your references hold up, I'm going to give you this job. I won't fire you. The only one who can fire you is yourself if you don't produce." He then started to talk about the company with an almost religious fervour. He said this was the greatest job in the world. That food was a necessity and was therefore one of the easiest things to sell. The company dealt with products of only the highest quality and 87 per cent of the business came from repeat customers. His last point impressed me. He said, "It's not like selling in a shop. You get in your truck, pick out a territory and sell for as long as you want. You are the store. You set store policy. When a shop is closed, your business is closed. In this company, you close only when you want to. Business is always open. There are no ceilings here."

'I remembered how excited Victor was when he met his first boss at Lever Brothers, Keith Porter. Porter was apparently one ball of fire. His enthusiasm was so contagious and his ideas so innovative, Victor couldn't wait to work for him. Well, I thought, it looks like I just found my Keith Porter. He turned out to be everything I expected and the company really was a

great place to work. My fellow employees couldn't be a more
terrific group of guys.'

Just like Remington, Sean's new employer had an incentive
system. 'If you sold fifty boxes of food in one week, you got a
bonus. Once you hit fifty, each additional ten boxes sold earns
you another bonus. That extra money was a great motivator,
but I had set my own goals. First they were small. An expensive
leather jacket I had eyed for some time, a new watch, that sort
of thing. I got those in the first couple of weeks. Then I set my
sights higher. I realized Victor was right. The entrepreneur is
interested in more than just monetary gain. I wanted to make
this business go as best I could. My job was a line position,
something Mr Kiam talked about. Being a salesman in a sales
company, it led straight to the top. I wanted to move into
management. The only way to accomplish this was to stand out
and *Going For It!* gave me the ammunition to do exactly that.'

The first thing Sean did was make it a point to show up at
work forty-five minutes ahead of schedule. This gave him time
to gear up mentally for the coming day and also let him be
among the first to hit the roads with his products. In addition,
it offered him an opportunity to brainstorm with his boss.
This was very important. The entrepreneur understands that
business is a game. You play it to win. Your sweat and toil are
the keys to getting ahead of your competitors. But hard work
is not enough. In order to move up, you have to get recognition
for your labour. Sean's early arrival showed a strong commitment to the company and his job. The ideas he offered in these
morning sessions illustrated that the company's welfare was
uppermost in his mind.

Since a lack of confidence was still an issue for him, Sean
attacked this problem daily. He practised his pitch in a mirror
making sure to keep constant eye contact. He used a tape
machine to iron out the verbal wrinkles in his presentation.
Sean also took pressure off himself by designating the first few
selling weeks as practice runs. Getting the order was important,
but it was more vital for him to learn how to communicate with
people. He wanted them to share his enthusiasm for his product.

At the end of each selling day, he drew up a list. It was another version of the Balance Sheet. In one column, he recorded all his successful sales. The other side of the ledger contained his misses. He would analyze this breakdown to see what had worked for him and what had gone awry. The next day he would apply the information to all his calls.

He also learned everything he could about the products he was selling. For instance, he could tell a customer why Ecuadoran shrimp was superior to shrimp bred in the Atlantic Ocean. Sean had discovered that most chefs preferred it because it showed less shrinkage in cooking. He could explain the difference between a Black Angus steak and a piece of Grade A beef. The more Sean added to his presentation, the greater his success. The hard work was paying off and it created the most pleasant of synergies. Each sale was another boost for Sean's confidence. The rejections hardly got him down. He welcomed them as an opportunity to refine his pitch further.

This doesn't mean he didn't have his down days. Everyone does. But he was building an entrepreneurial resilience that made it impossible to keep him down. For instance, one day, he says, 'I had put in nine hours on the road and I hadn't made a sale. I was so frustrated I pulled the truck over to the side of the road, got out, slammed the door shut, and took a long walk. I just had to let off steam. When I got back I found I had locked the keys in my truck. I had to walk a mile to a gas station, get a mechanic, and have him pick my lock. I had hardly any money on me so I had to pay the guy off with a box of shrimp. That capped off everything. I had worked my tail off, hadn't made a cent, and now I was out the money for the shrimp. I was operating at a loss!

'If this had happened a few weeks before, I might have chucked the whole thing. But I had learned something: *failure quits in the face of persistence.* I was tired and my persistence had been close to running empty. But that mishap jump-started my engine. I got back in the truck and called on the first house I came upon. I was resolved to get an order and it fed my enthusiasm. A housewife answered the door and I started painting my vista. I'll tell you she caught my fire. She not only bought a couple of boxes, she rang the doorbells of her neighbours and had them come out to see what I was offering. I made enough money from those sales to cover my losses and put $100 in my pocket. That episode taught me one more thing about selling. *No matter how badly things are going, take it all in your stride. There is always one more bell to ring.*'

With his confidence now in place, Sean turned his attention to marketing his company's product. He did not have an extravagant budget or the services of some Madison Avenue ad agency. If you're an entrepreneur you can get along without those things. What he had was his own creativity. Says Sean, 'I remember borrowing an idea from Remington. Every now and then I would come across a fence-straddler, a first-time customer who was leaning towards buying, but needed a gentle nudge. I would offer them my version of the money-back guarantee. They would post-date their cheque by a few days and sample the order I left them. If it wasn't up to their expectations, they could cancel the cheque and return the unused portion. I knew they would fall in love with this food once they tasted it and I was right. I have yet to see a single return. This offer helped me build up my customer base and created a trust between me and my customers. That's invaluable in any enterprise, especially the food business.'

Sean also tried other ideas. There was one particularly wealthy neighbourhood that looked like a promising territory. However, the area had a large Jewish population and most of these people wanted only kosher food. Sean's company didn't supply that. Consequently, most of his colleagues stayed out of that neighbourhood after a few unsuccessful tries. Sean followed their example. Until the Christmas season. Then he drove his truck around on a Sunday evening and jotted down the address of every house that was adorned by Christmas lights. He assumed kosher food wouldn't be an issue in those homes. The following week, he returned to those households and came away with a new crop of customers.

Thanksgiving posed another problem. Sean's company didn't

sell turkeys. This made that holiday week a particularly dead period. However, Sean realized that they did sell appetizers that would make suitable accompaniments to a turkey dinner. He printed up a list of each one of these items and handed them out to his customers. He did an extraordinary business in a week that most people would have written off.

When Sean's company brought out a line of cakes, he bought several, sliced them, and handed out free samples to his customers. He was showing his appreciation for their business and introducing them to another product. He started passing out recipes showcasing his company's wares. Whenever the temperature dropped below freezing, he ignored the discomfort: 'I made extra certain to put in a full day. I knew this was my time to sell. People didn't want to go out to shop so my service was that much more valuable. Also, many of them had been cooped up at home all day with no one to talk to. When they see my smiling face come through the door with this beautiful food, I invariably get a warm welcome.'

This from a fellow who used to lack confidence. Boy, I'm glad he's not in the shaver business, or I'd be in big trouble. I have a feeling this young man is going to surpass any goal he sets for himself. He proves that anyone can be an entrepreneur. Everything he has accomplished is the product of hard work and his powers of observation. Even his vision and creativity were talents that were honed. You don't need the right genes, a PhD a pinstripe suit, or a fancy business card to live the entrepreneurial life. Take it from me, entrepreneurs are rarely extraordinarily gifted. Like the subjects in this chapter, they are merely people who are not content to watch things happen; they make things happen. Creating and building an enterprise is their main goal. The financial rewards are wonderful, but they aren't all important. Their success comes from proving something can be done well and on their own terms. They have no time for the commonplace or second rate. They prove that all you really need to succeed is a dream and the courage to grab it with both hands. Their lives are vivid testimonies that anyone can win as long as they keep going for it.